Supply Ship Operations

D1242703

Supply Ship Operations

Vic Gibson

Newnes
An imprint of Butterworth-Heinemann Ltd
Linacre House, Jordan Hill, Oxford OX2 8DP

 PART OF REED INTERNATIONAL BOOKS

OXFORD   LONDON   BOSTON
MUNICH   NEW DELHI   SINGAPORE   SYDNEY
TOKYO   TORONTO   WELLINGTON

First published 1992

© Vic Gibson 1992

British Library Cataloguing in Publication Data
Gibson, Vic.
  Supply Ship Operations
  I. Title
  623.8

ISBN 0 7506 0780 7

Library of Congress Cataloguing in Publication Data
Gibson, Vic.
  Supply ship operations/Vic Gibson.
  p.   cm.
  Includes index.
  ISBN 0 7506 0780 7
  1. Offshore support vessels.   I. Title.
  VM466.035G53
  359.8′345−dc20
                                    92−2461
                                      CIP

**Printed and bound in Great Britain by
Thomson Litho Ltd, East Kilbride, Scotland**

Contents

Foreword

The offshore industry depends upon supply vessels for logistic support. However, ships do not have the permanence, size or significance of a major production platform and it is all too easy to overlook the contribution of shipping to offshore development.

I am pleased to write the foreword to this first comprehensive book on supply vessel operations because it is a specialized sector of the maritime industry and one which has sustained a remarkable record of service. Having said that, there are clearly good practices and bad ones. There are charterers and managers who make impossible demands and seafarers who make decisions in the field which, on reflection, they would probably judge to have been unwise. A careful reading of this text will help all concerned to optimize the performance of their vessels.

This book, which examines the history and evolution of offshore support vessels, takes the reader through the complex tasks undertaken to meet different specialist applications — these may be anchor handling, seismic surveying or diving support — and in so doing provides excellent professional advice to those operating the vessels.

The book also fulfils another important function in that it gives an insight into the practicalities of supply vessel operation which can be read and studied by crane drivers, barge masters, offshore installation managers and of course charterers, shippers and contractors. The author has written a book which is not only technically accurate but he has also written it in an up-to-date and easily readable style.

A publication on this subject is long overdue and I would like to congratulate Captain Gibson on his lucid and informative text.

Captain P. Boyle, FNI
President, The Nautical
Institute
20 August 1992

Preface

This book is intended to accomplish three things: firstly, to provide a starting point for anyone entering, or considering entering, the industry; secondly, to provide an alternative view for those already working offshore; thirdly, to convey some of the excitement and satisfaction there is in working in one of the last marine areas where traditional seamanship in all its forms still exists.

Everyone is still learning, from the tow master to the supply ship deckhand, and this book is intended to provide a basis for this learning process so that the reader may more easily contribute to the collective experience of the marine offshore industry in the future.

I make no apology for having been unable to cover every possible procedure and eventuality, since I feel that the explanations of the fundamentals of supply ship operations will be sufficient to give the reader a real insight into what is a very exciting and progressive marine activity. I hope I have been able to convey the genuine enthusiasm and interest which all mariners involved with the offshore industry feel for the business — and to encourage those thinking of entering it.

It is a different and vital world: if those involved in it give of their best, it will return a wealth of experience and job satisfaction. The supply vessel master really is the captain of his own ship. He makes on-the-spot decisions that will influence the course of events in operations costing enormous sums, and is personally able to enhance the reputation of both his ship and his company.

I once opened a children's book on ships in our local library. On the page depicting an offshore supply vessel an OSA anchor handler was portrayed diving into an enormous swell, the spray flying high into the air and obscuring the whole forepart of the craft. 'These ships supply offshore oil rigs', read the caption; 'They require very skillful captains to drive them'. What further endorsement could a seafarer require?

Vic Gibson
February 1992

Acknowledgements

My thanks are due to a number of current and former supply ship masters who have helped to fill in the gaps in my own knowledge: in particular, Captain Mark Nicholson who spent two years towing barges round the world on the *Invincible*, and Captain George Craigen, whose computer programming skills have allowed me to include an invaluable stability program to assist those ship masters whose owners do not recognize the importance of professional stability programming.

I am grateful to Captain Mike Hancox and to the Norwegian Maritime Directorate for permission to reproduce the documents in Appendix 6. I am also indebted to the following for information, access to their vessels or data about their products:
Farstad UK
Sea Information Systems
Karmfork
Ulstein
Tidewater
Balmoral.

V.R.G.

Introduction

During the early 1970s I was working as a cargo superintendent and suffering the standard malaise of all former seafarers in this position: working long hours for little reward and longing for better things. One of the few tangible benefits was easy access to Lloyds List, and in those days every week saw a profile of a new supply vessel which had just rolled off the stocks, in Appledore for Offshore Marine, Drypool Engineering for Seaforth or from Holland for OIL. I used to look at these plans and descriptions and think what a wonderfully seamanlike task operating these craft must be.

In the summer of 1975 my youngest son was born. I was still rising before dawn and returning home long after the kids had gone to bed, and getting more and more fed up. That summer was also a big season for pipe-laying in the North Sea, and a vessel which had won a number of major contracts was the pipe-laying barge *Viking Piper*. This particular barge was for its time extremely advanced, being a semi-submersible rather than a conventional monohull, and also being serviced by its own purpose-built pipe carrier, the *Oil Challenger*.

Almost immediately after the *Viking Piper* went into service it suffered a major anchor winch failure which necessitated a return to drydock in Holland and a loss for its owners of a great deal of time and therefore of money. The incident was noteworthy for me because for the first time an aspect of marine activity offshore was written up in the national press: I actually got an idea of what was going on. This incident decided me and, reasoning that I would at least be seeing my family half of the time, in November I joined the OIL well-testing vessel *Oil Dragon* in the Arabian Gulf, and entered a new world.

Years later I found myself at the controls of the Star Offshore anchor handler *Star Aquarius*, loading pennants and buoys while going astern at 3 knots. The after end of our ship was between the pontoons of a semi-submersible under tow, and in the midst of the churning white water we were preparing to lay the first anchor during the approach to the location. Beside me on the bridge I heard a new crew member, who had been detailed to watch the first operation, mutter 'If I hadn't seen it I would not have believed it'.

That was how I felt as the days passed on the *Oil Dragon*. The master, John de Barr, was an old North Sea hand, extremely experienced and totally unflappable. The ship's task was to pick up a bow mooring and then back up to the small Gulf

Oil platforms, tie up aft and test the flow of oil through the well with on-board equipment. This could be done twice and sometimes three times in a day, with total mastery, in tides of up to 2 knots and frequently with only one main engine working. I was astounded, and full of admiration for the captain who, it seemed to me, handled the ship with almost magical skill.

Most of this operation was carried out with me on the bridge operating the controls and the master on the stern with a two-way radio; as a result, I was under constant ship handling instruction. This was to stand me in good stead later.

I moved on from there to the North Sea where I began to learn the skills required to carry out the many and varied tasks given to mariners by the offshore industry, and eventually found myself passing on these skills to others. I also learnt that, no matter what one's experience, the job is so varied that mariners in the industry are constantly faced with completely new activities. What is required is the ability to visualize what one's ship is doing, and will do with the application of any force. It is also a help to be able to visualize what is likely to be happening under the water and on the seabed.

Our job can be said to have been in existence since the *Ebb Tide* berthed in Morgan City on its way to the *Mr Charlie* for the first time — a mere forty years. Over the whole period new equipment has been presented to the mariner, and he has had to learn how to use it in the field. This will continue to happen. The evolution of the supply ship and the techniques required to operate it have been exhilaratingly rapid and, after a period in the doldrums, exploration and platform development are picking up again and new supply ships are being built.

The techniques used to carry out the various supply ship functions are the result of the accumulated experience of supply ship masters since 1954 and as new experience is gained all aspects of offshore operations will improve. My explanations in the following pages are the result of what I was taught, onto which is imposed my own experience. These techniques all worked for me, but they are probably not the only effective ways of carrying out the tasks of the supply ship.

<table>
<tr><td>**1**</td><td># The job of the supply ship</td></tr>
</table>

How it all started

At the turn of this century the southward movement of oil exploration across the Mississippi delta made the eventual search for hydrocarbons under the sea inevitable, and in 1923 the first offshore exploration took place in the state of Louisiana.

The drilling derricks were set on platforms which in turn were supported by piles driven into the mud of the Mississippi delta. It was not long before these structures were being erected just off the shore, and by 1930 the oil companies were using derricks mounted on barges which were sunk to the seabed on the location. However this technique limited the depth of water in which the operation could take place to something slightly less than the depth of the barge from deck to keel. Despite the first allocation of offshore leases in 1945, because of the extremely shallow waters of the Gulf coast this situation persisted until 1954 when the first revolution in offshore drilling took place: the submersible drilling barge *Mr Charlie*.

This vessel was the brainchild of Alden J. 'Doc' Laborde who, while employed by the oil company Kerr-McGee, came to the logical conclusion that since the depth of a drilling barge limited the depth of water in which offshore exploration could take place, the barge should be capable of being submerged. Hence the *Mr Charlie* consisted of a barge on which ten legs were mounted which in turn supported the deck on which the derrick and living quarters were positioned. This enabled the craft to drill in water depths of 40 ft (12 m), far in excess of anything which had previously been possible.

Up to this time the offshore units had been supported by whatever vessels were available, the majority of the work being carried out by shrimp boats and tugs and, after the Second World War, by government surplus LCTs. These ships were the first to provide a large uncluttered area of open deck, ideal for the carriage of drill-pipe and similar awkward components of drilling hardware.

The *Mr Charlie* spudded its first well for Shell on 24 June 1954, and Doc Laborde, now Chief Executive of ODECO, the company formed to build and market *Mr Charlie*, turned his attention to the support of his baby.

What was required was a vessel with the maximum of available open deck commensurate with the size of the craft, and since all ships need a bow which, besides being pointed, must carry the windlass, anchors and cable stowage, it seemed a good idea to add the pilot house and accommodation, thereby allowing the rest of the deck to be available for cargo.

He transferred his idea from his head to the back of an envelope and propounded it to Bill LeBlanc, then port captain for Kerr McGee, who felt that the design was impractical because it would 'pound the crew unmercifully'. It says something for Bill LeBlanc's immediate grasp of the vessel's potential qualities that no one who has ever sailed on a supply ship would be likely to dispute the statement.

However, Doc LaBorde was undeterred by any prospective limitations to crew comfort and, in the same month that the *Mr Charlie* commenced operations for Shell, gathered a group of potential investors at the offices of the Alexander Shipyard in New Orleans. The result of this meeting was the formation of Tidewater Marine Services, and the company immediately commissioned the yard to build a ship along the lines of Doc's concept.

The yard refined the idea into formal drawings, which the board members criticized until everyone was satisfied, the result being a vessel 120 ft (36.5 m) long, having a clear deck area aft of 90 ft (27 m), the only intrusion into this area being two squat funnels positioned at either side through which the engine exhaust gases were routed. This feature of supply ship design was not to change for nearly twenty years until oil exploration began to take place in more hostile waters.

The other important dimensions were a deck width of 27 ft (8.2 m), a light draft of 5 ft (1.5 m) and a loaded draft of 8 ft 6 in (2.6 m). Twin GM diesel engines with a total of 600 bhp (450 kW), provided second hand by one of the board members, Don Durant, gave a top speed of 10 knots. The wheelhouse was also second hand, being scavenged from an old tug, the *Navajo*. The liquid capacities of the ship were 330 tonnes of ballast and 110 tonnes of fuel.

As was expected, before the ship was delivered to the owners it was chartered by ODECO, and at this point, to avoid a conflict of interests, Alden LaBorde withdrew from Tidewater. However, the company, learning that Shell was interested in chartering a similar ship, immediately ordered a second vessel.

On 25 March 1955 the *Ebb Tide* left the Alexander Shipyard and sailed down the Mississippi to Morgan City, presenting its un-nautical shape (Figure 1) to public gaze for the first time. It is a shape which has changed little over the years, and even today's North Sea superships are little different. The *Ebb Tide* was rapidly followed by two sister ships, starting a continuous process of building and development which continued from that date until the 1985 oil crash which effectively halted the building of supply ships except in the USSR.

The first supply vessels were able to lie alongside the *Mr Charlie* and the barges and piled structures then in use, so their ability to manoeuvre was limited to the requirement of most ships, the need to be able to get close enough in to make fast; it was only the arrival of the jack-up, where the hull of the rig was raised above the water, leaving only the legs at sea level, which necessitated a change of the operating techniques of supply ships. It was now required that they let go an anchor and tie up stern to the rig in a type of Mediterranean moor.

In the early 1960s the jack-up and its attendant supply vessels began to migrate to other parts of the world — notably the Arabian Gulf and the southern North Sea where the oil companies began to drill for gas, soon making discoveries off

Figure 1   *The world's first supply ship, the* Ebb Tide

the coast of Holland. In 1966 the *Mr Cap* became the first jack-up to commence drilling in the British sector of the North Sea.

The increasing number of jack-ups in the North Sea were still supplied mainly by American vessels from the Gulf of Mexico, but both British and European shipping companies, alive to the new opportunities, began to build their own supply vessels, much in the style of their American counterparts and still powered by two engines each of about 500 bhp (375 kW), with twin rudders. The only serious concession to the rather unusual work being carried out was the provision of a large window at the after end of the bridge to allow the captain to see out.

Meanwhile, back in the Gulf of Mexico, ODECO had developed the first column-stabilized semi-submersible drilling rig, building on the experience gained with the *Mr Charlie* which showed that stability could be maintained even when the barge was not actually resting on the seabed. This provided another problem for the supply ship: the requirement to lay anchors.

In the Gulf of Mexico small rollers were added to the stern of some supply ships, and a diesel powered winch bolted to the afterdeck. In Europe some supply ships were fitted with large A-frames at the stern, so that the anchors could be lifted clear of the water and then dragged aboard. However the A-frame was soon dispensed with and rollers became de rigueur. In Europe the winches were soon being housed under cover at the after end of the accommodation and engine power began to increase in order that anchors could be pulled further away from the rig.

Concurrently with this development, new buildings were fitted with tunnel thrusters in the bow to increase manoeuvrability, and a set of engine and rudder controls facing aft, at the after window of the wheelhouse. This enabled the master to control the vessel and to see what was going on at the same time; also, once the ability of the supply ship to tow had been accepted, it became necessary to move the funnels forward, off the deck to the after end of the accommodation. It was also necessary to make them higher to keep the exhausts clear of the waves in the more unpleasant sea conditions in the North Sea.

Figure 2 *The anchor handler* Oil Supplier *built in 1972, with a 45 tonne bollard pull*

By 1972 the shape of the supply ship had been more or less established (Figure 2). They were vessels of about 4000 bhp (3000 kW) and a bollard pull of 45 tonnes, with a 500 bhp (375 kW) tunnel thruster in the bow. They could carry fresh water, drill water and fuel in limited quantities, and had a massive ballast capability so that they would remain stable regardless of cargo requirements. Cement and other bulk powders were stored in cylindrical tanks below deck and *blown* up to the installations by compressed air at rates of between 10 and 20 tonnes per hour.

The propellers were driven through clutches and gearboxes and the speed and direction of the screws controlled by air controls on the bridge, the forward and after controls usually being connected by chains under the deck of the wheelhouse. The bow thruster was controlled by a combined direction and speed lever and was usually powered by a diesel engine in a compartment directly under the accommodation.

Using the early semi-submersibles, supported by these somewhat primitive craft, all the major discoveries in the North Sea were made. The problems of shifting the rigs were considerable and were compounded by the limited accuracy of the position fixing systems available at the time, the best being Decca Pulse 8.

The accommodation available on these craft was more akin to that on the fishing vessels built previously by the yards now turning them out, than to the deep sea ships previously sailed on by most of the crews, though the unusual and difficult form of work and the general lack of legislation brought in crews from a variety of sources. Many early vessels were commanded by former fishing skippers and coastal masters, who did not have the same fear of approaching fixed objects that is part of the mental make-up of the deep sea ship master. Engineer officers were likewise taken on more for their willingness to 'get stuck in' than for their qualifications, and usually sailed by courtesy of a Department of Transport dispensation.

Early 'anchor jobs', as rig shifts are known throughout the business, were fraught with danger and difficulty. At the best of times the ships had very little freeboard, and it was necessary to keep them ballasted down to ensure that the rudders and screws remained under water. In quite moderate seas, waves would be constantly sweeping over the decks to wash the legs from any unwary seaman or to trap him behind a floating object. This, combined with an unhealthy contempt for hard hats, made every aspect of the work a hazardous business.

Because of the low power of the ships it was often necessary for one to connect to the bow of another and for them to pull the anchor out in tandem; when a back-up or second anchor was required, two ships would line up side by side, one with the main anchor on deck, and one with the back-up. They would then connect the two with a pennant and lower them to the seabed at the same time. This technique resulted in much contact damage, which is hardly surprising.

New techniques were developed for the day-to-day supplying of the rigs and one unusual but logical change was the increased amount of anchor cable carried by the ships. By 1972 the North Sea supply ships were carrying about 15 shackles of cable, and were dropping anchors and tying up to rigs in up to 600 ft (183 m) of water.

The rigs were also making more use of the increasing ability of the ships to remain within the radius of the crane, purely by manoeuvring with the engines and the thruster. This was, and still is, known as 'snatching', a term which no doubt derived from the time when ships could do no more than drift slowly past while a single urgent lift has hooked on during the moments when the stern was within range of the crane. When the weather was too rough to allow tying up it became commonplace for the ships to manoeuvre under the crane while complete deck cargoes were discharged and loaded, and by the mid-1970s bulk cargoes were also being discharged while the ships kept within range of lengthened hoses.

To carry out this form of operation it was necessary for the ships fitted with fixed-pitch propellers to have one engine going ahead and one astern at all times. This was due to the inordinate time it took for an engine to clutch in — 8 seconds while the ship is within a couple of metres of a rig leg can seem like an eternity. The tendency for the stern to swing was countered by the application of opposite rudder, and the bow was held in place by the application of suitable thrust. It was a natural progression therefore that supply ships should be provided with controllable-pitch propellers which cut out the clutching-in problems.

By 1975 several major fields in the North Sea were under development, and their associated pipelines were being planned. To fulfil the demands of this phase, specialized pipe carriers and platform supply ships were beginning to come into service. The move into platform and pipeline development also required vessels to carry manned submersibles and divers.

Several former tankers became heavy lift ships by the simple addition of a large crane, and updated and new designs of semi-submersibles made their appearance, some with large blocks of accommodation to house the workers required to carry out the construction work. These are known as 'flotels'.

Notable among the pipe carriers available in the mid-1970s was the *Oil Challenger*, probably the only supply ship to be produced with the accommodation aft.

Unfortunately it did not prove successful in operation due to its inability to lie alongside the pipe-laying barge *Viking Piper* without causing considerable damage to both. Its owners made attempts to market it in other fields but the essentially conservative approach of the oil majors made it more or less inoperable, and it was subsequently sold to Heerama.

It quickly became evident that the pipe carrier market was becoming overtonnaged and several of these vessels were converted into diving ships, with a single moonpool, two thrusters forward and one aft, saturation diving chambers and dynamic positioning systems. Some large trawlers and one or two supply vessels were also converted into diving ships.

During the 1970s the popularity of the manned submersible was also at its zenith and several types of ship were converted to carry these craft, including supply vessels, trawlers and small ferries. This was generally a simple process requiring the addition of a thruster, an A-frame on the stern, and a hanger for the submarine (or submarines, since some of the larger vessels carried two).

Throughout the period the marine industry was supplying more and more sophisticated anchor handlers and by 1976 there were several boasting an available power of more than 8000 bhp (6000 kW). The increase in power of North Sea supply ships was also to lead to an increase in power of the ships built in the United States, though of a lesser order. In Europe the supply ship was moving further and further away from the original Gulf of Mexico concept, the first thing to change being the shallow draft. To convert the extra power into bollard pull, large screws were required which naturally increased the amount of the hull under the water, as did the constantly increasing requirement for carrying capacity.

Systems for the carriage of bulk cargoes were also developed. The early horizontal cement tanks were being superseded by vertical hoppers with higher pressure pumping systems capable of discharging up to 30 tonnes per hour. Development in this area has continued, and in the 1980s pumping rates of up to 80 tonnes per hour became commonplace. This completely takes the pain out of bulk powder operations. Dedicated tanks for the unusual fluids used in the drilling operation also began to appear, and ballast tanks capable of doubling as rig chain lockers were fitted to the anchor handlers.

The control systems of all types of vessel were also becoming more sophisticated with the greater use of electronics, and with the requirement for ships to spend more time snatching came the single stick or 'joystick' control. This allowed the master to control all thrusters, engines and rudders with one handle — the ultimate video game.

Another marine activity going through rapid technical change was the seismic work. Most seismic vessels were, and still are, either converted trawlers or supply ships, only a very small number being constructed for the purpose. Until recently the ship could be of any type large enough to carry the equipment and the twenty or so men required to operate it; however, recent developments in the seismic gun arrays and the cables carrying the geophones have begun to make it necessary for seismic vessels to be dimensionally large and to have formidable bollard pull. Navigation systems are also constantly becoming more accurate, the latest available, the Differential GPS system, possibly being the ultimate.

This constant improvement in the equipment means that, even though most of the major potential oil-bearing areas of the world are already criss-crossed by survey lines, all areas are constantly being resurveyed as the oil companies update their material.

Figure 3 *A group of modern American supply vessels in Morgan City. Note that the funnels are still on the main deck*

A new impetus in the operation of offshore vessels has resulted from the *Piper Alpha* disaster, and the resulting Cullen Enquiry and report. This has focused attention on the operation of the standby vessel which, all over the North Sea, is required to stand by in the area of each offshore installation to take on survivors of a disaster, or to recover men from the water. The Cullen Enquiry found the standby vessel at the Piper A lacking in all sorts of ways, so that finally in the summer of 1991 the Department of Transport and the Health and Safety Executive issued a new set of regulations for the construction and operation of standby vessels.

These ships are really outside the scope of this book, but the change in regulations has resulted in numbers of older supply ships being converted to this new role, and eventually virtually all the old side trawlers which have given so many years of faithful service will be put out to pasture. Some supply ship owners have, as a result of this change, become standby vessel owners and therefore it seems that the standby ship may well take a place in the promotion structure of the industry.

The past decade has seen other traumatic changes in the industry, with the general reduction in the price of crude oil slowing down field development and reducing the level of exploration. This effectively halted the construction, and therefore the development, of the supply ship world wide, except in the USSR, and it was not until 1989 that any new orders were placed. The existing world fleet is continuing to move between markets, the large North Sea vessels venturing out to the Far East, China and Brazil, and the less sophisticated Gulf of Mexico craft moving to the Arabian Gulf and the Continent of Africa.

From survey to oilfield

What then are the various stages required to move from an area of virgin seabed to the final production of oil from an offshore installation?

Seismic exploration

The process starts with the acquisition of seismic data. It is common for seismic companies to run long, widely spaced lines over likely areas that are due to be auctioned and to sell these to any oil company who may have an interest. This allows the company to make a more positive analysis of the value of the block on offer. These lines can be 30 km long and several kilometres apart, intended only to confirm the geologist's ideas of the formation of the substrata.

In the simplest terms, they are searching for a dome-shaped substructure holding beneath it the oil-bearing rock, in fact a reservoir (Figure 4); in the event of preliminary surveys giving this impression, more detailed seismic work is carried out using shorter lines, closer together. They may be 10 km long and 1 km apart, and may be run in several directions.

This data is then analysed by the oil company's geological team and, assuming that they still consider the area productive, they will identify a spot where an initial hole is to be drilled. This will usually be where they consider the centre of the field to be.

Exploration drilling

An exploration rig will then be hired, or taken from another area on completion of its work there, and towed into the precise position defined by the geologists. It will then be sunk to the seabed and jacked up on its legs or anchored, depending on what type of rig it is; the type used obviously depends on the depth of water.

Assuming that the first hole is productive, the rig may then be moved to other spots in the field to attempt to discover the actual structure, and the more complex the structure the more holes have to be drilled. In the event of a particularly worth-while field, more than one rig may be used, and drilling will continue until the company is satisfied that they know exactly what lies beneath the earth's crust.

Reservoirs may be found at any depth up to 20 000 ft (6 km) and the speed with which drilling takes place depends on the hardness of the strata being penetrated. Complete holes take anything from six weeks to three months, so that the exploration of a field may be measured in years in some cases.

Once the company has decided that the field will be productive, they will go through the process of applying to the government under whose jurisdiction the area of the seabed lies for permission to develop it, and will decide what sort of means are to be used to extract the oil, process it and transport it.

Bringing a field into production

The criteria used here are the potential recoverable quantities of oil. Large fields are likely to be provided with platforms piled into the seabed with a pipeline to some suitable point on the mainland; smaller fields may be provided with floating

A dry hole

A productive well

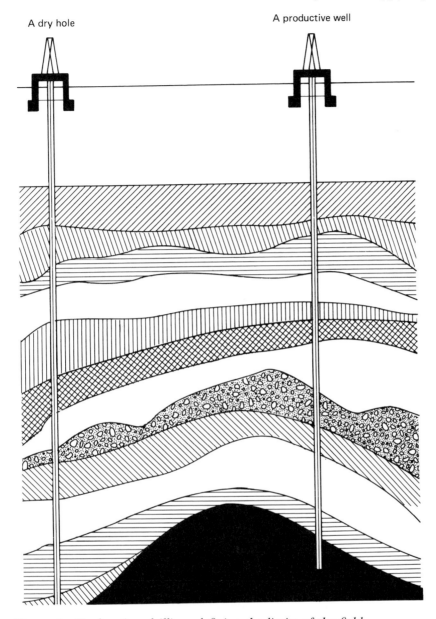

Figure 4 *Exploration drilling: defining the limits of the field*

facilities, usually converted semi-submersibles, and tanker mooring facilities. There are various combinations such as tension leg platforms and floating storage units, all of them finally providing a means of recovering the oil in the cheapest possible manner.

Today sub-sea completions are also in use. These are recovery systems on the seabed, usually linked to an existing platform close by. New ideas for the recovery of oil from marginal fields also include SWOPS vessels which are able to link remotely to wellheads on the seabed, fill themselves up and them sail off to a refinery to be discharged.

The oil company will also decide at an early stage how many wells are to be drilled and the manner in which this is to be done. For this purpose a technique known as deviated drilling is used, so that the oil can be recovered from all areas of the field. The collection point of the well may end up a mile away from the point of origin. Satellite wells may also be drilled at further distances, the wellheads being connected to the platform by lines on the surface.

Positioning platforms

In the early days it was normal for the jacket, or base, of the platform to be sunk into position, the superstructure or 'topsides' built onto it, and then for the drilling operation to commence. However, it has become more usual for a rig to be placed in the platform position and for the drilling to be done while the structure is being manufactured, thereby saving a considerable amount of time. This and the ability of modern heavy lift cranes to position much heavier weights, and so allow the construction of much larger topsides units ashore, has considerably reduced the time taken between discovery and start-up.

In some cases the platforms arrive on location completed, with their topsides already in position. This is always the case with concrete platforms and also, uniquely, in the case of the *Maureen* platform, which is a steel jacket, but which was towed to location vertically with the topsides in position, buoyancy being achieved by flotation units.

Tension leg platforms

Tension leg platforms are also an obvious development which ensure that the structure can be completed close to the shore and then towed out into position. So far the only one in the North Sea, the *Hutton* TLP, has proved successful and is likely to be the prototype for others worldwide, particularly in the deeper waters of the Gulf of Mexico.

Figure 5   Brent Bravo, *a typical concrete platform.* Charlie *and* Delta *can be seen in the background*

Once in position and operating, platforms need to be supplied with all the requirements of the drilling rig — food, water, bulk powders, tubulars and drilling fluids — so every platform increased the requirement for supply ships.

Maintenance of platforms

The platforms also need to be maintained, and for this purpose the oil companies employ diving ships, most of the larger fields having one continuously on location. Shell and BP have their own semi-submersibles employed on the Brent and Forties Fields respectively, the *Stadive* and the *Iolair*. As well as providing diving services, these vessels are capable of carrying out firefighting duties and can provide accommodation for overflows of workers. The *Tharos*, a similar craft employed by Occidental, became briefly famous during the *Piper Alpha* disaster in June 1988.

Platform removal

No well-defined marine procedures have yet been established for platform removal. The techniques used in the future will hinge on whether they are to be completely removed, or allowed to remain on location, but horizontal on the seabed, or whether a combination of the two will be required. There seems to be a good chance that what is done will depend on water depth, since the shallower the water the more danger there will be to shipping. In deeper water the only hazard caused by the remnants of a platform lying on the seabed is to the trawls of fishing vessels, something which the fishermen may well be pleased to tolerate since the structures will provide breeding grounds for fish.

It would therefore be reasonable to suggest that platforms sited in water depths of less than 200 ft (60 m) are likely to have to be removed complete, while those in greater depths may be allowed to be toppled by the use of explosives. There is also the chance that those in deeper water will have to have their topsides removed before the jacket is toppled.

This removal work is likely to provide charters for the crane barges with high lifting capacity for some time.

Chartering practices

Throughout the various activities described, the oil company charters the ships used to carry out all the marine operations. The supply ship is obviously chartered in the greatest numbers, and different oil companies adopt different policies, mainly to carry out the marine operations at the best possible price.

Larger companies who run extensive drilling programmes together with numbers of platforms will usually employ a mix of platform ships and anchor handlers, their length of charter depending on the prevailing prices on the spot market, and the direction in which the price is likely to go.

There is obviously a tendency for oil companies in the UK to charter for long periods on a rising market and for short periods on a falling market, and indeed when the market is at rock bottom some operators take all their ships all the time off the spot.

In Norway the operators tend towards very long term charters, and they will often take a ship for five years straight from the builders. Such a policy gives both the ship owner and the operator stability and results in good service. The operator may pay more for some of the time for the ship than he might have done by playing the market, but it will not be more than he can afford, and similarly the ship owner will receive a proper return for his investment which will enable him to keep his ship maintained and his crews keen, well trained, and suitably recompensed for their labours.

Charters for single wells are common, without a specified duration, though it will be indicated how many days this is likely to be; options are often given to extend charters by one well, one year, or whatever the parties agree. In most charter parties there is also a clause allowing the operator to give the ship owner 30 days notice of termination. This does not make for a secure situation.

All operators also make up their numbers of craft from the spot market. This may be to enhance the anchor handling capability of their fleet, to fill in for ship's tank cleaning, to supplement regular platform supply craft or to keep the service running during periods of bad weather. Vessels on the spot market are usually on one hour's notice, and it is not infrequent for them to be dispatched straight from their layby berth to a rig they have never seen before to assist in a complex anchor handling operation, the full ramifications of which are only made clear when they actually arrive on the location.

Charters of other vessels

Diving ships are usually chartered by the season, i.e. for the summer months, and each spring the diving ship owners vie for the contracts after the long period of winter lay-up.

Seismic ships are usually chartered for very long periods by the seismic companies, some of whom also own their own ships, and are paid by the kilometre for the seismic data.

The whole chartering process keeps numbers of shipbrokers in work and gives the ship owners a continual task of tendering for work as it arises.

The exploration hole

Before moving on to the meat of the business, the operation of marine craft in the offshore industry, it is worth while to go through the cycle of the operation of a semi-submersible for the drilling of a single hole, and see how the operation requires various services from the marine craft associated with it.

The rig will be towed onto location by one or two ships, depending on the requirements of the operators and the insurers, some of whom stipulate a minimum engine power, and there will be waiting on the location one or two other anchor handlers to assist with the duties associated with placing the rig in position.

The rig's anchors will then be deployed using all the anchor handlers on location — a process usually taking about 24 hours, but at times becoming a seemingly endless task if problems with the bottom or with any of the systems involved occur. Once the anchors are deployed they are usually allowed to soak, or settle into the seabed, for a time; this again may be a period of 24 hours if the bottom is particularly soft.

The anchors are then tensioned up to a predetermined level. To carry out this operation, opposite anchors are tensioned against each other. If they do not drag, the tension is reduced to a working level and then the next pair is tested. In the event of any anchor not holding it may be rerun or a back-up or piggy-back may be added using one of the anchor handlers. In particularly soft conditions two or even three back-ups may have to be attached. Finally, the tow master will be satisfied with the rig's position, all anchors will have been tested and the tension reduced to working level. Drilling operations can then commence.

The drilling operation

The rig can then spud in, and for this purpose extends a 36 in (0.9 m) drill bit on the end of the drill string to the seabed and drills a hole deep enough to receive about 300 ft (91 m) of 30 in (762 mm) casing. The carriage of this casing and the marine riser, of which more shortly, is the first supply task to be carried out by one of the operator's chartered vessels, and these may be lifted aboard the rig while the initial hole is being drilled.

Once the 30 in casing is lowered into position, the 'Christmas tree', which can be described as the seabed valve system connecting the rig to the hole, is added. This unit contains the blow-out preventer and the pipework to allow for the circulation of the drilling fluid. Once this is in position, the marine riser can be attached.

The marine riser consists of enough lengths of 30 in pipe to reach from the drill floor to the Christmas tree. The sections are bolted together, having along their exterior the additional pipework required to receive the drilling fluids. They are always painted white and, because they are flanged at the ends, are difficult for the supply vessels to carry. Indeed, complete riser systems have been lost over the stern of anchor handlers in heavy weather.

The other requirements needed at the start on the hole must also be transported to the rig. These consist of cement, oil-based mud and drill water, as well as 1000 ft (305 m) of 20 in and about 4000 ft (1220 m) of $13\frac{3}{8}$ in casing.

On board the rig, the drilling cycle proper commences. A 26 in (660 mm) drill bit is used to drill 1000 ft (305 m) into the substrata, then the drill string is pulled out of the hole and the casing run. The casing lines the hole and, when it is positioned, cement is pumped from the bottom up so that it is firmly held in position. Then a $17\frac{1}{2}$ in (445 mm) bit is used and drilling starts in earnest. As the drill bit rotates, oil-based mud is pumped down the centre of the drill string and is allowed to flow back up the outside, carrying with it the debris and providing a hydrostatic head (Figure 6). The usual drilling fluid requirement is about 2000 barrels, hence modern supply ships are designed to carry this amount. Should the ships on charter be unable to fulfil this requirement, two ships must be available on the location at the same time, carrying the total quantity required.

Oil-based mud, currently the favoured drilling fluid, consists of gas oil with as many of the toxic constituents removed as possible, to which chemicals are added to raise the viscosity so that it can hold in suspension the quantity of barytes required to provide the weight. As well as providing good lubrication it has other essential qualities, the primary one being that it does not react with any of the substrata as water-based mud sometimes does.

Once drilling is under way the ships have the task of keeping the rig supplied with the basics of living: food, potable water and fuel for the generators. The drillers also call for special chemicals to add to the drilling fluid and special tools to assist in the drilling operation. The ships are sailed out with these items usually on a fairly ad hoc basis, and if they are part of larger operations may call at the rig as part of a run which involves discharge and loading at several locations.

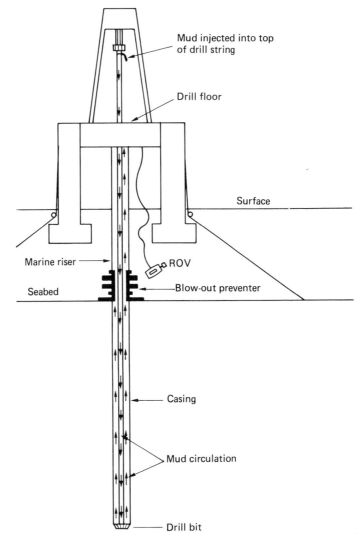

Figure 6   *A semi-submersible and drill hole*

When drilling has reached a depth of about 4000 ft (1220 m) the drillers will call for $9\frac{5}{8}$ in casing. Being loaded with casing used to be the cause of considerable distress aboard the supply ships, for two reasons. Firstly, it was usually called for far in advance of the time when it would be required, necessitating the ship remaining on the location for long periods while space was made on the rig; secondly, all casing must be measured individually so that the exact length will be known to the drillers when it is connected together and lowered into the hole. Because of the limited deck space available on the rig, it was customary for each length to be measured during unloading from the supply ship, making the discharge time extremely lengthy, i.e. between 12 and 24 hours. If the master was lucky he might be able to tie up, and if even more fortunate the weather might remain calm. However, the more likely event was interminably long periods of snatching.

Today it is more usual for the rig to make space and to discharge all the casing from the ship at once, and measure it later.

Drilling continues and once a depth of about 10 000 ft (3000 m) has been reached the $9\frac{5}{8}$ in (245 mm) casing is run. After this, drilling resumes with an $8\frac{1}{2}$ in (190 mm) drill bit to a depth of up to 17 000 ft (5000 m), when the same procedure is carried out with 7 in (178 mm) casing.

It is possible that by now the well has been assessed as being dry, or that oil has been struck. If it is still felt that the oil bearing strata lie beneath the level which has been reached, a down-hole survey may be carried out.

Down-hole survey

This operation will involve one of the supply vessels which will be loaded with a position-fixing system, the necessary computers and a means of detonating under-water explosions, usually an air-gun. The ship will be required to operate from a fixed position at a distance from the rig, firing the air-gun when required; meanwhile, on the rig the signal reflected from the substrata is received by geophones lowered down the hole.

Testing the flow

If oil has been discovered, a supply ship will be required to transport quantities of equipment to allow for the rate of flow of oil to be tested. While the oil is flowing it will be burnt off using flare booms which the rig deploys. Once this is done, the well can be capped and the rig is ready to move on. If the hole turns out to be dry, it is plugged with cement and the top section of casing blown off with explosives and retrieved, leaving the seabed level.

Now the anchor handlers are recalled and the anchors recovered, and the rig is towed away to another location. The procedure for a jack-up is of course similar except that, instead of the anchors being deployed, the rig must be held in the correct position while the legs are jacked down onto the seabed. Jack-ups also use smaller craft for towing, since they are dimensionally much smaller than semi's; however, from there on the process is the same.

From the foregoing it can be seen that marine support is essential to every stage of the hole and that effectiveness of the supply operation is as important as efficiency on the drill floor. That being said, the drill floor always has priority in the allocation of crane time: understandable, but frustrating for the ships. In this area the accountants have come to the aid of the supply ship crews so that the rig crews have become aware of the financial penalties of holding ships alongside unnecessarily, so some sort of balance is being reached.

2 Ship handling

Introduction

In the world of the supply vessel, ship handling bears little relationship to conventional practice. To start with, the majority of ship handling is done with the vessel stationary rather than moving; secondly, it is mainly carried out with the operator facing astern. On supply vessels ship handling is known as driving, and this is what it is called in this book. There is nothing illogical in the term: it simply indicates that the operator is continuously handling the controls in order to achieve the desired response from the vessel.

Propulsion configurations

In this chapter all types of ships with most known configurations will be dealt with.

The simplest modern supply ship has a single tunnel thruster forward with twin CP propellers and conventional rudders. Possible variations on this are the addition of Becker rudders, some of which can be split, an azimuthing thruster instead of the tunnel thruster, twin bow thrusters, twin bow thrusters and a stern thruster, or even twin azimuthing thrusters. Vessels are still in service with fixed-pitch propellers, the change of direction of the propellers being achieved by clutches and gearboxes. There is very little advantage to the operator in this configuration but it does have some advantages due to simplicity and cost savings.

Unfortunately for those who consider that there are already enough variations, the situation is further complicated: by the presence or absence of Kort nozzles on the anchor handlers; where Kort nozzles are not present, whether the screws turn inward or outward; and when considering the effect of the screw rotation, whether the ship is fitted with CP or fixed-pitch propellers.

From very early in the development of the North Sea supply ship the Norwegians opted for CP propellers and a single tunnel thruster, whereas the British at the same time were building ships with fixed-pitch propellers and a forward azimuthing

Figure 7   *The screws of an anchor handler, CP propellers, Kort nozzles and Becker flap rudders. Note the position of this equipment in relation to the stern*

thruster or even a tunnel thruster. These early anchor handlers were usually about 5000 or 6000 bhp (3750 or 4500 kW).

Typical British anchor handlers of the early 1970s were powered by two Allen diesel engines developing 5700 bhp with a Gill-jet azimuthing thruster, itself powered by a 500 bhp (375 kW) Caterpillar in the bow-thruster room under the accommodation. The twin rudders were — or are — controlled by a single lever on the console. Most of these ships are still in service somewhere in the world.

Essentially, the manoeuvring tasks required of the supply ship are:

• to be able to move in any direction on any heading;
• to be able to berth alongside in spaces no greater in length than the length of the ship;
• to be able to maintain a stationary position within the radius of an offshore crane;
• to be able to manoeuvre reasonably while restricted by tow-wires, rig anchors and cables, the vessel's own anchor and cable, or any other restriction one's charterer may think of.

Indeed sometimes it appears that some sort of cosmic game is being played with the supply ship master who, on apparently achieving the impossible, is almost immediately faced with something even more difficult.

The basic trick in supply ship driving is the balance of the engines and thruster, so that they all may be producing thrust but this is balanced so that the ship does not move. This is apparently not unlike the technique required to fly a helicopter, where the pilot's main endeavour is to stop it rotating in the direction opposite to the main rotor.

The class of vessel which has just been described includes such venerable craft as the *Oil Venturer*, the *Oil Discoverer*, the *Cromarty Service*, *Forties Service* and others built in 1973 and 1974. It also includes some of the Stirling platform supply

Figure 8   *The aft controls of a UT708*
Right: tiller, engine controls, rudder indicator, deck tannoy
Centre: joystick
Left: forward thrusters, aft thrusters, ER telephone, VHF radio

ships built in the late 1970s and even a class of TNT vessels including the *TNT Lion* and *TNT Tiger* which were built to a Stirling design in 1983.

The controls available to the master of this class of vessel are in most cases a pair of throttles which usually have a neutral and an astern setting, i.e. a combined throttle and direction control. I have avoided the use of the word 'combinator' since this term is generally used in relation to CP controls, described later. There will be, in the case of the Gill-jet or other type of azimuthing thruster, a direction control and a throttle control, and a rudder control. Instrumentation should consist of rudder indicators, and rev counters for the main engines and for the bow thruster.

Inward turning and outward turning screws

Before entering into the details of actual control it may be worth while to discuss the effects on the ship of inward turning and outward turning screws. With a single screw there is a thrust in one direction which is overcome when the ship is moving forward by the rudder, but takes effect when the ship is moving astern.

On twin screw vessels, when one engine is set ahead and the other is set astern the stern will tend to move in the direction of the ahead engine, or towards the side of the ahead engine, because of the turning effect due to the screws being off centre. If the screws are outward turning when the ship is moving ahead then, when one engine is ahead and one astern on a ship with fixed-pitch propellers, both screws will be turning the same way and both screws will be contributing to the turning effect.

In the event of the screws being inward turning, the screw effect will counter the tendency of the ship to turn due to the off-centre position of the screws. The effect will be different on CP ships since the screws will always turn the same way and therefore will always cancel each other out, whether the engines are going ahead or astern. However, should the vessel be operating on one engine, this effect needs to be taken into consideration. If the screw turns outwards then the screw effect will add to the tendency of the ship to turn due to the position of the screw; if it is inward turning it will tend to reduce it. The effects will be opposite if the ship is going astern.

The effect of feathering CP propellers

A more important effect of CP propellers is the change of direction which results if the pitch is returned to zero while the ship still has way on. This is a well-known effect with single screw ships, and is less appreciated but just the same with twin screw ships. If one screw is feathered the ship will tend to move in the direction of the side on which the screw is feathered.

Moving sideways

Moving sideways with the screws only

On a ship with outward turning screws it is supposed to be possible to make the ship move sideways, or 'crab', without the assistance of a bow thruster. In fact the Becker rudder is said to have been developed for just this purpose for marine operations completely unrelated to the oil industry.

The principle is that, even though the rudders and the screws are close together, they still create a lever. If the rudders are placed amidships and the engines are set to cant the stern away from the quay, then if the correct rudder setting is put on in the opposite direction the ship should move out bodily. If too much rudder is put on, the stern will begin to swing back, though the bow will be swinging out.

Few of these effects apply to vessels with Kort nozzles, since virtually all the transverse effect is masked. However, feathering the screws with way on will have an effect and feathering a single screw will drag the stern over.

Driving the ship facing the stern

We have yet to consider the effect of the rudders on the transverse movement of the stern, and at this point it seems a good idea to provide a few hints as to how to deal with the curious situation resulting from having to learn to drive the ship facing both forwards and backwards.

Before operation of the controls becomes a natural response it is helpful to visualize the jets of water resulting from the propeller and thruster movements. This automatically indicates what is likely to happen to the ship and makes it easy to assess the effect of application of rudder. It also makes it possible to visualize what is likely to happen to the ship regardless of the direction in which the driver

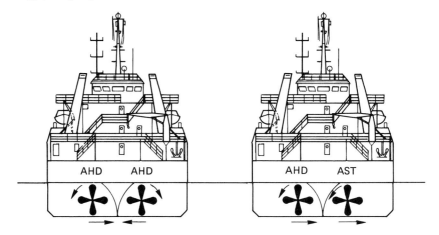

Fixed pitch propellers — outward turning screws:
Transverse thrust assists the turning effect

(a)

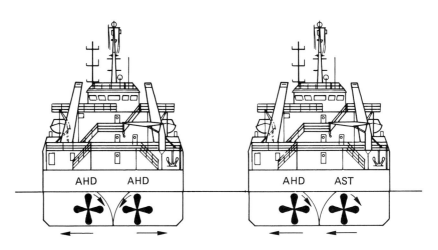

Fixed pitch propellers — inward turning screws:
Transverse thrust reduces the turning effect

(b)

Figure 9 *The effects of inward turning and outward turning screws*

is facing, and makes it unnecessary to remember which side is port and which is starboard.

Moving sideways: effect of rudder position

Visualizing the streams of water beneath the ship, one engine should be put ahead and the other astern. Having got the stern moving sideways by dint of crossing the

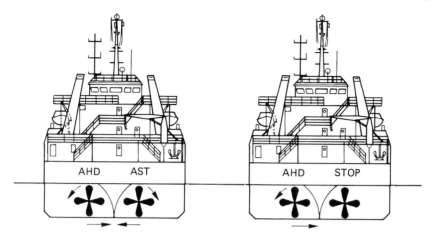

CP propellers — outward turning screws:
Only with one engine stopped does
transverse thrust help the turning effect

(c)

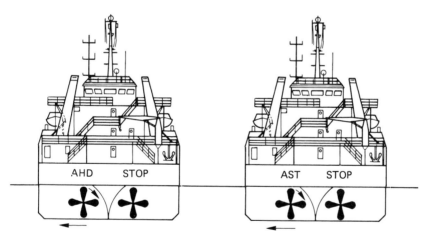

CP propellers — inward turning screws:
With one engine stopped going ahead reduces the
turning effect, going astern increases it

(d)

sticks, this movement may be augmented or reduced by positioning the rudders, the result depending somewhat on what type are fitted. The sideways movement due to rudder position is virtually unaffected by the presence of Kort nozzles.

To augment the speed of the sideways movement of the stern, the rudder should be put over so that the stream of water being projected astern from the ahead engine is deflected past the other screw; the speed of movement can then be increased or reduced by altering the rudder angle.

Once the rudders are put over in the opposite direction so that the stream of water from the ahead engine is directed against the movement of the stern, the swing will be slowed down. If they are put far enough over there is a chance that the swing may be countered altogether, and where Becker rudders are fitted it is likely that, despite the position of the screws, the stern may move slowly in the opposite direction. However, it should be remembered that, when using Becker rudders in the hard-over position, so much of the water flow is directed sideways that some adjustment to the engines may be required to stop the ship moving astern.

The ability of the rudders to stop the sideways movement of the stern is an essential ingredient in the process of manoeuvring ships with fixed-pitch propellers, since the sideways movement may be stopped without declutching the engines. This saves the operator from the stress of having to wait for eight seconds while the engines clutch in in the opposite direction: eight seconds can seem like a lifetime in the close proximity of an offshore installation with the crane hooked onto a lift on the deck.

In the logical process of things the stern of a supply ship may be moved in either direction by crossing the engines, and the speed of that movement altered by using the rudders. In still water the astern engine will require slightly higher revs or more pitch to stop the ship from moving forward, and if the rudders are hard over the astern component may need to be reduced because of the deflection of the flow of water from the ahead engine.   .

To move the ship sideways it is now purely a matter of applying bow thrust to keep the bow moving at the same speed as the stern, so with little effort the basic and most used supply ship manoeuvre has been achieved. In general, on ships with a single bow thruster, whether it be an azimuthing thruster or a tunnel thruster, the stern can be moved sideways faster than the bow. On this type of craft, if maximum bow thrust is applied, the stern can keep pace with the bow using about half power on both the ahead and the astern engines with the rudders hard over. Hence it is bow thruster power which is the key to ease of manoeuvring in bad weather conditions.

Use of azimuthing thrusters

While the azimuthing thruster has some advantages over the tunnel thruster, when it comes to power output for any given engine power the azimuthing thruster is less effective since the jet from it is directed at an angle downwards, and there is therefore a vertical component. In an attempt to overcome this disadvantage, azimuthing thrusters have been developed which are lowered below the hull or, more recently, hinged down from the hull. While they perform better offshore it is not possible to use them in port, because they add a metre or so to the draught, and have a tendency to get bent on the seabed.

What then is the advantage of the azimuthing thruster? The answer is that by themselves they can propel the ship in any direction. This is not much of an advantage on ships fitted with CP propellers, but can be a great help on ships with fixed-pitch propellers. The main engines on vessels with fixed-pitch propellers have a minimum speed, and one engine on the 5700 bhp (4275 kW) anchor handler will propel the ship at a minimum speed of four knots. Therefore if one engine is down the ship can be manoeuvred with the thruster, certainly up and down the quay, and it can be of considerable help berthing and unberthing. In calm weather offshore it can be used to manoeuvre under the cranes. In the event of total engine failure it can be used to drive the ship along.

Multiple thrusters

For some time ship owners and builders have been aware of the potential weakness in a ship's manoeuvring capability due to lack of thruster power. Since the size of a single thruster is limited by noise and vibration, many ships are now fitted with twin thrusters to increase the total side thrust available. These can usually be operated either individually or with a single control. A typical installation would be two 700 bhp thrusters, giving 1400 bhp (1050 kW) in all. At this point it is worth remembering that some of the early anchor handlers had only 2000 bhp (1500 kW) available for the main engines.

Stern thrusters are also fitted on some of the more powerful anchor handlers and on virtually all modern platform supply vessels. The presence of a stern thruster makes manoeuvring a supply vessel sideways an extremely simple matter: one is required solely to set the thrust at one end and adjust the thrust at the other to suit.

We can now move on to some of the actual manoeuvres that supply ships are required to carry out.

Berthing and unberthing

Supply ships are usually required to berth and unberth in extremely restricted areas. North Sea ports are used as examples, because they provide a number of variations of conditions, will be familiar to many and there is no doubt that their idiosyncrasies must be duplicated elsewhere, particularly since there is a tendency for port operators to allocate supply ships to the older parts of their domains, where the water is shallower and the berths are shorter.

There is a tendency for new supply ship masters to be so entranced with their new-found ability to go sideways that, particularly in port, they forget that the quickest way to move a ship is forwards or backwards. Hence the first maxim must be that the berth is approached as closely as possible before moving sideways.

On more powerful ships there is also a tendency to fail to take into account current or wind direction, and while the required result can usually be achieved in the long run, considerable time and energy can be expended pushing the ship sideways into a current. On river berths such as those in the River Tay the ship may be put alongside by holding it against the current and then angling the bow in slightly towards the quay. She will then drift inward until she is alongside. At the Oil (former Norscott) Base at Lerwick there are usually miles of open quay, but unless the berth is approached closely in a conventional manner it can take an age to put the ship alongside. This is because the tide flows under the quay and then back out into the harbour, pushing the ship away.

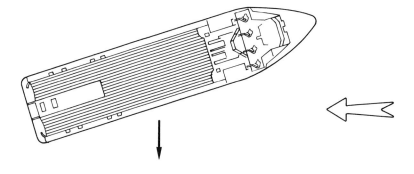

Ship pushed away from quay by waterflow

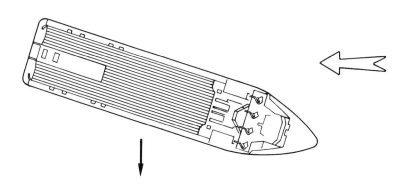

Ship pushed towards quay by waterflow

Figure 10   *The effect of waterflow when putting the ship alongside*

Much more of a supply ship is visible from the after control position than the forward one, so masters tend to move about astern when it would be more efficient to move ahead. Before the inner dock entrance was widened in Aberdeen ships could frequently be seen going through the cut astern. In this way the masters had more of the ship ahead of them. They then turned in the restricted area of the inner dock.

However, despite the fact that there is very little of the ship ahead of the wheelhouse, it only takes a little practice to steer the ship through quite narrow passages. If the cut to be steered through is really narrow it is worth while to pick the course off the chart since, while it is easy enough to steer the forward end of the vessel for the centre, checking the course ensures that the rest of the ship behind is not trailing along at an angle. This technique is also useful when entering drydocks.

It is also important to remember the result of using the engines and bow thruster for turning in restricted areas. If only the bow thruster is used the ship will appear to be turning round a central point, but actually the turning centre is closer to the stern. Likewise with the engines: while the vessel may appear to be turning on the spot, in fact the turning centre is closer to the bow.

Berthing alongside other vessels

Supply ships are frequently required to berth alongside each other. There is no hazard attached to this. They all have suitable hull strengthening and are well fendered. However, should a supply ship be required to berth alongside a conventional ship, some care should be taken.

When going alongside another supply vessel the ship should be facing the same way as the ship to be berthed against. If it is not in sight and if it is positioned in a restricted area it will be worth asking the harbour control which way round it is so that the approach can be made facing in the correct direction. When berthing against a conventional ship the chances are that it will be an all-aft coaster. It may then be worth considering berthing bow to stern, since the general form of the two vessels will then match. Coasters are usually unfendered and there is a possibility, if a coaster is low in the water, that the fendering of a large supply vessel may foul its rails. There is no way to avoid this except not to berth against it.

High speed manoeuvring

Almost all manoeuvring in port can be done at slow speed. High speed manoeuvres are unlikely to save time, and vastly increase the potential for doing damage to one's own or other craft. An extra two minutes spent coming alongside can save hours of paperwork.

There are exceptions and these should be recognized. It is, for instance, necessary to enter Torry Dock at Aberdeen at a reasonable speed. This dock lies at an angle of about 70 degrees to the river Dee which always flows fairly rapidly towards the sea. The outflow can be very strong after heavy rain or when the snow is melting in the hills. Any vessel turning out of the river into the dock must therefore do so at sufficient speed to avoid getting set down by the current onto the corner of the downstream side of the dock or, even worse, onto a ship, if there is one lying alongside.

It is also necessary to be positive when steaming with the tide in the Yarmouth river, or any other fast-flowing estuary. It is essential to maintain steerage way even though this may seem to be incredibly fast. It is unnerving to see the ships alongside flashing past at 6–8 knots, but even worse to find oneself heading towards one, or becoming jammed across the river. The azimuthing thruster comes into its own here. If it is set so that it would in theory propel the ship astern, this will slow down the ship without reducing its steering capability. Of course the tunnel thruster may also be used to assist with steering, though it should be used in conjunction with the rudders, not instead of them.

Those unfamiliar with supply ships may be wondering what the pilot is up to during these activities; the answer is, probably nothing. Supply ship masters tend not to use pilots if they have the choice, and indeed may be discouraged from doing so by their charterers, since pilots' services are not cheap. In addition, the rules concerning the use of pilots vary from place to place, but whether they are on board or not the only function they serve is that of adviser on local conditions. Pilots almost never function as ship handlers on supply ships.

In general it is probably a good idea to take a pilot at unfamiliar ports whose local conditions are not obvious from the chart, or where there is no indication as to where the ship is to berth.

Snatching

Snatching cargo at offshore installations has now become the rule rather than the exception, though in the early days it was, as the term implies, an emergency procedure to be used only when the vessel was unable to tie up and an urgent lift was required. Due to the limited manoeuvring capability of the ships, not least that they had no thrusters, they would try to get within range of the crane and drift slowly past. During this transit the crane would lower its hook and the lift would be attached and then lifted off. With the advent of the bow thruster it became possible to hold the ship under the crane for quite long periods, or at least to get the stern within the arc of the boom at frequent intervals. By pulling lifts down the deck with the tugger winches it became possible to discharge most or all of the deck cargo in this way.

As platforms began to be installed in the northern North Sea it became more essential to snatch cargo, since many of the installations started off without mooring systems, and some of them, such as the *Thistle* platform, never had any fitted. It therefore became necessary to discharge not only deck cargo in this manner, but also bulk cargoes. To facilitate this part of the operation the platforms simply extended their hoses to give the supply ships longer scope.

Snatching has therefore tended to become the norm rather than the exception and much of the manoeuvring capability fitted to supply ships is installed with this activity in mind. For this reason the funnels of most ships have gradually been moved forward until they come up on either side of the bridge, or in some cases through the centre of the wheelhouse. On old designs such as the Ulstein 704 the funnels have been cut off so that the driver can see over the top of them.

Remaining within the range of the crane boom is therefore probably the most important supply ship activity. Fortunately the offshore cranes have also developed with this in mind, and the cranes on more modern platforms can reach any part of the vessel while it stands off at a reasonable distance. Rig cranes, however, are still limited, and there are some extremely short jibs still in service. Indeed, it is sad to report that some unmanned platforms are being built with crane jibs so short that when the supply ship is within range of them, the driver cannot see the deck: a banksman has to be used to guide the crane.

Figure 11 *A small anchor handler snatching at* Ninian Central. *The pipe-laying barge* Viking Piper *is in the background*

Positioning the ship for snatching

Given freedom of choice the first thing to decide is which side of the installation to work, and all things being equal the obvious choice is the lee side. The classic snatching position is on the lee side of the installation with the vessel at right angles to the rig, so that the crane jibs out over the deck when at right angles to the side of the installation.

This position gives the best view from the bridge regardless of the position of the funnels. It also provides the quickest means of escape from the locality of the installation.

Working with the wind astern

To work in this position with the wind astern is very simple for the driver. On a vessel with CP propellers it is solely a matter of putting sufficient astern power on both engines to hold up against the wind and then steering with the bow thruster. Alternatively it is usually possible to manoeuvre the stern without using the thruster, by putting the engines astern individually.

On a vessel with fixed-pitch propellers it would be unusual to be able to put both engines astern for reasons already described. Hence it is still necessary to put one engine ahead and the other astern, obviously with much more power on the astern engine. By putting the rudders over against the engines it may be possible to cancel the sideways movement, but if not the ship should be canted slightly across the wind to cancel out the sideways movement, and then balanced using the bow thruster.

Most ships are fitted with compass repeaters at the after driving position. Without one the driver is deprived of an essential and relatively cheap aide, and ship owners who do not fit them should be persuaded to do so. Knowledge of the ship's head is invaluable when carrying out manoeuvres offshore.

Holding position

Having achieved a comfortable position for the ship, its relationship with the legs of the installation should be fixed in the mind, together with the ship's compass heading. Gradually as time passes it will become automatic to restore the ship to the correct position if it starts to drift off, as it will to maintain the correct heading. If the heading is not kept in mind it is very easy to drift round gradually to an entirely unsuitable heading, until one finds oneself drifting away, or in trouble.

Of course, the position just described is not suitable at all times. For a variety of reasons the ship may be required to work on the windward side. It may be that the lee crane is out of order ('down' in the vernacular), that the installation has to work its cargo on that side, that the hoses are on that side, or sometimes that there are waves sweeping up the deck which will be avoided if the ship is head to wind.

When is it safe to work?

This last situation raises the question, 'When is it not safe to work, and who decides?' In general it is left to the master to decide, and the first criterion is whether the crew will be safe on the deck, hence consideration as to whether the ship might be able to work head to wind. If it is considered that the men can work on the deck it must then be decided whether the ship can manoeuvred safely in the proximity of the installation. In most cases this second consideration becomes unnecessary, but on ships with tanks round the cargo deck and multi-thrusters it is a situation which may have to be considered. Should the master say that it is not

Figure 12 *A sea rushing up the deck of an anchor handler. This might have been avoided by ballasting up*

possible to work, the installation is bound to accept this, and if there is no great urgency there is unlikely to be any problem. However, in the event of urgent lifts being required the ship may be pressured into doing something. In this situation unfortunately commercial considerations come into play. Even if the weather makes work totally impossible it is important to show willing and go in and test the conditions.

Unfortunately from this point it is impossible to give further guidance. It really is in the hands of the master. The ship should be placed in the best possible position and then the opinion sought of those who have to go out on the deck.

Having said all this, with the increase in size and power of the modern supply vessel it is becoming more and more common for the installation management to call a halt before the ship does. Many installations will not operate their cranes in wind speeds in excess of 45 knots, which in itself limits their ability to work.

Some operators are also beginning to define precise limits to working conditions, particularly where wave-measuring devices are present. They are also limiting weather-side working to lower wave heights than lee-side working. Obviously these limits differ, but rules of about 4 metres significant wave height to leeward and 3 metres to windward seem to be coming more and more common. These values equate to about 6.5 m maximum and 4.5 m maximum wave height.

Heavy lifts

Special thought should be given to working with heavy lifts, which for most installations are anything over 8 tonnes, since these require the cranes to use their double blocks and also restrict the radius. Obviously if the crane radius is restricted the ship must be closer to the installation than would otherwise be required. On most rigs the heavy lift radius requires that the ship be extremely close, and that the lift be placed as far aft as possible. On platforms the crane will usually plumb about halfway up the deck in the heavy lift mode with the vessel stern on.

Consideration must also be given to the vertical movement of the ship. The big block is always extremely slow, so the crane driver cannot follow the movement of the ship. Hence it is possible for a lift to land heavily enough to damage the deck or some part of the deck structure.

Working head to wind

In the head-to-wind position, stern to the rig or platform, the ship is obviously being set back all the time (Figure 13). In theory it is possible to set the engines ahead to counter the wave action and keep the head directly into the wind by steering with the bow thruster. Again, having noted the wind direction, the after compass repeater should be used for this purpose. If there is also a head swell the task becomes less simple, since swells tend to pick up the ship and roll it along bodily.

The best way of dealing with swells is to put plenty of ahead power on as the bow of the ship is lifted and then take it off as the swell rolls past the stern. In fact some astern power may be needed at this moment because the ship will tend to slide down the back of the swell.

If possible, snatching to windward on a ship with fixed-pitch propellers should be avoided. Having the ship immobile for eight seconds if one feels the need to change engines may be more than the nerves can stand. However, there may be masters of ships with fixed-pitch propellers who have developed a technique for

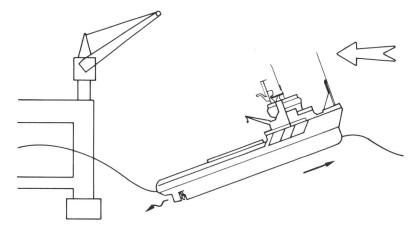

Head to wind in rough weather:
Go ahead to counter swell effect

Figure 13 *Head to wind in rough weather: go ahead to counter the swell effect*

coping with this situation. One of the great joys of the supply boat business is that there is no limit to innovation.

The stern-on position developed because it allowed the vessel to escape in the event of any difficulty, particularly the failure of an engine or a thruster. With the ship on the lee side it would be expected to drift away, therefore putting neither it or the installation in danger.

The design of the early North Sea supply ships tended to encourage them to lie in this position since most of them had funnels placed aft of the bridge, on either side of the winch. Although this gave a clear view of the stern, large areas on the quarters were obscured. As time has passed the funnels have gradually crept forward from their original position on either side of the working deck aft until, on the modern ships, they are usually located on either side of the bridge, or sometimes through the centre so that the driver gets a clear view from forward of the beam to astern.

Working beam-on

It is now the norm that supply ships may take up any position which may be convenient either for themselves or the platform, so given the option it is good policy to lie stern to wind even if this results in the ship lying parallel to the platform. However, if the captain is given the choice he should opt for the side that provides the easiest escape. There is usually one side that allows the bow to be clear of the installation because of the position of the crane, flare boom etc.

Being beam-on to the installation does allow the driver to judge the distance off much more accurately and if hoses are attached to the ship they can be seen more easily. This is particularly true of many modern platform supply ships with tanks round the cargo deck, where distance off cannot be estimated by judging the amount of sea visible between the stern and the legs of the installation.

Many installations also favour beam-on working because it allows them to pick out individual lifts from anywhere on the deck.

Figure 14 *A PSV close to the legs of the* Montrose A. *The platform does not look likely to be able to withstand heavy impact*

Having achieved the correct position beam-on to the installation, the driver should once more check the heading and note the position of the ship against the legs through the side windows of the bridge. It is then easy to see whether the ship is moving forward or aft.

If the ship is required to lie head to wind, beam-on, it is a good idea to put the wind slightly on one bow so that if the head falls off it will do so away from the structure. This naturally requires the driver to be pushing the ship towards the installation all the time, and if he stops doing so the ship should drift away as well as astern. Should he need to escape ahead then the ship should be moving away from the structure.

Unfortunately this advice placed the drivers of ships with fixed-pitch propellers in something of a Catch 22 situation. If it is really necessary to work head to wind on one of these ships it would be most prudent to have the engines crossed so that the ship naturally moves sideways away from the platform, but if it is so positioned that the wind will tend to blow it away from the structure then the controls are set to move the ship the wrong way.

It is possible that the problem can be solved by crossing the engines to push the stern away and then putting the rudders hard over in the opposite direction and balancing with the bowthruster accordingly, though this solution would not be open to vessels with Kort nozzles and without Becker rudders.

Many modern supply ships are fitted with two bow thrusters and a stern thruster and it is possible to put then into any position alongside structures in wind speeds up to about 30 knots. However, they are still vulnerable to being swept sideways by big swells, since thruster response is much slower than main engine response. It is also an unalterable fact that a ship to windward is going to be in big trouble in the event of any mechanical failure. It is this possibility which constantly exercises the minds of the marine departments of most of the operators.

Recently platform operators have become much more sensitive about ships working to windward as the result of a Department of Trade investigation which discovered that a 2000 tonne supply vessel hitting a platform at 2 knots could be expected to do sufficient structural damage to make the platform unsafe. This has given rise to a spate of instructions to ships and to the resurrection of in-field mooring projects which have been gathering dust for years.

Possibly another cardinal rule for the supply ship driver should be 'I will not be the one to test the 2000 tonne theory'.

The joystick

Single-stick manoeuvring capability is now a requirement for virtually all vessels operating in the North Sea, essentially to allow cargo operations to take place without the use of ropes, and to allow the master to handle the ship for very long periods.

In essence, the joystick (Figure 15) is connected to a computer which is interfaced with the gyro-compass to maintain the set heading. When the stick is moved in any direction the computer activates the engines, thrusters and rudders to move the ship in that direction. This would appear to simplify the task to the point where little thought is needed. However, the reality is rather different.

The basic ability of the system to maintain the heading is its most useful component, and beyond this the ease of use depends on the ship's hardware, engines thrusters and rudders, the sensitivity which is designed into the control, and the programming of the software.

Figure 15 *Operating the joystick. Also visible ahead of the driver are three rudder controls, two rudder indicators and the gyro repeater*

Programming

The computer is fitted with an Eprom, a programmable chip, which will sub-sequently respond to specific movements of the stick, and this programming is usually carried out when the vessel is on sea trials. Needless to say this activity may well come bottom of the list of necessary operations, so the master on board the vessel at this time should ensure that the programming is carried out properly, both for his own benefit and that of subsequent incumbents of his position.

Before programming commences the master should ensure that when the main engine controls are in the neutral position the propellers are feathered. This will provide the programmer with proper references.

The programmer will probably have existing data available which will allow him to put in a basic program which should operate the ship effectively. The stick should then be tried out to see if it responds correctly in all directions.

Full speed ahead and astern are the easiest positions, and if a 'Low Gain' control is fitted the manoeuvring speed ahead and astern are obviously the easiest to define. The only rudder or thruster inputs likely to occur are those which will maintain the heading.

Next, the full sideways positions should be set up. Here the thrusters or thruster/rudder combinations must be adjusted so that the bow and stern are balanced. This must be done with the gyro interface disconnected, otherwise this balance will automatically be readjusted.

Similarly the diagonals must be set up without the gyro input so that the ship will maintain its heading while moving at 45 degrees to it, either astern or ahead. The ahead diagonal is particularly difficult to set up on vessels with low thruster power forward, since the increasing forward speed will often cause the rudders to take over so that the ship describes a circle. It is worth putting in time to getting this right, since incorrect setting up will be a cross the ship is likely to have to bear for ever afterwards.

Using the joystick

Most joysticks have no point of reference on them so the probable operating technique is for the master to place the ship in the correct position under the crane and then switch controls. The system will immediately take over the main-tenance of the heading and in all but totally calm and tide-free conditions the ship will gradually begin to drift away from the correct position. The master will then put the stick over in the opposite direction to the ship's natural movement, and the thrusters and engines will bring it back into position. The action must be taken gently and cautiously so that the ship does not move past the correct position in the opposite direction. The stick is then returned to the central position.

Only on units where the position of the stick is marked by indicators may it be possible to adjust the power so that the ship exactly counters the effect of wind and tide. Curiously, this allows the master to duplicate almost exactly the operation of thrusters and engines manually, but in this case the computer maintains the heading.

Anchoring in confined waters
One of the problems of supply vessels at anchor is their tendency to sail back and

forth in the wind. This makes it difficult to tell whether the ship is dragging and, if several ships are anchored in close proximity, increases the danger of their touching each other.

It may be difficult to visualize the situation where a vessel could find itself so constrained, but nevertheless it does occur. If the period at anchor is not to be too long, the ship's thrusters can be left running and the joystick switched on. The heading will then be maintained and the ship will lie quietly at anchor.

Tying up to offshore installations

It will be apparent to the reader from the preceding section that tying up is becoming less and less common as time passes, and even if weather conditions are favourable and ropes are available many masters prefer to snatch. This is certainly true of the North Sea, although tying up may still be common in other parts of the world.

This is probably because there is a certain amount of preparation involved; however, if the weather is good and such a facility is available then it should be used. The result is a great reduction in concentration and the inevitable fatigue that snatching involves. Delays for helicopters and deck lifts are of no consequence, and multiple hoses may be passed down to the ship, all of which may save time in the long run.

The manner of tying up in the North Sea has always been to put an anchor down forward and tie up astern with two ropes which are attached to the legs of the installation (Figure 16). In extremely calm offshore waters, such as Lake Maracaibo and the Gulf of Mexico, the installations have facilities for supply ships to tie up alongside.

Before supply ships were fitted with thrusters, tying up was almost essential. The ships dropped an anchor some way off the installation and then backed up into the wind or current until they were within range of the crane.

As ships developed it became common practice for them to drop an anchor and then approach the rig bow on. This technique was used principally because it seemed possible to lay the cable straighter with a reasonable amount of way on the vessel.

The distance away from the rig at which the anchor is let go depends principally on the amount of cable carried by the ship, since in any depth of water the objective is to lay as much cable as possible. This rule can be said to apply to about 600 ft (185 m) since it is uncommon to anchor in greater depths. If one were to consider anchoring in water depths greater than this some thought should be given to whether the windlass is capable of recovering the cable.

If fifteen shackles of cable are fitted to the ship then the anchor should be let go at one and a half cables. If twenty or more shackles are fitted, the anchor should be let go at two cables.

Running in bow-to

The sequence of operations to anchor at an offshore installation, approaching it with the ship going ahead, is as follows.

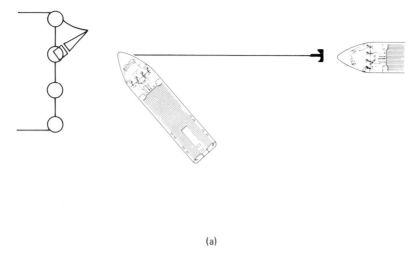

(a)

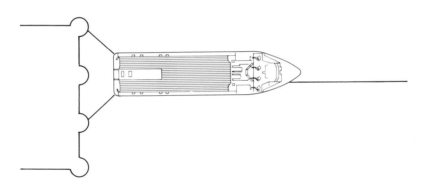

(b)

Figure 16   *(a) A supply vessel swinging into position to tie up to a semi-submersible*
(b) All fast: the crane will reach one-third of the distance up the deck

1 Arrange for a set of whistle signals for use between the bridge and the forecastle, unless the windlass can be operated from the bridge. Traditionally these signals are one blast to let go, two blasts to stop, three blasts to heave away.
2 The ship should be taken out to a position slightly further away than the drop point and the anchor walked back to a depth which leaves approximately one shackle clear of the seabed.
3 The vessel should be aligned on the correct heading. This is usually done by

lining up the legs of the installation under the crane, though some platforms are fitted with sectored lights so that the ship anchoring avoids pipelines.

4 The course should be set for the installation at a speed of between 2 and 4 knots, depending on the speed at which the cable is likely to be paid out. At the let go position one blast should be blown on the whistle. The brake should then be taken off the windlass and the cable allowed to run out.

Any officer entering the supply ship industry is likely to be faced with a number of experiences which are initially terrifying. Letting an anchor go when approaching a rig is one of the worst. The chain appears to describe an arc from the gypsy to the hawse pipe, scattering rust, smoke and sparks in all directions. The temptation is therefore to put the brake on in an attempt to slow down the gypsy. This should be done with caution. To stop paying out the cable may well result in the anchor being dragged along the seabed and the ship being pulled off the correct heading. This will incur the wrath of the master. On the other hand, if too much cable is let out this may result in build-up on the seabed and, if the windlass is not powerful enough to pull them out, the ship will be insecure when tied up.

The ship must be kept going ahead until the bow is as close to the installation as prudence will allow, and the cable should be paid out until the last moment to get it as close as possible to up and down. Only then should the signal be given to stop paying out and the ship turned stern to the installation. While the ship is turning, the officer on the forecastle should be putting the windlass in gear in preparation for heaving away.

It is almost inevitable that during the turn the ship will be pulled away from the structure so, once stern-to, it will be necessary to back up into position. When the stern is facing the rig the ship should be manoeuvred to place the quarter to which the rope is to be made fast as close as possible to the leg to which that rope is secured. This means really close. This will normally be the windward or up-current leg. The crane will lower the end of the rope onto the deck and the crew may detach the hook.

Unless the capstans are particularly well positioned it is usual to heave the rope in by hand until it is as tight as possible and then to turn it down on the bitts. In all cases the maximum number of turns should be put on.

Once the first rope is fast, a crew member should indicate that this is so and then the stern can be manoeuvred across to the other leg, again placing the quarter as close as possible. This can be done quite slowly, since it will take some time for the installation deck crew to get to the second rope and hook it onto the crane.

For the ship to get to the second leg there must be some slack left in the first rope, and fortunately this is usually just the amount which will be available if the first rope was made fast with a bight trailing in the water. Hence, as the first rope tightens up, the other quarter should be close to the second leg. The crane will lower away the second rope and the crew may detach it from the hook. They should then make the second rope fast in the same way as the first, tightening it up as much as possible.

Once both ropes are fast, the master should give the signal to the forecastle for the cable to be heaved in.

It is not yet possible to relax, since there will for some time be sufficient slack in the cable for the ship to touch the installation unless the position is maintained with the engines. Gradually, as the cable begins to take the weight, the ropes will tighten up. On older ships the windlass may be kept going until it is not possible to heave in any more, but with modern high-speed windlasses it is possible to put too much strain on the ropes. The officer on the forecastle should gauge the amount of weight by checking on the catenary of the cable.

Running in stern-to

The technique of running in bow-to was developed because the early supply ships did not have bow thrusters, but since all modern supply ships are so fitted an alternative technique is available.

There is absolutely nothing to stop the master putting the stern of the ship to the rig at the drop position and letting the cable out using the windlass until it is on the bottom. At this moment he can start moving astern at a speed commensurate with the speed of the windlass, which may be quite fast on modern ships. The ship is steered with the bow thruster, and the cable will be laid out on the bottom in a perfectly straight line.

While the actual approach may be slower than that which can be achieved bow-on, once the rig is approached there is no time lost turning round and repositioning the vessel.

As the first leg is approached, the rope will be passed down and the rest of the tie-up will be carried out in a conventional manner.

The advantage of this method is that the cable invariably gets laid out straight on the bottom, with no slack and no kinks, and the officer on the bow will not experience the terror induced by the other method.

Mooring systems

Obviously there are endless variations in mooring systems, water depths and holding ground. There are a number of different make-ups and types of rope, and it must be said that very little thought has gone into mooring systems. It now seems unlikely that they will ever be the subject of genuine improvement since it is becoming less and less common to use them.

Mooring lines may be made of nylon, polypropylene or a combination of nylon and wire. The ends of the ropes may be attached to the legs with chains, chains via shock absorbers, or sometimes rubber tyres. All systems have their own problems. Where connections are made in the lines using links or shackles, the result may be a rope which is so heavy that the tugger winch or capstan must be used to heave it in. This is most frequently the case with systems using wire tails, though once fast these are the most secure.

Polypropylene is the least suitable since, in addition to its vulnerability to sunlight, it chafes very easily. When it was in common use some supply ships had their bitts sleeved with stainless steel in an attempt to reduce this. Should a polypropylene rope be attached to the leg, using a rubber tyre, it can sometimes chaff at that end: should it break, the whole length of rope will fall into the water in close proximity to the stern. Unfortunately, when a rope breaks there is an immediate reaction to go astern, thereby increasing the possibility of putting the rope round the screw.

Systems which are made up of a nylon rope with a wire tail are usually so constructed that when the ship is correctly positioned the connection is just outside the rail. In the event of a ship regularly supplying an installation it is useful to fit a rope tail at the connection between the nylon and the wire. If this is done, when the rope is lowered down, the tail can be secured to the ship's rail and the mooring rope turned up on the bitts. The tail can then be let go.

There are some installations where it is necessary to cross the ropes. Sometimes it is because the horizontal distance between the ropes is small, sometimes because the ropes are connected to the legs at a great height, and sometimes because the manner in which the mooring system has been designed requires it.

Sometimes the mooring rope is connected to a web of two or sometimes three other ropes under or on the other side of the installation. Particularly memorable examples of this arrangement can be found on cruciform rigs such as the *Ocean Kokuei* and the *Sindbad Saxon*. On these rigs the ropes lead from somewhere across the other side of the installation and to stop lateral movement of the stern they must be crossed and tightened up using the tuggers or capstans.

Training in ship handling

Most deck officers join the supply ship industry from the deep sea shipping industry. With very few exceptions they will have no experience at all of ship handling, and their training will be limited to the tying up of theoretical single-screw ships to theoretical quaysides. For the purposes of their future as supply ship officers this is as good as nothing.

Masters must make a positive effort to train their officers to drive their ships, overcoming the natural reluctance to allow others to handle their vessels. In the long term such training will be of personal benefit to them, since on many occasions they will be able to hand over the controls and take a rest.

There will be many times when the ship is doing nothing except drifting about on location, while the rig deck crew have lunch, while waiting for the first anchor, or while another vessel is engaged in some activity at the installation. The temptation is to switch off the thrusters and leave the officer of the watch on the bridge steaming about slowly and waiting for the next move.

The alternative, if it is during the day, and no sleep is going to be disturbed by thruster movements, is to leave the officer of the watch with all the systems operating and tell him to go to the nearest buoy and practice keeping close to it. The officer of the watch can then spend some constructive hours finding out how the ship responds to each control and getting used to operating the ship while facing the stern. It is to be hoped that by now he has read this volume and has the basic concepts in his mind, or that the master has already briefed him with some equivalently suitable means of visualizing what is happening beneath the water.

Once this has been done on a number of occasions the officer will be ready to make his first approach to an installation. The essentials are good weather, no tide, and preferably a single lift to a large platform.

The master should talk the officer through the operation, telling him where to place the ship, and what heading to be on, but should not instruct him as to the actual positions of the controls unless absolutely necessary. An order such as 'Port 30 with the rudders' will switch the learner's mind into neutral and he will just wait for the next command, whereas 'Give it a little more port rudder', will keep him thinking.

Once a single lift has been achieved, the worst is over for the trainee. He has approached a platform and carried out the task. He may now be assigned snatching operations in good weather and no tide. Masters should not miss these opportunities in the North Sea since they are the exception rather than the rule.

When the ability to snatch has been mastered, the trainee may be given tasks such as controlling the vessel with hoses connected up, and as he gains confidence the master will be more able to relax. In addition, the enthusiasm of supply vessel mates to drive the ship is usually such that they will take much of the drudgery of prolonged pumping operations from the master, allowing him to relax for more onerous tasks.

How far the Master may go in delegating the responsibility of shiphandling at offshore installations is discussed in Chapter 8.

Of course, to be able to train a mate in ship handling the ship really needs to have a master and two mates. If the master only has one mate to assist him he inevitably will be doing all the driving while the mate will be working on deck, asleep, or on the bridge while the ship is on passage. It is even unlikely that the mate will be able to have any training in port, since the ship will need two men forward and two aft to tie up.

Ship handling training in port is as important as that offshore, and the mate should be trained in the whole range of activities, from port approach and picking up the pilot to controlling the ship to the berth and putting her alongside. Once more the process may be gradual, starting off with a move from one berth to another, where the quaysides are clear and there are no pressures such as the presence of a pilot to reduce concentration, to the point where the mate can carry out the whole operation and berth the ship anywhere no matter what the challenge.

<table>
<tr><td>

3</td><td>

Anchor handling</td></tr>
</table>

The anchor handler's job

Anchor handling has gained a certain aura over the years: those involved have become members of a 'club' into which one is initiated on one's first anchor job. This must be in some way similar to being a member of the select group who have sailed round the Horn, or who fought in the Battle of Britain. Before that first experience, the terms and tales are at best only imperfectly understood, and at worst a complete mystery. After initiation it is possible to take part in the tales of daring and courage which echo round the walls of hostelries frequented by supply boat men the world over.

There is no mystery to the basic requirement. An exploration rig is held in its drilling position by a spread of eight or ten anchors (Figure 17), and it must remain in that position for the duration of the hole. Obviously it cannot lay the anchors itself, so once it is in position the anchor handlers must run the anchors out from the rig and position them on the sea bed at the correct distance. From this position they must be capable of being recovered and returned to the rig. This chapter deals with the actual mechanics of this exercise.

It is probably easiest to imagine an exploration rig in its drilling position with all anchors out. It will usually be headed in the direction of the prevailing wind, which is north west in the North Sea, and the anchor pattern will be spread out from it, each anchor at 45 degrees from its fellows, so that if the anchors are numbered clockwise from the starboard bow No. 1 will bear 338 degrees, No. 2 will bear 023 degrees, and so on. If the rig mooring system uses wires the anchors will be 1500 metres — close to a mile — from the rig. If chain is being used they will be about half a mile away.

If a system of pennants and buoys is used to mark and recover the anchors, each will be marked with a surface buoy. If a chasing system is used there will be no indication of the anchor positions.

The anchor string

The individual anchor may be dug into the seabed some 800 metres from the rig

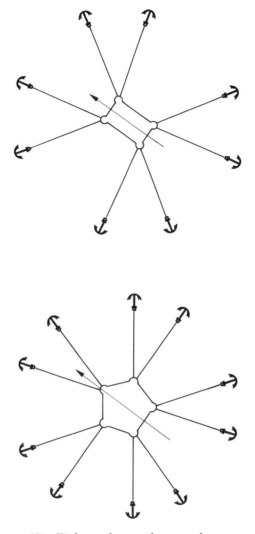

Figure 17   *Eight-anchor and ten-anchor spreads*

but connected to it by 3 inch, $3\frac{1}{4}$ inch or $3\frac{1}{2}$ inch chain. From its crown there will be a short length of chain, and connected to that a number of pennants (wires with a hard eye in either end), the length and number depending on the water depth.

Eacn pennant is usually of 56 mm diameter, and is connected to the next by a 75 tonne D-shackle. The pennant nearest to the surface is connected to a short wire known as the pigtail, and this in turn is connected to the surface buoy. Most traditional anchors weigh about 15 tonnes, the most common type in this category being LWT or Vicenay, as they are often known after their most prolific manufacturer. It is the task of the anchor handler to recover the buoy and reel in the pennants until the anchor is at the stern, then to allow the rig to heave in its cable until the anchor can be lowered away and stowed on its bolster. It is then said to be 'racked'.

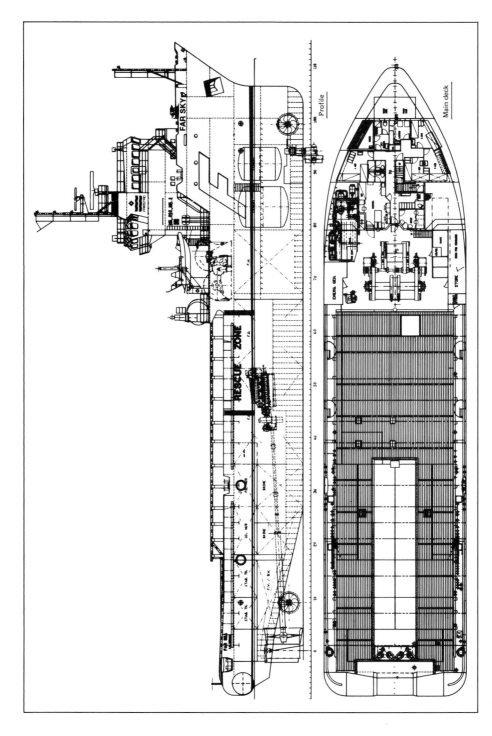

Figure 18 *The ME303 Mk II* Far Sky

Anchor handling gear

The ships must be provided with a means of securing the wires on the deck, and a winch for heaving up the anchors. They also need a healthy bollard pull for pulling the anchors out to the correct positions and for towing the rigs when required.

The earliest supply ships were intended only to service jack-ups and were therefore not provided with any means of towing or anchor handling. They had a clear deck for cargo and a number of tanks below deck for liquid and solid bulk cargo.

When the jack-ups needed to move they were assisted by tugs. However, the advent of the semi-submersible in the early 1960s required that supply ships should be able to lay and recover the rig anchors, and so they were provided with winches and rollers on the stern, and a means of stoppering off the wires on the deck. In the North Sea, where most of the semis were operating, virtually all the supply ships built were capable of handling anchors as well.

The earliest British anchor handlers has as little as 2000 bhp (1500 kW) available, with a bollard pull of 30 tonnes and winches capable of lifting no more than 50 tonnes. By 1972 the ships had become a little larger, the then most powerful ships in the world being the OIL Mark Is with 4500 bhp (3375 kW) available, giving them a bollard pull of 45 tonnes. The most recent anchor handlers, the ME303 MkIIs built for Farstad and Viking, have four engines producing 14 400 bhp (10 800 kW), giving a continuous 150 tonnes bollard pull.

Means of stoppering off the wires were borrowed from conventional marine anchoring and towing systems of the time, finally centring on Smitlocks and pelican hooks. Using Smitlocks the wires centred themselves on the deck, which was useful, but finally the industry adopted the pelican hook (Figure 19), despite the dangers when connecting and releasing it, mainly because there was nothing better available.

Figure 19   *The pelican hook*

With the passing of time a number of marine equipment manufacturers have put their minds to improving on the pelican hook, and as a result a number of hydraulically operated systems are available. They all incorporate a pair of hydraulic posts which lift from the deck and trap the wire between them, some of these having plates on the top which turn inwards, preventing the wire from escape. The posts are known as 'towing pins' or 'pop-ups', and the plates on the top as 'elephants' feet'.

The three commonest forms of securing system are the Ulstein 'Shark's Jaw', the Karmfork and 'Triplex gear'. In all cases the wire is first of all trapped between the towing pins; then, in the case of the Shark's Jaw (Figure 20), the operator standing behind the crash barrier raises the jaw and captures the wire, then closes the jaw. Once this has been done the wire is slackened off and the ferrule on the first splice comes up against the face of the jaw. The wire can then be worked on.

The jaw is pinned in the closed position so that in the event of hydraulic failure the wire is not lost, nor is the crew on the deck hazarded; however, it is set centrally between the towing pins and therefore the wire may need to be moved by some means to position it above the jaw. To make the change from wire to chain, the central part of the jaw must be replaced, making it difficult to change from one to the other.

Karmforks (Figure 21) consist of a pair of slotted tubes which are positioned one in line with each 'pop-up'. Therefore, as long as the incoming wire is positioned against the post, it will be picked up by the Karmfork which rises out of the deck and collects it in a slot in the top. The wire enters the slot and when fully in position passes a latch which will be released only if the fork is retracted into the deck.

The system is therefore very simple and, when weather conditions allow good manoeuvring, one fork can be set up for wire and the other for chain. The

Figure 20 *The Ulstein Shark's Jaw in the 'open' position*

Figure 21   *A pair of Karmforks, one fitted for chain, the other for wire*

drawback of the system is that in the event of hydraulic failure the forks will gradually retract into the deck, opening the latch and eventually releasing the wire.

Triplex gear (Figure 22) is probably the most elaborate of the systems and consists of two triangular plates, set into the deck, which hinge forward

Figure 22   *Triplex gear: the posts hold the line securely. The small post in the centre lifts the connection for ease of working*

hydraulically, thereby creating a vertical slot in which the wire or chain is trapped. The big advantage of this equipment is that it will gather the wire into the slot no matter where it lies between the pop-ups.

All three systems have advantages; the most effective is probably the Karmfork, which is simple in operation, raises the wire above the deck so that it can be worked on, and can easily be adapted for either chain or wire. Its only failing is its release of the wire on hydraulic failure.

Despite the advantages and efficiency of these modern systems the pelican hook should be available to deal with emergencies and hydraulic failure. While this is a simple instruction, it should be considered that the same hydraulics usually operate the wire securing system and the posts, and that without a post it is very dangerous to use the pelican hook. Ship's officers should consider the task of operating the pelican hook without hydraulics and if necessary persuade their owners to fit a suitable socket and provide a suitable post so that they can work anchors even if the hydraulics fail.

Recovering a buoyed anchor

It is probably simplest to start with a conventional pennant and buoy system and its recovery. The function of the master in this operation is primarily to place the ship in the best position to carry out the task, and then to remain calm while the work on deck is being carried out.

The activity can be divided into several distinct parts which must be individually reported to the rig, and be recorded in the ship's log book. These are as follows:

Approach to the buoy
Lassoing the buoy
Bringing the buoy on deck. Record in log and report to the rig
Disconnect the buoy pennant
Connect the workwire
Heave the anchor off the bottom. Record and report to the rig
Heave the anchor to the roller. Record and report to rig
Be heaved in to rig. Record in log book
Lower anchor for racking
Disconnect pennant
Return pennant to rig. Record in log book

In all these parts every action must be as effective and rapid as can be managed while remaining in control and safe. There is always healthy competition between the various vessels carrying out the task, particularly if they are of different nationalities, and in the initial stages the speed of operations on each vessel is visible to the rig, and therefore the charterers. However, as the shift progresses the different efficiencies of the vessels become less obvious, and it is only in the event of one making an error, or being unfortunate enough to be involved in any sort of accident, that a particular vessel will be highlighted.

As in most other areas of the industry, the master and crew should make great efforts to present themselves in a positive manner to the rig and its manpower. If the ship is on a long-term charter there is every possibility that those on the ship will be familiar with those on the rig, and so they will be on first name terms and will know each other quite well. This is a great advantage in times of difficulty, when it is most important that people have some rapport with each other.

Working with an unknown rig

What is more likely is that one's ship will be picked up off the spot market to take part in the rig shift, and one will arrive on the location probably never having seen the rig or spoken to any of the rig or oil company personnel before. In this situation it is most important to give an impression of experience, reliability and competence, and this is done by using one's ship to the best advantage, and making sure that the crew work together and plan ahead. Some hints as to how this may be done follow.

As the moment to start the anchor job comes closer the anchor handlers will close in to the buoy pattern, waiting for the instruction to 'go' to be given. When this happens each ship will be given an anchor buoy to lift, and should proceed to it immediately.

Preparation

As the ship is proceeding in the direction of the first buoy the deck crew should be checking that all is ready. The tools should have been collected in a bucket or fish basket, and should consist of at least the following:

Lump hammer
Chisel
Very large Stilsons
Pliers
Punches

A complete list of the equipment that should be carried by every anchor handler is as follows:

2×5 ft crowbars
1×14 lb sledge hammer
1×7 lb Monday hammer
1×14 lb lump hammer
2×2 lb ballpane hammers
1×24 in Stilson
1×36 in Stilson
2×1 in hardened steel cold chisels
1×7 in angle grinder
$1 \times$ cold set
1 set 30 in bolt cutters
2 marlin spikes
Punches: $\frac{1}{8}$ drift punch
          $\frac{1}{2}$ in drift punch
          $\frac{3}{8}$ in drift punch
          $\frac{1}{2}$ in Kenter link punch

Pliers

2 fish box hooks (these are heavy wire hooks on long handles, which enable the
   crew to pull things about on the deck from the standing position. They can
   obviously be made up from any heavy duty wire)

1 hacksaw

2 aluminium boathooks

2 builders shovels

Spare shafts for hammers

2 chain stoppers

2 lassoes

The lasso should be shackled onto one workwire, or if the ship has only one
workdrum, to a pennant on the end of the tow-wire and this shackle should be
well over the outer periphery of the roller. This is to ensure that the lasso does
not come up short and close before it reaches the buoy. The other wire should be
on hand to one side, so that as soon as the buoy has been disconnected it can be
brought in and connected up.

The approach

As the ship approaches the buoy, speed should be reduced and it should be
allowed to pass close down one side. It is all too easy to make the approach to the
buoy too fast so that the ship must go astern for a long time before the deck crew
is in a position to lasso.

   Once the buoy is visible from the after controls it is a good idea to start going
astern, so that as the buoy approaches the stern the ship is stationary. By moving
the stern sideways the buoy can be placed just aft of the ship. Very slight stern
power should be maintained if possible to keep the buoy actually touching the
stern of the ship. The bow thruster/s can be used to keep the stern pointing
towards the buoy, and if this is done the ship will naturally turn until it is stern to
the prevailing external force, whether it is the wind or tide, or a combination of
both.

   Ahead power should be used as little as possible, since the wash will push the
buoy away, frustrating any attempt to lasso it.

   On modern anchor handlers the buoy will probably be out of sight from the
bridge when it is close up, so it is sometimes necessary for the mate at the stern to
indicate to the bridge its actual position. Alternatively it is often possible for the
master to get an idea of the position of the buoy from the movement of the
lassoing team, who will naturally move from one side of the roller to the other as
they follow it. If they stop moving and stand dejectedly doing nothing it means
that the ship has drifted away. If they become stationary and begin swinging the
lasso it means that the ship is correctly positioned.

   When they judge the moment appropriate they will swing the lasso and let it
go. The lasso will disappear over the stern, and until some further reaction is seen
it is essential to maintain the position because, if they have missed, they should be
able to recover the lasso and immediately try again.

   If total success is achieved — the lasso completely over the buoy — they will be
seen running away from the stern gesticulating. If the lasso has partly lodged over
the buoy one of them will grab a boathook and try to push it the rest of the way.

   There are now some anchor handlers which are so large, and have rollers of
such a diameter, that the buoy cannot even be seen from the stern when it is in

position under the roller. This is a very real problem in the operation of these large vessels since they have been designed to operate with modern chasing systems. The only logical means of achieving reasonable success is for the master to line the buoy up with the centre of the roller and to move slowly astern until it disappears from view between the two men with the lasso standing on the roller. They in turn will see it disappear and when they judge that it has touched the stern they should launch the lasso. They will only know that they have been successful when the ship drifts away and the buoy returns into view.

If this continues to be a problem then some other means may be discovered to lasso the buoys, possibly by placing the vessel alongside the buoy and lassoing over the side of the ship. It is difficult to know whether this would be a practical alternative until it is tried.

Heaving the buoy aboard

Once the bridge has received a signal from the deck crew that the buoy is properly lassoed, the winch driver (usually the chief engineer, also more often than not on the bridge) puts the winch into gear and heaves the buoy aboard. The master should now be attempting to maintain the ship's position close to the now imaginary spot in the water where the buoy used to be, and must continue to do this until the first pennant is secured in the anchor-handling tong. Once the wire is secured he can, unless the weather is really unpleasant, stop the engines and allow the ship to hang stern-to on the rig anchor.

Disconnecting the anchor

During this phase of the operation there is little for the master to do, other than wait for the task to be carried out. The deck crew will disconnect the pigtail (the short pennant from the buoy to the first anchor pennant) and will shackle on the work-wire. In the event of D-shackles being used the D should face the stern of the ship. This reduces the possibility of the shackles being snagged under the turns when reeling off at a later time.

The deck crew will heave the buoy into the ship's side with a tugger and indicate to the bridge that all is ready to heave away. Before taking any further steps the master should ask the rig for permission to lift the anchor.

Lifting the anchor

On receiving the affirmative the chief engineer will be instructed to commence heaving away. The pennant will gradually tighten up and a steady increase in weight will be seen on the winch gauges. The ship will be heaved directly over the top of the anchor and will break it out from the seabed. The weight will be seen to fall off, and the master should inform the rig that the anchor is off the bottom.

In the event of any sort of swell running it is at the point of breaking out that the anchor pennants part, as the waves lift the stern of the ship and place an unacceptable strain on the wire. In these conditions the ship should be driven slowly ahead so as to keep a constant weight on the pennant string.

As the pennants are reeled onto the workdrum it is essential to both count them and note their length. This is done both on the deck and on the bridge. It is particularly important if the pennants making up the string are of differing

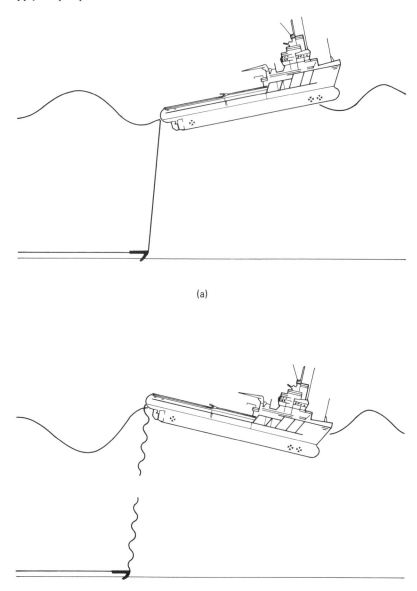

(a)

(b)

Figure 23 *(a) An anchor handler over an anchor in rough weather*
(b) The stern lifts on a swell and breaks the pennant

lengths, since on arrival at the new location the ship may be required to make up an entirely different pennant string, and if a good record is not maintained the only course of action is to reel the complete drum over the stern and start again.

Depending on the depth of water and the speed of the winch, after some minutes the anchor will come up to the stern roller. On its approach, the mate on the deck should sight it to ensure that it is in good condition and that the crown chain is not snagged round the flukes. If all is well he should indicate the same to the bridge and the anchor should be lowered back in the water.

During the reeling in of the anchor pennants every effort should be made to ensure that the wire covers the drum evenly. This is sometimes done by the deck crew who use a 70 tonne shackle over the pennant wire connected to both tuggers. The wire can then be guided from side to side as required.

The master can achieve the same result: by putting the ship on a heading with the stern to the rig and going slowly ahead, there is a little weight on the pennant string; then by steering to starboard the wire will move to the port side of the roller, and hence be reeled onto the port side of the drum. Steering to port has the opposite effect.

The moment of sighting the anchor is always fraught with tension, since the revelation of any problems can mean hours of work on the deck. Anchors have appeared in a veritable ball of pennant wire, all of which will have to be laboriously removed before the operation can continue. On some occasions only parts of the anchor have emerged from the water, flukes or stabilizing bars having dropped off at some point in the operation.

Once the bridge has received an indication that all is well, the master can inform the rig that the anchor is at the roller, and will be informed in turn that recovery of the rig anchor cable has commenced.

In the event of the moorings being chain, the master can relax, the ship being held in position by the weight of the chain, and allow events to take their course. If wire is used it will be necessary to keep a check on the ship's position since it could drift away from the correct line, taking the wire with it. In this situation it may be prudent to drive the ship very slowly ahead, applying suitable rudder to ensure that it remains on the correct line.

Assuming that no winch failures occur, the ship should find itself approaching the leg where the anchor is to be housed between thirty minutes and an hour after the reeling-in operation commenced. At this time it is essential that the master position the ship both on the correct heading and in the correct position in relation to the leg. This will allow the anchor to be racked on its bolster.

When the ship is about 100 metres away the anchor should be lowered until the weight is transferred from the pennant to the anchor cable. The anchor will then be hanging below the rig.

Now the last pennant may be gripped in the shark's jaw and unshackled from the next. The ship should now be very close to the leg, so that there is plenty of slack in the pennant, ensuring that the anchor is not pulled over the bolster. The chain will be heaved in very slowly, the rig's deck crew looking down at the bolster to ensure that the anchor is correctly housed. It is a time of particular tension since the ship is now securely attached to the rig by a 50 metre pennant, and if any weight is put on the anchor it may be displaced in some way.

To make matters worse, the crane will now swing over with a short wire on the hook, and this must be passed through the eye of the pennant and the eye put over the hook. At this moment not only is the ship secured to the installation, the crane is secured to the ship, sometimes at the full extent of the jib. However the pennant can now be released, freeing the pennant from the ship and completing the operation. The ship may then pull away, and the master will be instructed to proceed to the next anchor.

In an ideal situation each of the anchors will be recovered in a similar manner until all are racked. When half or more of the anchors have been recovered, one

Figure 24 *An anchor handler returning an anchor to a semi-submersible*

of the anchor handlers will be designated to take up the tow, and this vessel may be joined by a second during the final stages of anchor recovery. The rig may then be towed to its new location. Towing is dealt with in Chapter 5.

The rig has now arrived on its new location, and the anchors must be run so that drilling can commence on the new hole.

Anchoring in the new location

The approach

It is common practice for the rig to drop the first anchor as it passes over the first anchor position at the new location, and of course this anchor must be buoyed like the others. Preparing this anchor is a particularly exciting operation.

It is best for the designated anchor handler to get ahead of the rig, slightly to one side of the approach, and turn so that it is going astern at the same speed as the rig. At this time the speed with probably be between 2 and 3 knots.

The rig should be allowed to pass and the ship should tuck itself in astern in a position where it can be reached by the rig crane. Some rigs have a crane actually at the stern whose principal purpose is to assist with anchor handling. In this case the ship can come up between the aft pontoons, and the master will find that in this position the ship is being dragged along and virtually held in position by interaction with the rig. The rig crane will then pass down the buoy, and then the anchor pennant. The pennant can be secured in the jaw and the crane released. As soon as the pennant is connected to the string on the workdrum, the ship can begin to slacken off the string and drop back from the rig.

The pennant string should be counted and when it is in the water the buoy can be connected and launched. The rig will then be approaching the anchor drop position with the anchor hanging below the bolster and the complete pennant string with its buoy trailing astern.

Running a buoyed anchor

Once the rig has arrived at the new location, usually with the first anchor down and now being held in position by the towing vessels, laying of the remaining anchors may commence.

The anchor handlers will be assigned their anchors and should approach the relevant leg. The crane will lower the end of the anchor pennant and the deck crew should secure the thimble to the end of the tugger wire, take the weight and release the crane hook. The tugger can then be used to heave the end of the pennant past the anchor handling tong, and as long as the wire is between the towing pins the tong can easily be raised to grasp it.

The tugger can then be slacked back and removed, and the last pennant on the workdrum shackled on. The tong or Karmfork can then be lowered out of the way. Now by cooperation between the rig and the ship the anchor will be lowered off the bolster and the workdrum turned until the anchor is at the stern of the ship. It should then be sighted once more to ensure that it is clear of turns or defects.

Having been given the bearing and distance on which to run, the master should align the head of the vessel and on instruction from the rig slowly move away. The anchor cable or wire will be seen being lowered away and the ship will steadily move off in the direction of the anchor position.

Once the ship is on its way it is usual for the mate in charge of the deck to come up to the bridge to assist the master with the run out.

The basic technique for maintaining direction during the run is to use the autopilot, and for the mate to monitor the ship's position using the radar. He can ensure that the bearing of the rig remains correct and can check on distance to the drop position.

The master usually remains at the aft controls and is able to check on the deck and vary the speed of the ship if necessary. In this a doppler log can be a great help. If the autopilot is effective the mate will be able to steer the ship and monitor the position. Alternatively, if the joystick is provided with an autopilot setting this may be used so that the course remains under the control of the master. The normal manoeuvring joystick may not be used, since even though it can be put into a forward mode it may well vary the engine speed to keep on the correct course.

Given some practice, and a compass repeater at the aft end, the master may steer the ship manually, but it should be remembered that all steering conventions are reversed.

Today running an anchor is a fairly sedate operation carried out at between 1 and 3 knots. High-power ships are able to pull the cable out as far as required with the rig winch in gear. This is something of a contrast to the sort of starting-gate techniques used when anchor handlers were of lower power. On getting the word to go, the master would put the controls to full ahead and the winchman on board the rig would release the break, the method being to get up enough momentum while the ship was close to the rig to pull the cable out as far as possible, usually until the ship was pulled to a halt, with the engines still pounding away, the engine room full of smoke and all the fire alarms going off. This method was extremely destructive to anchors and cables and often ineffective, the ships being reeled in for another go if they did not get far enough.

During today's sedate progress towards the dropping position the mate will read out the distance so that the master may make any necessary adjustments to the power, and as the position is reached power should be reduced to ensure that the pennants do not part when the winch brake is put on. The winchmen on the rig usually rely on the ships to do this and will seldom give any verbal indication that they are about to stop the cable from running.

Once in position, the anchor may be lowered away. During this a constant check must be maintained of the ship's position to ensure that it does not drift away. Once off station with the anchor cable at full stretch it is difficult to recover, and lack of care at this time sometimes results in anchors being incorrectly laid. In addition, if the master realizes that his position is wrong, and makes violent alterations of heading in an attempt to get back, pennant strings may well ride up over the towing pins and end up round the side of the ship. Except in the calmest weather conditions it is very difficult to get the pennant string back round the stern.

Once the anchor is on the bottom the master should inform the rig, and, in good weather, may relax while the deck crew make preparations to launch the buoy.

When everyone is satisfied that the correct number of pennants of the correct length are in the water, the deck crew should secure the end of the last pennant in the anchor handling tong and unshackle it from the string on the workdrum. The buoy should then be dragged down the deck, past the anchor handling tong and into a position to one side of the roller. The buoy pigtail can then be shackled onto the pennant, and permission obtained for the release.

All tools should be cleared from the area, the towing pins retracted and all personnel should retire behind the crash barrier. The anchor handling tong should then be lowered. In the case of a Shark's Jaw, the jaw should be opened just as the wire is at deck level. The buoy will then disappear over the stern and enter the water with a satisfactory splash. The ship is then free for its next task.

Permanent chasers

Running an anchor with a permanent chaser

Unfortunately anchor buoys are vulnerable to being damaged by passing ships since they are not lit, and if a rig remains in one position for a long period they may be lost due to mooring failure. These anchors are recovered using the shepherd's crook or J-hook, but it is becoming more common to use permanent chasers in order to avoid these problems altogether. These are of various designs but basically consist of a collar or ring round the anchor chain or wire, to which a pennant is attached. When the anchor is housed, the collar rests round the shank.

To deploy these anchors the pennant is passed to the supply vessels in the usual way and the anchor brought to the stern. During this part of the operation the catenary of the cable should be kept shallow to ensure that the collar remains on the shank, and that the anchor does not turn as it passes through the wash of the anchor handler.

The ship should then proceed to the anchor position and, once there, the anchor may be lowered away. It is recommended, though not always possible, that the engines be stopped as the anchor passes through the wash zone, once more to ensure that it does not turn and put twists into the cable.

Figure 25   *A J-hook on the deck of an anchor handler, and a couple of pennants ready for spooling on*

While lowering, the engines should be kept turning slowly ahead, and sufficient wire paid out until a length of between one and a half and twice the water depth has passed over the stern. This is likely to involve between 200 and 700 metres of wire, hence the ship should have been suitably equipped before the start of the operation. This is not always the case and it is sometimes necessary to make up wires of the correct length from pennants supplied by the rig.

Once the anchor is on the bottom the ship should prepare to strip the chaser back to the rig (Figure 26). The cable should not be tensioned up since this tends to jam the chaser on the shank.

The recommended technique is for the ship to proceed astern, directly over the anchor position, towards the rig. This method is effective, and any master who feels that there is some danger to the screws should draw a scale diagram, allowing for the depth of water and the position of the screws and rudders in relation to the stern: the reality is that the screws are set sufficiently well forward for the wire to remain clear of them.

Progress towards the rig should be steady and continuous, the ship gradually slowing down as it approaches the leg. From this point the operation does not differ from returning the last pennant after the anchor has been housed, except that at all times the weight of the collar remains. This makes release more difficult and puts more strain on the crane as it takes the weight.

The end of the pennant will be guided by the rig crew into a holster, and the ship may then proceed to the next anchor.

Recovering an anchor with a permanent chaser

To recover anchors with permanent chasers the ship should run out on the correct heading, paying out the work-wire until a length equal to at least twice the water depth is over the stern. It may be possible to manage with less, but the likelihood

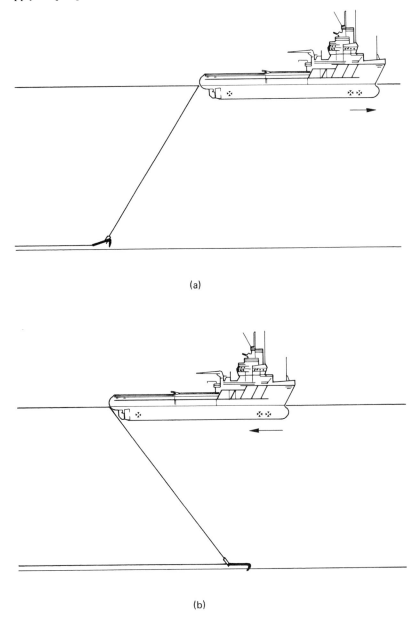

(a)

(b)

Figure 26 *(a) Lowering an anchor with permanent chase to the seabed*
(b) Commencing the strip back to the rig

of the collar picking up a kink in the cable, bringing every thing to a halt, or of
the collar failing to make its way up the shank of the anchor, is increased.

   In either of these cases the ship will appear to have reached its final position
but, when the chasing wire is heaved in, a bight of chain will appear on the deck.
There will probably be no indication which end leads to the rig and which to the
anchor.

   Many masters are tempted to carry out elaborate manoeuvres and have much work done on deck in an effort to get the bight to slide through the collar, so that the anchor will eventually end up at the stern. There is seldom much point to this, the best option being to lower the cable back to the seabed and have the rig tension up to remove the kinks. The only case for not doing this is where the anchor is known to be off the bottom.

Here the rig may heave the ship in until the chasing wire can be paid out to allow the anchor to hang below the leg. The collar will then run down the chain onto the shank and the anchor may be housed in a conventional manner. If there are any problems with the anchor it may also be heaved back on board the supply vessel for attention.

Back-up anchors or piggy-backs

The job of the back-up anchor

We have described the ideal rig shift where all the anchors are laid and in position. The next task is to tension them up. To do this, opposite pairs of anchors are tensioned up to 200 kips and then reduced to the working tension. (A kip or kilopound is equal to 1000 lbf or 4.45 kN.)

If either of the anchors drags out of position it must be rerun, or a back-up anchor added. Which option is taken will often depend on the surveyed seabed conditions. If the holding ground is good, the anchor may be rerun on the premise that it had not held properly the first time. If the holding ground is poor, a back-up may immediately be added.

To add a back-up to a conventional buoyed anchor the buoy must first be recovered and removed from the pennant string. The piggy-back anchor will then be added to the last pennant, and the first pennant of a string of equal length attached to the crown. To do this the ship must first have an anchor on the deck, which may have been loaded from the rig or, if the operation has been well planned, from the shore. It is also essential that the ship has a pennant string of the correct length made up on the workdrum.

It is sometimes easiest to connect the pennant string on the workdrum to the crown of the piggy-back and then drag it aft towards the stern with the tuggers. In this way, if the flukes of the anchor get stuck into the deck, the workdrum may be turned to pull it out.

Once the anchor has been connected up at either end the workdrum can be turned to tighten up the whole set, and the Shark's Jaw, or other securing device, can be lowered out of the way. The towing pins must also be retracted to clear the afterdeck and allow the piggy-back to slide aft.

At this moment the wire is not secured in any way into the middle of the deck, being held in position by the weight of the anchor and the direction of the ship. It is absolutely essential that the ship be aligned exactly stern to the rig so that the anchor will move down the centre of the deck. There comes a point, as the anchor lifts over the roller, when the wires may well be above the level of the crash barriers, so that if the ship moves off line for any reason the anchor will slide across the roller and may enter the water over the quarter. The pennant between the anchor and the workdrum will then slide up the side of the ship and, if there are no stag horns fitted on the crash barrier, come to rest just aft of the accommodation. If the ship is fitted with a pilot access in the bulwark the wire may well

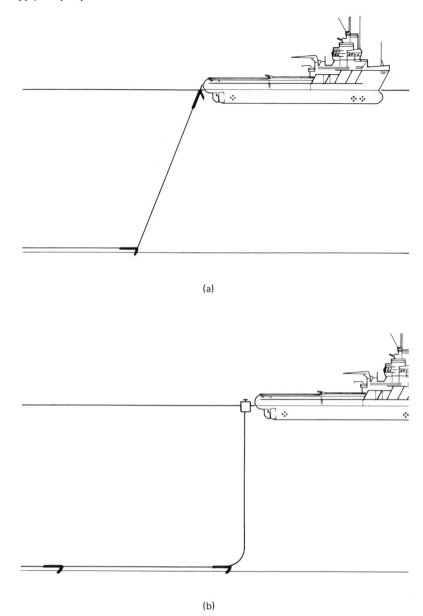

(a)

(b)

Figure 27   *(a) Lowering the piggy-back over the stern*
(b)Launching the buoy

end up hanging through it, with the anchor suspended somewhere below the ship, forward of the centre-line. It is very difficult to sort this problem out.

There is a tendency for the winch driver to respond to this moment of tension by letting the anchor go very slowly over the stern, which really makes things worse. This is possibly a moment when the master may give himself permission to shout: if the anchor goes over fast no damage will result, it will just make a bigger splash.

Once the piggy-back is on the bottom, the buoy may be reconnected and launched in a conventional manner.

In the event of a back-up being required on an anchor which is fitted with a permanent chaser, it is usual to attach the pennant string to the chaser which will have been run up the shank of the anchor once more, and the string buoyed off.

Most locations will require one or two back-ups and in particularly soft bottom conditions large numbers may be needed, possibly two on every main anchor.

A variety of anchors are available, most designs seeking to improve the holding power for a given weight. The best known is the Bruce anchor, and an earlier Vryhof anchor, the Stevin, is still much used as a piggy-back.

High holding power anchors

In some situations the main anchors may be replaced with high holding power anchors of Bruce or Vryhof designs to avoid the use of piggy-backs altogether. Some are so large that they have to be physically climbed on the deck of the ship to connect them up. They are also extremely difficult to return to the water, unless the recommended technique of launching them on their backs is followed.

If it is necessary to launch them fluke/s down, during their slide towards the stern they may rip up sections of the deck; sometimes, if the point of a fluke becomes jammed, it may pierce the deck, usually in the area of the steering gear.

Master's involvement

During anchor work it is essential that the master remain patient. What seems obvious to him from the wheelhouse may not be so obvious to those on the deck. However, he should be sparing with advice to the crew shouted through the loud-hailer, since it is also unlikely that from such a distant and elevated position the size and weight of the equipment and wires being handled can really be appreciated.

Figure 28   *Bruce anchor being launched on its back*

Figure 29 *Deck crew working on a Bruce fabricated anchor recovered from deep water. They are restoring the chaser system which can be seen round the shank*

It is therefore essential to weigh words carefully and only to advise when absolutely necessary, otherwise the deck crew will become irritated and, regardless of how helpful any instructions may be, will carry them out with a bad grace. The result will be the destruction of the rhythm of the job, eventually leaving the master in charge from a distance — an unsatisfactory state of affairs.

Recovering a back-up anchor

To recover a back-up anchor no special changes are made to recover the buoy and bring the anchor to the stern. However, getting the anchor from the stern to the deck requires the same approach as the techniques for putting the anchor in the water.

When bringing the anchor aboard high tensions can occur as it comes over the roller, so the winch operator should take this into consideration, as well as the anxiety of the master. Once on the deck it should be heaved rapidly past the towing pins and these raised to trap the pennant string. Nearly all anchor handlers are fitted with steel deck-plating around the anchor handling tong and to the stern, and if the ship is rolling the anchor may crash from side to side on the plating.

If this plating extends over the majority of the width of the deck the stabilizing bars may start to remove sections of crash barrier, and sometimes tank vents. Hence the anchor should be heaved up onto the wooden sheathing, when it will stop moving, and the Shark's Jaw or other wire securing device may be raised to grasp the wire. Then the anchor may be slackened back down the deck until it is held against the anchor handling tong. The anchor itself may then be secured by tugger winch wires before the pennant is released.

Use of the J-hook

One of the drawbacks of the conventional buoy and pennant system is the tendency for buoys to be lost. Sometimes the shackles may work loose and a pin drop out, but more commonly the last pennant will break due to chafe on the bottom, despite the presence of the crown chain. The buoy will then drift away, but will usually be spotted and recovered before it has gone too far. Unfortunately this leaves a specialized recovery operation to be carried out when the rig is moved, and involves the use of the J-hook or shepherd's crook.

This object, as its name implies, is shaped like a J. It weighs about two tonnes and must be lowered over the stern of the ship which is to recover the errant anchor.

When the rig comes to be moved it is normal for the anchors that need to be chased to be lifted first, or at least for a vessel to start chasing for them first.

The J-hook will be craned onto the after deck of the anchor handler designated to carry out the task, and it is first necessary for the crew to get it over the stern attached to one or more long pennants on the workdrum. No matter what the temptations, the tow-wire should not be used for this or any other anchor handling task.

Once the pennant has been shackled on, the J-hook may be manoeuvred over the stern using the tuggers. This is not easy to do, since there is nowhere over the stern to put a snatch block; nevertheless, it is possible and it is quite a good way of getting the crew tuned up to the work to come, and used to working together.

If the master does not wish to put his team through this character-building experience he may use a second and easier method. The deck crew should make up a loop of rope and put this round the hook. This can then be connected to the hook of the rig crane which will lift the J-hook over the stern. When the crane lowers away, the pennant takes the weight, the J-hook turns the right way up and the rope slips off. Alternatively it may slip up the pennant where it can be removed on the deck. If neither of these things happens, the rope will break.

Once the J-hook is in the water, the depth of the wire or chain must be calculated by reading the draft of the rig and then lowering the J-hook to a depth of between 20 and 40 metres more. The length of wire paid out may be measured by painting the wire at the winch with a white mark. This will usually be about 35 metres. Hence, by paying out about two deck lengths, the hook should end up at the right depth.

The rig should slacken down the wire or chain next to the one to be chased, which should be kept under tension so that it is easy to pick up.

A number of techniques may be used to pick up the mooring, all of them involving the work-wire making contact with it. At that time, the wire will be seen to move on the deck, and often an observer on the rig will be able to see the wire deflecting at the stern, and will report this on the radio.

One method is then to reel in the work-wire until the hook passes the chain and, hopefully, hooks on to it. The difficulty with this technique is that it is impossible to see whether the wire is still in contact since it will be jumping about as it is reeled in.

A second method is to steam slowly at right-angles to the mooring so that the J-hook will pass over it. However, it will sometimes jump right over, and not hook on. A variation on this is to attempt to get the depth just right while passing the stern backwards and forwards over the mooring position.

In the opinion of the writer, the best method is to align the ship with the direction of the cable, move sideways until the wire can be seen to be in contact with it, and then steam out very slowly in the direction of the anchor, making sure that contact can be maintained. Obviously there will come a time when the J-hook makes direct contact with the wire or chain and it should then naturally hook onto it.

Running out

Once this has happened the work-wire will tighten up, and an indication of success will probably be given from the rig. The ship should then start steaming out, ensuring that some weight remains on the work-wire, but at the same time gradually paying out, since, when the anchor position is reached, there should be considerably more wire out than the depth of water.

Despite the potential and actual difficulties, there will come a time when the ship is running at the correct speed with the correct length of wire between the stern and the hook. The whole ship can be felt vibrating rhythmically as the hook passes over each link of the cable, indicating that all is well.

As this is happening, the distance from the rig must be measured on the radar and, as the ship approaches the anchor, some reduction in speed may be necessary. Once more, this is a matter of judgement. Too great a reduction and the ship will stop, not enough and too much stress will be placed on the work-wire when contact is made. However, probably a speed of about 1 knot is suitable.

When the J-hook reaches the anchor it will ride up the shank until it comes to the crown, the wire will tighten up and the stern will be pulled down. The ship will then come to a dead stop and engine power may be reduced until there is a limited tension in the work-wire.

The anchor may now be heaved to the surface, over the roller and onto the deck. If the vessel is operating in particularly deep water, or if the winch is not very powerful, it may be difficult to heave the anchor and J-hook over the roller. This is because the shank of the anchor becomes a lever with the anchor cable on the end of it. To get over this problem, the anchor should be lowered back into the water and the ship turned until it is facing the rig. The anchor and the J-hook will now form a curve in the same plane as the roller, and so they may easily be heaved onto the deck (Figure 30).

Once on the deck, the anchor cable should be secured and the J-hook recovered. New pennants or whatever else is needed may now be attached and the anchor returned to the rig.

Recovering the anchor

When the hook is judged to be round the shank of the anchor, the work-wire should be heaved in while a low tension is maintained using the engines. If the run-out has not been undertaken positively there is once more the possibility that a bight will be heaved onto the deck, and again there is the temptation to get the chain to run through the hook until the anchor is reached. This will not be successful, but if there is a bight on the deck, the distance from the rig should be measured to see if the anchor is off the bottom.

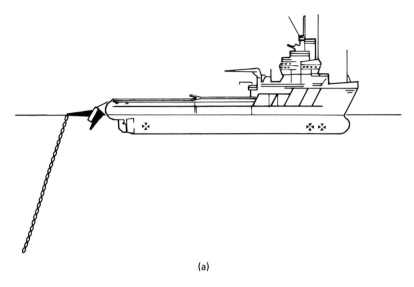

(a)

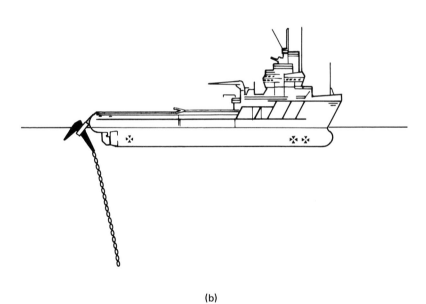

(b)

Figure 30   *(a) The lever created by anchor shank and chain*
(b) Turned the other way round, no lever is created

If this is the case the ship should be heaved in until it is fairly close to the rig, when the bight may be lowered over the stern. When the work-wire is paid out, the J-hook will run vertically down the cable until it is on the shank of the anchor. The work-wire may then be heaved in and the anchor brought onto the deck, where a new crown pennant may be attached before it is handed back to the rig.

In the event of the vessel being too far from the anchor for it to be anything other than on the seabed, the bight of the cable should be lowered to the bottom once more, then the cable tightened up from the rig. The ship should ensure that sufficient wire is paid out, if possible twice the water depth, then progress towards the anchor resumed.

Once more it is necessary to be positive with speed and direction. The master must ensure that he moves directly along the probable direction of the cable. Starting off too slowly may cause the hook to pick up a bight again and the vessel will not get far before coming to a halt. The whole process will then have to be repeated.

Chasing a piggy-back

When a back-up anchor has lost its anchor buoy there are obviously added complications involved in the recovery process, and sometimes a grapnel is used to pick up the pennant string between the two anchors. Both the recovery of the pennant wire and the heaving in of the anchors are complex processes and so it seems simpler to chase with the J-hook for the main anchor.

Once the main anchor has been pulled onto the deck it will lie athwartships with the rig mooring going off one quarter from the shank and the wire to the piggy-back going off the other quarter from the crown.

The anchor should be manoeuvred so that the rig mooring can be secured in the anchor handling tong, and if a second tong is not available, the pennant string should be secured using the pelican hook. The securing point for the pelican should be chosen so that the tension comes onto it before the tension on the mooring. The pennant string to the back-up may then be disconnected and a buoy attached, which should then be launched. This leaves the piggy-back buoyed off on the seabed and releases the main anchor, which may have a new pennant attached for return to the rig.

Once the deck is free the ship may return to collect the back-up, or if another ship is free it may be used to tidy up this part of the job.

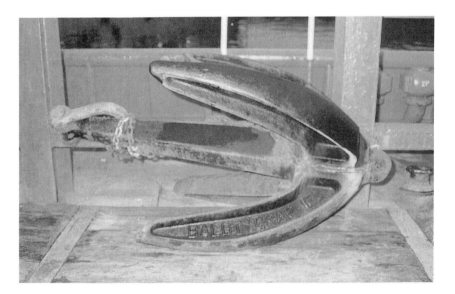

Figure 31 *A grapnel*

Deepwater anchor handling

In water depths of over 350 metres many additional problems occur in the deployment and recovery of anchors, which obviously become greater as the water depth increases. To date the deepest water in which a rig has been anchored is about 700 metres. The limitations to this activity are really the length of the rig chain and the amount of wire that can be stored on the supply vessels.

Obviously the deeper the water the longer the catenary of the cable and therefore the less cable there will be lying in the seabed to secure the rig in position. Hence most modern semi-submersibles are provided with sufficient cable to anchor in 700 metres.

In such depths permanent chasers are of limited use because of the length of the work-wire required and it is normal to use anchor buoys, or submerged buoys which return to the surface (hopefully) on receiving a radio signal from the anchor handler.

Because it would not be possible for the anchor buoys to support the weight of pennant wire required to reach from the seabed to the surface, a smaller wire, usually 32 mm, is used from the end of the pennant string to the surface buoy. The anchor handler must therefore have enough reel space to hold several hundred metres of pennant wire plus large quantities of smaller diameter wire.

Preparing ships for deepwater work

For this reason, before embarking on a deepwater job the ships are usually prepared in port, frequently by removing the tow-wires and spare tow-wires. This is done by contractors employed by the oil company, who in conjunction with the ship owners have determined how many anchors each ship is going to lift, defined the wire storage space, and decided how many ships are to be used in total.

It is also normal to designate one vessel as the towing vessel, and this craft may not carry out any anchor handling duties at all since its wires must remain in place.

Removal of the tow-wires is straightforward. The contractors place a powered reel at the after end of the vessel and guide the tow-wires onto it while the ship slowly pays them out. When the reels are full they are craned onto road transport and taken away.

Replacing the wires after the job is a more complex business and can easily go wrong, or be a prolonged and frustrating operation. If the contractors lack experience they have a tendency to place the reel in the same position which was used to remove the cables, re-attach the end to the tow drums and expect the cable to reel back into place without problems. The tendency is for the turns to be travelling across the portable reel at a different rate to the turns going onto the tow drum, and therefore the wire is constantly riding over itself or leaving spaces, and even guiding the wire with the tuggers may prove to be inadequate.

A better method is to place the portable reel at the forward end of the deck and lead the tow-wire round one of the after anchor handling posts and then back to the two drum. The lead of the wire is then constant, making it simple to guide it into position on the tow drum.

An even better technique is to place the portable reel at the after end, and then lead the tow-wire round the workdrum, having removed the work-wire, back down the deck, round a post and then to the tow drum. If a couple of turns are taken round the workdrum this creates sufficient tension to reel the wire tightly into position, and avoids problems with loose turns at a later date.

However, back to the job in hand: each ship which is to carry out anchor handling will be allocated enough wire to lay a designated number of anchors, depending on water depth. The most likely numbers are two or three anchors, requiring up to 2100 metres of 72 mm wire and 2100 metres of 32 mm wire to be stored on the ship's drums. Given time and forethought this wire may be shipped by the same contractor who removed the tow-wires and powered reels used to position it on the vessel. In less fortunate circumstances a primitive frame and a large number of cable drums may be dumped on the vessel just before sailing, and instructions given to have them in position by the time the ship reaches location.

In either case, the first thing to do is to calculate the maximum length of wire that can be reeled onto each drum, and if possible allocate one complete pennant length including the lightweight wire to each one. If this does not seem possible then all the thin wire should be allocated to a single drum and an attempt be made to fit a complete pennant length of 72 mm wire to the remaining drums. Obviously it is more difficult to reel on wire with little weight on it, since no matter how carefully the job is done it will take up more space.

Removing loose turns

Supply ship crews may spend hours carefully reeling on wire, and making sure that there are no spaces between the turns, only to find that as soon as any weight is put on the drum a turn will completely bury itself, sometimes necessitating hours of work to free it. This inevitably holds up the anchor deployment and results in acrimony between the rig master and the supply vessel.

Therefore, no matter how tidy the drums look, if it is possible an opportunity should be taken to pay them out and then reel them back onto the drums under tension. A technique sometimes used is to carry out this operation while the ship is steaming at full speed, but while this may result in a small improvement it is unlikely to be totally effective.

If the ship is left with one drum free, the wire may be reeled off one drum and onto another under tension; on occasion an opportunity occurs during the preparation for the location of the rig to retension the wires, or at least some of them. Sometimes a vessel may be allocated to slowing the rig down, involving attaching one of the after anchor pennants to a pennant string and using it all as a tow-wire. This makes it easy to reel out most of the wire and then to recover it under tension.

On occasion it may also be possible to do the same thing while attached to a rig anchor but awaiting instructions to run, and in extremis it is not beyond the bounds of credibility to get permission from the rig to carry out the operation: they are as aware of the problems created by buried turns as you are.

Pulling the anchors out

When laying anchors in deep water it is obviously necessary for the anchor handler to pull the rig chain as far out as possible so that there is sufficient cable on the seabed to provide good holding. Opinions as to the power required to carry out this part of the operation differ, but it can be reckoned that a vessel with 100 tonnes bollard pull is capable of laying rig anchors in 700 metres of water.

This is a fairly minimal requirement which can be met by almost all modern anchor handlers, but it is the higher powered vessels that are more likely to have the wire storage space, and also a winch capable of lowering the anchor to the seabed.

High power vessels running anchors using most of their power often find that the tension on the workdrum brake becomes excessive, and that they experience problems as they attempt to lower the anchors to the seabed, since obviously power must be maintained to stop the catenary of the cable pulling the ship back towards the rig.

The reason for this problem is that the tension is exerted at the periphery of the workdrum, since due to the length of wire it is absolutely full, and hence the tension on the brake may be reduced by paying out at least part of the pennant string during the initial stages of the run. This means that although the tension in the wire will be the same, the weight on the drum brake, and on the hydraulics during the paying out process, will be reduced by the reduction in the diameter of the wire on the drum.

It may, therefore, be possible to improve this situation by paying out part of the pennant string before the run-out commences, though this will naturally increase the possibility of the catenary touching the seabed, and therefore increasing the drag on the cable.

Recovering anchors in deep water

As already described, the anchor handlers will arrive on the location of the rig with tow wires removed from both the tow drum and the spare drum, and the absolute minimum of spare pennants.

The anchor buoys will either be conventional surface buoys or else they will be sub-sea buoys which will be released by radio signal and bob to the surface. In either case, typically the wire make-up will be a length of 32 mm wire greater than the water depth followed by a 72 mm pennant of similar length.

If the workdrum is large enough it is usually preferable to pick up the buoy and recover the whole of the two lengths of wire onto one drum. Even on vessels with only one workdrum there will be two drums available, the workdrum and the tow drum. Hence the first anchor should be recovered onto the tow drum.

From the outset the master should ensure that the wire is laid onto the drum evenly, and in these sort of depths may have no option but to cant the stern one way and the other to make the wire move across. The alternative technique of pulling it across with the tuggers may not work as the wire gets shorter, and the weight of the chain beneath the ship increases.

As the drum fills up, the weight on the winch will increase as the anchor and the increasing length of chain hang beneath the vessel. Finally the anchor will hang just below the stern.

In deep water it is often required that the ship take the anchor aboard, either to change it, or the pennant string, or the method of anchor recovery, usually from pennant and buoy to permanent chaser. The moment when the anchor is pulled over the stern places the greatest strain on the winch and the pennant string, and in some cases it may not be within the capability of the winch to carry out the task. Firstly the master must ensure that the anchor is correctly orientated if any sort of fabricated design is being used.

If attempting to heave the anchor aboard seems to be creating a lever, the ship should be turned to face the rig, and thereafter the anchor will slide on board in the correct manner. If it still refuses to come up over the roller, other action may have to be considered.

It may well be possible for the winch to pull the Telurit splice out of the end of the pennant if the anchor is stuck over the roller for any reason. Rollers which are not free may cause this to happen, and the result is of course the loss of the anchor to the seabed, so that, if it is not close enough to the rig, the anchor will have to be recovered with a J-hook.

If the winch refuses to pull the anchor aboard and the pennant does not pull out, the use of a second drum if available should be considered. The anchor should be stoppered off at the crown pennant and a second work-wire connected to it. If this is the actual work-wire the deck crew should first ensure that it is well secured to the drum since the weight, when it comes on, may be sufficient to pull the end out so that the anchor and the work-wire will be lost. This is because there will not be sufficient turns on the drum to reduce the weight on the securing point.

Once all these problems have been overcome, the anchor can be decked and any work necessary carried out on it. It may then be returned to the water, and the conventional return to the rig carried out.

The number of anchors that each ship has to recover will already have been determined, and therefore the crew will know whether they have to reel off wires onto storage drums before the next one is to be tackled. If this is to be done, the ship should pull out of the buoy pattern, reel the wire onto a storage drum and then be prepared to re-enter the fray.

Conclusion

It is inevitable that anchor handling activities will develop to accommodate any new requirements of the industry, the increasing amount of drilling in deep water, and the special anchors and equipment developed to carry out this task. There are also other forms of anchor handling activity which have not been covered in this chapter; however what is written probably forms the basis for the more elaborate anchor handling activities.

4 | The carriage of cargo

Deck cargo

Stowing cargo in port

Compared with cargo stowage on deep sea vessels, the stowage of deck cargo on offshore supply vessels appears to be simplicity itself. All cargo arrives in some form of unitized state and all is pre-slung, so that it may be removed from the vessel in a seaway with reasonable ease.

The basic unit of cargo is the container. Containers come in a number of sizes, from those with internal dimensions of a 40 × 48 inch (1016 × 1219 mm) pallet, mainly for the carriage of drilling chemicals, to 20 ft (6 m) full height containers. In between there are larger 8 × 8 ft and 8 × 10 ft containers for general cargo, and food containers usually of similar dimensions.

Non-standard loads are frequently presented and these include well testing and flaring equipment, generators, scaffolding, half-height open top containers and builders' skips, though there are moves afoot to ban skips because of the dangers in lifting them when full.

Manifests and cargo plans

Before loading begins, the mate of the vessel will sometimes receive a list of the cargo that is coming to the vessel during the following few hours, though it must be said that not all operators are able to supply this very necessary aid.

Loading lists are really presented on a need-to-know basis. If the operator is sending the ship to a number of installations he will almost always be sufficiently well organized to present the list to the mate, which allows the ship to plan the positions of the lifts for the different locations.

If the operator is sending the ship to a single installation, usually a drilling rig, the initial implication is that this installation is the sole place being serviced in the area, and therefore that the operator is going through the first phase of its activity — exploration. This in turn implies a small operation with minimum manpower and limited organization. The ship is therefore unlikely to get a loading list: they are just not that well organized.

However, here the loading list, though very useful, is not so necessary as it is

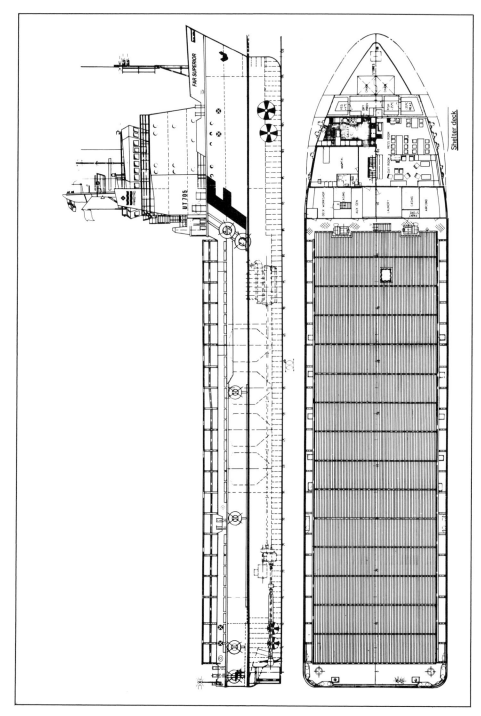

Figure 32 *A modern cargo carrier: the UT705 Far Superior*

for multiple discharge points. In this case the operator will normally indicate to the ship that loading is to commence at *x* hours, and at that time the dockers will stumble aboard, the crane will come alongside, and a number of lorries will be lined up with the cargo on them. It is often possible to see what is going to be loaded just by walking down the line of trailers.

Before any cargo is loaded onto the deck, the area should be prepared by stringing a chain or wire across the aft end so that space is left to allow the crew to walk easily from one side of the ship to the other, service the after ropes, make hoses fast etc.

On many vessels the chain or wire is placed in position and left there as a permanent part of the deck fittings. It is also common practice to paint a line across the forward end of the deck about 10 ft (3 m) from the accommodation to indicate the point beyond which no cargo may be loaded. This gives the crew access to both sides of the ship at the fore end of the deck, and also gives the crane drivers a point to work to, which may stop lifts hitting the aft end of the accommodation.

Where no loading list has been provided, loading will normally be started by butting containers against the after chain or wire, and working from side to side on the deck, moving forward. In most North Sea ports the dockers are aware of the systems employed and will load the ship in this way without any special instructions.

Tubulars

It is absolutely imperative, whether a loading list is provided or no, that the ship receive prior notice of the potential arrival of any tubulars. Tubulars include casing of all sizes, drill pipe, sections of marine riser, and sometimes piles. They also include pipe for pipebarges laying pipelines on the seabed, but it is customary for vessels employed to supply the barges to carry pipe only.

Figure 33 *Dockers loading a supply ship*

When casing is to be carried the deck must first be prepared by laying old mooring rope back and forth from crash barrier to crash barrier, to give the bottom tier something to bed into, and so to prevent it from rolling about during discharge.

The casing is loaded in convenient bundles to be handled by the crane offshore, i.e. singly for 30 in (762 mm) casing and in multiples for smaller sizes. The bundles are loaded across the deck one tier at a time, and built up probably to the level of the crash barrier. If the level of the top of the crash barrier is reached it is unlikely that a second tier will be started at the fore end of the deck because convention dictates that tubulars should be easily available for discharge; if they were to be discharged from the fore end, the ship would have to be sideways to the installation, and therefore under some circumstances might not be able to be discharged.

Casing has to be measured individually, and on some rigs this is done during the discharge, which results in the supply vessel spending many hours alongside. However, as supply ship time becomes more valuable this practice is now in the decline and an effort is likely to be made to discharge the casing and then measure it on the deck of the rig by moving it from one place to another.

Modern rigs usually keep their drill pipe on board at all times, and it is therefore unlikely that a supply vessel will be required to carry any more than small quantities. However, there are still a few semi-submersibles which have to reduce their deck weight before ballasting up, and these rigs discharge all their drill pipe to the supply vessels, and have it taken into port, recalling it once they reach the new location. In this situation, where large quantities of drill pipe are to be carried, it should be treated in exactly the same way as casing.

During discharge of casing no problems are likely to occur until the bottom tier is reached, since each pipe rests between two beneath it. However, once one hoist from the bottom tier is removed the remaining pipes are likely to roll from side to side, despite the rope dunnage. Therefore the crew should be armed with large wooden wedges, which must be carried as part of the ship's cargo handling equipment: when the hoist of casing is lifted from the deck, a crew member should rush in from either end and chock the next hoist before it has started to roll. When the next hoist is lifted they should pick up the chocks and move them into position against the remaining pipes.

The marine riser is possibly the most unpleasant tubular which a supply ship can expect to carry. Once more, many modern rigs are able to keep their risers aboard during moves, but older ones will send them ashore. There are also locations that require special risers, and under these circumstances supply ships may find themselves with risers occupying large areas of the afterdeck.

The marine riser is a unique tubular as far as the ships are concerned, because each section is flanged at both ends and comes in a variety of lengths. Quite often the risers will be loaded in two tiers, with the flanges interlocking. It is essential to chain these pipes down, that is to say that the chains should lead athwartships over the cargo and be chained down to the deck at either side, rather than being secured at the same level to the crash barrier.

In either case, when the vessel is in a seaway, shorter lengths of riser have a tendency to slide up from the bottom tier into the top tier, creating a gap. The remaining sections on the bottom tier will then roll from side to side and, unless the chains are secured downwards, individual sections of riser will begin to climb towards the top of the crash barrier, and the looser sections on the bottom will begin to move forward or aft. Anchor handlers have been known to lose complete marine risers over the stern. Obviously, once one section has gone the remaining pieces have more room to move, and the more mobile the cargo is, the more dangerous it is to send men out onto the deck to resecure it.

As an aside, in difficult situations where cargo is moving towards the stern on an anchor handler it is a good idea to present the stern to the weather and back into the seas cautiously. In this way the cargo will be washed forward to safety by the water on the deck. Then, by running downwind, the crew can go on the deck to carry out the resecuring operation. With the wind astern and proceeding at a reasonable speed, no water will come onto the deck, and the pitching motion will be minimized.

Other special cargoes

Other cargoes worthy of special consideration are helifuel tanks, which are explosive and therefore to be sited as far from the accommodation as possible, and also segregated from other explosives. The aft end is usually a good place to put the helifuel tanks because they are often wanted urgently, and may need to be discharged in what is known as marginal weather to allow the helicopters to keep flying.

Food is in a similar category so should be placed towards the aft end of the vessel, but a reasonable distance from the helifuel tanks, to avoid any possibility of contamination. Offshore food containers are not yet sufficiently advanced to be provided with their own freezer units, but many have insulated compartments within them into which frozen products are loaded and then kept cold with dry ice. This naturally creates a situation of urgency offshore, and even in bad weather it is often necessary to make a valiant attempt to offload food containers.

Heavy lifts

Similarly, the ship should be advised of the potential loading of any heavy lifts — though it should also be noted that what is a heavy lift for one installation may well be able to be transported by the whipline of another. Hence it is advisable to be aware of the lifting capacities of each of the cranes at the installation being serviced, to allow a judgement to be made on board the vessel as to whether they are being presented with a heavy lift or not.

A heavy lift is one that requires the offshore crane to use its large block, and to reduce the radius at which it can lift. The large block moves slowly, and the reduced radius means that the vessel must be close to the installation. Hence whatever constitutes a heavy lift for the installation that the vessel is servicing must be placed at the stern.

Establishing priorities

The reader will have noticed by now that there may be several objects vying for position at the stern of the ship, and in this situation it is up to the mate to make the judgement as to what goes where.

For discharge to a single installation, all the cargo is loaded onto the deck, starting aft and working forward. Once the cargo has reached the forward line aft of the accommodation, the ship is full. This is an unlikely event for a single installation, but if it does happen the loading supervisor working on behalf of the oil company may offload some items to place more essential ones aboard, or else the ship may be able to assist by restowing certain items. For instance, if the after part of the deck is loaded with tubulars but they are not up to the top of the crash barrier, it may be possible to offload them and then to stow a line of containers alongside the barrier on one side, reloading the tubulars afterwards. This is not difficult, and does not take long: loading the deck of a supply vessel is a rapid operation.

It follows that a cargo plan is not really essential if the voyage is to a single location, but where multiple discharges are to take place a cargo plan becomes essential, and the position and number of each container should be marked on the plan. This can be related to the loading list, which should give the container numbers and contents for each location.

Securing the cargo

It has already been stated that a chain should be fixed across the aft end of the vessel for the cargo to be loaded against. It is also recommended by M Notice No 1231 that individual parcels of cargo for different installations be separately secured. This can be done with chains and chain tensioners, but in reality such a securing operation would probably require the cargo to be offloaded in specific order, or that large spaces be left between parcels on the deck. Neither of these options is attractive, so the directive is not followed.

Most commonly the cargo is loaded solidly from aft to forward and then secured at the fore end by running a tugger wire across it, attaching the hook to the crash barrier at one side and leading it through a snatch block at the other.

Part cargoes are most frequently loaded against one crash barrier and then secured with the tugger wires or by chaining them tightly using cargo chain and chain tensioners.

Offshore discharge

Preparation for discharge

On arrival at the offshore location the first thing to be done is to establish radio contact with the deck of the installation. Usually the calling and working frequencies of the installation will be known to the supply ship, either from previous experience or from the operating manual provided for the ship by the operator. If they are not known, the best communication link in the North Sea is the standby vessel, which listens to the rig's working frequency and channel 16. Elsewhere it may be necessary to call up the rig radio room on 2182 or VHF 16 or, if all fails, to steam slowly past waving from the wing of the bridge. The last course of action is very effective for semi-submersibles but less so for platforms.

Once contact has been established, the ship will be given a working channel for the deck foreman or the crane driver — who is sometimes also the deck foreman. A time for commencement of work will be established and the position in which it is to be done, taking into account the weather, the crane positions and whether they are working, and the best storage points for the cargo. This information will probably be received by the officer of the watch, who will then inform the engine-room, the crew and the master of the intended programme.

It is not unusual for a vessel to sail straight up to the installation and commence discharge of cargo. In this case it is essential to check that all systems are operating. The UKOOA/BOSVA Code (Appendix 2) contains a checklist which is as useful for self-checking as for reporting to the installation, thus avoiding the embarrass-

Figure 34 *Discharging deck cargo to a platform*

ment of initiating a manoeuvre close to the rig having forgotten to turn on the thrusters.

Once the ship is under the crane, an order of discharge for the deck cargo will be agreed. It may be that all the cargo is to be taken, or it may be that only the urgent lifts are to be removed.

The deck crew will assemble on deck wearing their safety gear, which will be at least steel-toecapped boots and safety helmets. There may still be a few brave men in the industry who will venture onto the deck without these protective items, but no wise master will allow it. Other gear will depend on weather conditions and the vessel. On low freeboard ships in the northern North Sea the deck crew will appear wearing a full set of oilskins with the bottoms of the legs of the trousers taped onto the seaboots with heavy duty adhesive.

The main danger to deck crews working on the deck during cargo work is the possibility of being crushed by containers. All cargo remains fairly well attached to the wooden deck planking even if the vessels are rolling, but in the event of a wave getting aboard the adhesion is reduced and heavy objects can easily move, to squash the unwary.

Various M Notices have been issued to attempt to deal with this problem, recommending the provision of a look-out to yell when a sea climbs aboard as well as the individual lashing of individual consignments of cargo. Sadly, neither of these recommendations has really proved practical, though the incidence of seas washing aboard has been much reduced as the size of supply vessels has increased worldwide. There are still some designs which are outstandingly wet, including the ME303 which, though its accommodation towers like an apartment block over the afterdeck, remains sufficiently wet on the deck to require old mooring rope to be laid even for ordinary containerized cargo.

Indeed, for cargo operations it is worth while for the master to check the loading of the ship to see whether more freeboard can be gained by removing ballast water or altering the trim. Stability tanks have a tendency to be either at the fore or after end of the vessel, and to be operated partially filled with ballast. In many situations, if these tanks are emptied, ballast may be removed from the other end of the vessel and the freeboard increased accordingly.

When working stern to the weather it is also sometimes worth trimming the ship slightly by the head, so raising the stern and reducing the possibility of waves climbing aboard. In an emergency the master should not hesitate to ask permission from the installation to discharge excess drill or potable water to increase the freeboard.

The discharge operation

When discharge commences the crane will come down with what is known in the dock industry as a 'leg' on the main hook of the whipline, and on the end of the leg will be a safety hook. The safety hook is operated usually by pushing up or down a short lever on the back which allows the jaw to open to be put round the ring on the container lifting gear.

Safety hooks ensure that the cargo does not fall off the hook while being lifted and, possibly more importantly, that the crane does not become attached to the vessel. This is possibly the worst fear for the crane driver. In the event of the hook becoming attached to the ship, the driver has the choice of remaining in the cab and letting out the whipline in the hope of allowing the deck crew to detach the hook, or else leaving the cab before the crane is pulled down into the sea. The latter event is not unknown, and has resulted in the loss of crane drivers and sometimes injuries or fatalities aboard the ship. It is therefore essential that the deck crew remain alert to this possibility and keep a good eye on the lift as it is taking place, and on the crane hook while it is being recovered by the crane for another lift.

In the event of the hook, or a lift, becoming permanently attached to the ship, if the driver sees that the crew are rushing forward to release it he may take the decision to remain in the cab, and therefore tragedy will be averted.

It is the writer's view that this problem could be averted by using lighter cargo handling equipment than is customary on offshore cranes. The crane leg and the crane hook normally have a safe working load of at least 20 tonnes, giving a breaking strain of about 120 tonnes. This is far in excess of what the crane jib is capable of dealing with. If a crane leg and safety hook were used commensurate with the weight of the lifts, this problem would occur less often. Crane legs and hook of, say, 5 tonnes safe working load would be easy to handle on the deck, and if the crane became attached to the ship would be more likely to break. Obviously such an arrangement would require some care and consideration in preparing the lifts, and the weight of each container would have to be noted and annotated on the manifest so that the ship would know when the crane leg and hook should be changed. This is conventional cargo handling practice and is as relevant to work offshore as in port.

It may be some time before such thinking becomes normal in the oil industry, and up to that time it will be necessary to continue to work with oversize equipment. So, when the hook comes down to the ship, one of the deck crew should grab it and open the hook, and a second member of the crew should offer the lifting ring on the container. The hook can then be attached with the minimum of delay.

It is important that the deck crew be trained to use hand signals to indicate to the driver what is going on. It is all too common for the crew to grab the hook, walk to a container, hook it on and then walk away, relying on the driver to know what is happening. In fact, as the hook is coming down they should point to the container which they intend to discharge so that the driver can land the hook next to it. Having hooked it on, they should then give a signal that the container is ready to be lifted. This can be a single arm raised above the head or both hands being swept upwards in a lifting motion. Whichever it is, if they use the same signal every time the driver will be confident that all is clear for him to take the container away. This may seem pedantic, but once a routine is established it will considerably speed up the rate of discharge.

Where discharge is taking place to offshore platforms events are seldom straight-forward. Platforms are usually limited for deck space and so will seldom be able to take all the cargo designated for them without first landing empty containers aboard the vessel. This has resulted in a technique known as 'one for one', now severely discouraged in the North Sea, but nevertheless sometimes unavoidable.

Usually the deck foreman on the platform will call the ship and ask for a specific container (herein showing the importance of a cargo plan — though some operators paint the container numbers on the top to ease the operation). To get to the designated container, the deck crew will have to climb onto the top of the cargo and stand on the container to hook it on. They are therefore unprotected, and may slip down onto the deck or even over the side.

The container will be lifted and an empty one lowered into the space from which it was taken. Hence it is essential to cross off the lift from the cargo plan so that the master will know what is going on. Complete cargoes are sometimes discharged in this fashion, and in rough weather it can be a slow and tedious operation.

Discharging tubulars

During the discharge of tubulars, the installation will frequently require that tag lines are attached so that the lifts can be guided into the correct positions on the

Figure 35 *Discharging tubulars at a semi-submersible*

rig deck. These lines tend to get caught in the ship's structure unless care is taken. For the discharge of tubulars, two legs are slung onto the main hook, and it is best to attach the tag lines to the shackle above each hook so that they do not have to be tied on to each lift.

As the hooks come down, two crew members should stand on the deck under the lowering point and, when they are able to reach the lines, grab one each and walk forward and aft to either end of the lift, taking in the lines as they go. They will then end up with a hook each which they can attach to the slings on either end of the lift. As the crane heaves away they should keep hold of the tag lines to ensure that they do not snag anything on the way up.

When backloading tubulars, the use of tag lines is really a matter of choice. It is not a good idea to get anywhere near tubulars in the air, and many crane drivers are skilled in swinging the crane booms so that the pipes align with the deck of the ship. They are then able to drop them into place, and once there is plenty of slack in the crane legs the crew can run forward to detach the hooks.

Bulk cargoes

Types of bulk cargo

A major proportion of the cargo carried to offshore installations is loaded within the tanks on board the ship and discharged by means of hoses. These cargoes include gas oil for running the installation generators, potable water for drinking on board, drill water for mixing with cement and barytes and dry bulk in the form of cement for securing the casing. The dry bulk tanks may also be used for other chemicals such as barytes for drilling fluid and bentonite, also used for the same purpose.

Most supply ships are also fitted with tanks in which to carry oil-based mud, the most commonly used drilling fluid, and for brine which has a similar use.

The carriage of gas oil presents few problems, though some vessels are fitted with meters to indicate the exact quantity of fuel discharged to the installation, in which case the discharge slip should be sent up at the end of the job. However, it is more usual to identify an individual tank which more or less fulfils the requirement of the installation, and discharge it until empty. This allows the ship to give an exact quantity discharged, and the result seldom gives reason for dispute.

Likewise, potable water creates few problems, and the only difference between potable water and drill water lies in the tanks in which they are carried. Since drill water is not used for consumption it can be carried in tanks which are also used for ballast, on older ships. On modern vessels there is often enough tankage to allow potable water to be carried in such large quantities that it can be used on board the rig for any purpose deemed fit.

Possibly the only serious consideration in the carriage of water is the length of time which it takes to load. Water pressure from the shore mains is often low, so the loading times can be extremely long. Hence it is a good idea for the ship to start loading water as soon as it gets alongside, without recourse to any special instructions from the charterers; in the event of the vessel eventually ending up overloaded, some water may be discharged.

Carriage of oil-based mud

The most difficult bulk cargo to carry is drilling fluid. This is a mixture of detoxified diesel oil in which barytes are suspended, and other chemicals added in mystic formulations which only the mud companies fully understand. It is known as oil-based mud or OBM.

Supply ship OBM tanks are either purpose built, in which case they are usually rectangular with no excessive projections or framing, or converted from fuel or water tanks. In the latter case they will probably contain obstructions of one sort or another which makes them difficult to clean.

Because the liquid is a suspension rather than a solution, some effort must be made to maintain the solids in suspension during carriage. This is done by fitting agitators or circulating pumps. Agitators are some form of propeller or vane system, which rotates under hydraulic power while the mud is in the tank, stirring it up and ensuring that there is not too much fallout. These propellers are fairly effective but are more expensive than the conventional circulating system.

Circulating systems consist of pumps which take the liquid from the main suctions and pump it back into the tank through pipes, hence keeping the liquid moving. The pipes from which the liquid is discharged back into the tank are usually fitted with nozzles and either extend along the top of the tank, or the bottom, and in some cases both. The mud is supposed to be sprayed from the nozzles to increase the agitation, but only too frequently these get blocked, and most ships have resorted to removing the ends so that the liquid just cascades out. From the foregoing it can be seen that the carriage of mud is by no means an exact science.

The specific gravity of the mud depends on the expected pressure which will be found down the well, and in extreme cases can exceed 2.0, and of course the greater the specific gravity the larger the amount of barytes in suspension and the greater the fallout.

Mud is an extremely expensive commodity and should be loaded with care. It usually comes in batches of 2000 bbls. The supply ship should designate the tanks to be loaded so as to conform as closely as possible to the total cargo, and should dip the tanks when each is completed to ensure that the correct quantity has been delivered. Discrepancies should not be accepted, and in the event of the mud company denying shortages the charterer should be contacted. Some operators use independent surveyors to ensure that the correct quantity of cargo is loaded, which of course reduces the immediate responsibility of the ship.

Brine cargoes are even more valuable and so should be measured with equal care.

Discharge of bulk cargoes

Obviously all bulk cargoes are discharged through hoses. There is no problem with the hoses if the vessel is tied up to the installation. Any number of hoses may be connected at once and all sent up at the same time. It has become common in some areas to use the joystick and in this case there may be a limit to how many hoses the ship will wish to have connected at the same time. Two is a good number.

When initiating the discharge of bulk it is a good idea to identify the cargo that is going to take longest, and connect this hose up first, and get the cargo going

Figure 36   *A 4 inch Weco connection — male*

before moving on to anything else. Water is the most obvious starter. The volume required by the installation is usually large, and the receiving rate on the installation may be low. There is at least one rig which can receive water at only 15 m^3 per hour, so it will take a long time to make the transfer.

There are a number of connections commonly used by the offshore industry, the most common being Weco or its clones, camlocks, and Avery-Hardoll for fuel. Wecos (Figure 36) are large screw connections fitted with lugs so that they can be hammered up tight. They are almost always 4 in or 5 in (102 or 127 mm) either way. Some ships are fitted with 5 in connections and lines as are some rigs, equally some ships have 4 in and so do some rigs. It is therefore a good idea for the ship to carry a reducer so that any combination can be catered for.

Camlocks are most commonly used in the transport industry, but some have strayed offshore. However they are now seldom used.

Avery-Hardolls (Figure 37) are connections used in the transport of fuel, and are designed to close up when disconnected. Once more, it is a good idea to carry a Weco to Avery-Hardoll connection so that rigs with this fitting can be serviced. It is probable that this type of connection will become more prevalent as the offshore industry becomes more aware of pollution and of the unsociability of showering the supply vessel with fuel when the hose is disconnected and recovered to the rig.

Dry bulk cargoes are probably the most difficult to deal with and, on older vessels which cannot produce high pressure air, their discharge is a long and tedious operation.

The most common manner in which dry bulk is carried is in hopper tanks with the discharge line running from the bottom. The tank is pressurized with air, so that when the discharge valves are opened the cement or other cargo is pushed along the line to the rig. The tanks are fitted with 'slides', which are fabric panels

Figure 37   *An Avery-Hardoll fuel connection*

in the cone through which air is pumped to keep the cement moving, and the lines are fitted with air injection points to push the bulk along. The trick of successful discharge is to balance the tank pressure and the line injection pressure. If too much air is injected into the line, little bulk will move up to the rig; if too little, the cargo will stop moving altogether and it will be very difficult to start up again.

Some modern systems operate in two stages, and use conventional rectangular tanks for carriage and hoppers for discharge. These may consist of four rectangular tanks and two hoppers. Cement is pumped into one of the hoppers. When it is full it is pressurized and discharged to the rig. While this is happening, cement is pumped into the second hopper. In this way continuous discharge can take place and, since the hoppers are smaller, discharge should be more rapid.

The first and most essential requirement for cement discharge is a clear line to the installation tank, and a vent from the tank so that the excess air can escape. Therefore, once the flexible hose has been connected, the ship will pump air for a few minutes to check the line. It is usually possible to see the air escaping from a line somewhere under the deck of the installation. Once this has been seen, and the vent has been visible to the person on the installation in charge of the reception of the bulk, discharge can start.

On older, low pressure systems the bulk hose will leap all over the deck as the cement passes through it. These older systems can usually discharge between 20 and 30 tonnes per hour. There is little hose movement visible on modern high pressure systems which can achieve discharge rates of between 80 and 100 tonnes per hour.

At the time of writing there is a move towards the use of coloured hoses which will be more visible during the hours of darkness, and flotation collars so that they do not get caught in the screws of the ships.

Safety considerations in loading and discharge of bulk cargoes

There are recurring problems in the loading, discharge and carriage of bulk cargoes which relate mainly to the complexity of the pipework within supply vessels. It is only too easy, if the operation is improperly supervised, to make errors which can result in accidental discharge of liquid or solids overside or of discharge of the wrong commodity to offshore installations.

Bunkering in port on all vessels may result in overflows which can contaminate dock areas and this now results in swingeing penalties for the master. Elsewhere, oil-based mud cargoes have been known to be discharged overside instead of being circulated, and brine cargoes can be contaminated by ballast water if the valves in the system are not kept in good condition. Hence it is important to have well laid down procedures for all bulk cargoes and these should be written for the individual vessels. They may be incorporated in the ship's operating manual if it is provided with one.

There follows an example of a bulk procedures guide for a specific vessel, in this case a typical modern anchor handler.

Bulk operating procedures guide

General

All discharge and loading lines should be colour coded as follows:

Heavy fuel and gas oil	Brown
Cement and dry bulk	Yellow
Oil-based mud/brine	Black
Potable water	Blue
Drill/Ballast/Brine	Green

This is particularly important on deck, where both the end caps and the Weco connections should be painted.

The joining chief engineer should check the use of all dual purpose tanks and the positions of the blanks in the loading/discharge lines.

Fuel oil: loading

Tanks available	Capacity
2DB P	73 m^3
2DB S	73 m^3
4DB P	44 m^3
4DB S	44 m^3
2W P	58 m^3
2W S	58 m^3
3W P	18 m^3
3W S	18 m^3
4DB C	107 m^3
3DB P	44 m^3
3DB S	44 m^3

In addition, the service and settling tanks are available but these are never used for bunkering.

Tanks should not be loaded to more than 90% capacity and if possible tanks which are empty should be filled.

At the commencement of bunkering the shore staff must be acquainted with the grade of fuel required and the quantity.

Procedures differ from port to port but in all cases the engineer on duty must ensure that the bunkering hose is correctly connected. Both the deck officer on watch and the engineer in charge of the bunkering must be aware of the positions of the stop valves on the quay and, if remote from the ship's side, acquaint themselves with the communications system in use.

The shore staff must agree at the outset on what the likely rate of loading is to be and the probable finishing time for each tank or set of tanks, and for the whole operation.

Within the limits of the stability of the vessel, all tanks to be filled should be loaded at once. Even if this cannot be done, empty wing tanks should be left open when double bottoms are being filled so as to take any overflow.

During loading the deck officer on watch must be aware of which tank, or set of tanks, is being loaded and has the particular duty of checking the shore meter against the tank soundings. The engineer on watch will make sure that the shipboard fuel meter coincides with the Pielo gauge soundings and, in consultation with the deck officer, ensure that the reading on the shore meter is compatible.

The deck officer on watch must be aware of the position of the sounding pipe in the tank and also the trim of the ship, so that he will be able to allow for the fact that the tank soundings will either lag behind or lead the actual depth of oil in the tank.

A plan of the sounding pipe positions is attached to this document.

The loading rate should be monitored to ensure that it does not increase and towards the end of the tank or tanks being filled the rate should be slowed down.

Fuel oil: discharge

This vessel is only capable of discharging gas oil to offshore installations, however it is possible to turn the IFO (heavy fuel) tanks into gas oil tanks by turning a blank in the pipelines.

The officer working on the deck should ensure that the installation fuel line is connected up to the correct discharge point: on this vessel, starboard aft.

On completion of the operation the quantity of fuel discharged must be agreed with the installation.

Bulk dry cargo: loading

This vessel has available four tanks each of 2000 cu ft capacity. They are normally loaded to 90% of the total volume, which gives the following capacities by weight per tank:

Commodity	Weight	
Cement	74.0	tonnes
Barytes	105.88	tonnes
Bentonite	49.9	tonnes
Gilsonite	36.7	tonnes
Grout	74.9	tonnes

Figure 38 *A mimic board for bulk load and discharge of four tanks. The gauges on the left show tank pressure, the one next to them line pressure*

On this vessel the filling lines are on the port side and the vent lines are on the starboard side. Since these lines are identical apart from the valves, vent lines may be used for filling, and vice versa. Before the loading of any tank commences it must be physically checked to make sure that it is empty. New cargoes should not be loaded on top of part cargoes remaining in the tanks.

Before the commencement of loading, when the valves are being set up on the mimic board, the tank contents notices should be checked. The operator must satisfy himself that there are no discrepancies between the actual contents of the tanks and what appears on the notice, before loading commences. Once loading is complete, the notices must be brought up to date.

Bulk dry cargo discharge

Prior to discharge the contents of the tanks should be checked to ensure that they are as indicated on the notices.

Careful note should be taken of the commodity and quantity requested by the installation.

This vessel has separate connections for the forward and aft tanks, both on the port side. The officer on the deck should ensure that the hose is connected to the correct outlet.

During the discharge operation the mimic board should be monitored by the officer of the watch to ensure that the tank pressure remains as expected for the job being carried out.

On completion of discharge, the quantity received by the installation must be verified. The tank should be opened to ensure that it is empty, or that the quantity remaining appears to be correct within the limitations of visual estimation. The notices on the mimic board should be brought up to date.

Bulk tank cleaning

When cleaning tanks and discharging the residues overside the actual blowing out of the tanks must be monitored. If the operation is being carried out in darkness at sea, assuming that weather conditions allow, sufficient lighting must be switched on to illuminate the after part of the vessel.

Brine: loading

Tanks available	Capacity
1DB P	75.6 m^3
1DB S	60.8 m^3
Chain Lkr P	102.9 m^3
Chain Lkr S	102.9 m^3

	90% capacity
1DB P	428 bbls
1DB S	344 bbls
Chain Lkr P	582 bbls
Chain Lkr S	582 bbls

Before loading commences, all tanks to be used should be opened and inspected. They should be dry and clean. As far as possible, loading lines should be drained.

Experience has shown that it is usually possible to exclude the chain lockers from the ballast requirements of the ship so that they remain as dedicated brine tanks. Therefore these tanks should be used in preference to No.1 DB tanks for part cargoes.

Loading takes place through the drill/ballast/brine connections on the starboard side. The lines must be checked carefully to ensure that only the correct valves are opened for the brine tanks to be loaded. All tanks to be loaded should be filled together and the levels monitored by means of hand soundings on deck.

Since brine loading is extremely rapid, if No.1 DB tanks are being used they should be shut in as they are being completed. As the chain lockers are approaching completion, the level should be checked visually by removing the spurling pipe/vent covers at the main winch.

The Pielo gauge readings should be checked on completion, and the quantity verified by calculation using the SG of the brine. The quantity loaded should agree with the shore meter reading, and if there is a discrepancy this should be brought to the attention of the brine company and the charterer's representative. A sample of the brine loaded should be retained on board.

Brine: carriage at sea

While brine is being carried, as far as possible no ballast should be taken on or discharged, and during the initial loading of the vessel this requirement should be borne in mind. This will ensure that, for whatever reason, the brine will not be diluted or accidentally discharged, also that the ballast system will remain empty.

Should ballasting or deballasting be absolutely essential the system must be thoroughly checked first and, prior to the arrival at the installation, the lines to be used for brine discharge should be drained.

Brine: discharge offshore

When setting up for brine discharge it is once more essential that the tank valves be carefully checked so as to be absolutely certain that only the brine tanks can be discharged.

There is only one brine/drillwater connection, which is on the starboard side aft. During the discharge the ship should, if possible, be trimmed by the stern and, as individual tanks approach completion, be listed in the direction of the suction.

Tanks should be sounded to ensure that they are empty, and the quantity received by the installation agreed. Serious discrepancies must be investigated by visually checking the chain lockers and sounding No.1 DBs.

Brine tanks: cleaning

After carrying brine do not, if possible, ballast the tanks prior to cleaning. They should be cleaned by hosing them down with fresh water, introducing a small quantity of fresh water into the bottom, pumping them out, and allowing them to dry.

Base oil and oil-based mud: loading

Tanks available	Capacity
Mud port	95.0 m^3
Mud starbd	95.0 m^3
Mud centre	136.2 m^3

	90% capacity
Mud port	538 bbls
Mud starbd	538 bbls
Mud centre	771 bbls

Prior to commencement of loading, the charterer's representative must be made aware of the state of the tanks, i.e. dirty, mud clean or brine clean. It will then be in the charterer's interest to improve the cleanliness of the tanks if he regards this as necessary.

If any mud tank already contains cargo, the tank valves should be carefully checked to ensure that only the designated tanks are filled.

Mud is loaded through the mud load/discharge connections midships and aft on the port side of the afterdeck.

During loading, the ship should be as close as possible to an even keel and the quantity loaded monitored by means of hand soundings in conjunction with the readings on the shore meter. Towards completion the rate of loading should be slowed down, and careful liaison with the mud company personnel ensured.

On completion, any serious discrepancy should be thoroughly investigated and the mud company and charterer's representatives made aware of any discrepancies. A sample of the mud loaded should be kept on board.

Mud: carriage at sea

At sea, mud should be circulated. On this vessel each tank can be circulated independently, and each tank should be circulated for not less than four hours per day, for as many days as the mud is present on the vessel.

It is essential that, while mud cargoes are on board, the deck is sufficiently illuminated at all times for the bridge watchkeeper to see any accidental overflow. On this vessel it is possible to illuminate the mud tank vents by means of the after gangway lights port and starboard.

Oil-based mud and base oil: discharge

The rig mud hose should be connected to the aft mud connection on the port side.

If more than one grade is being carried, it must be perfectly clear on the ship which grade has been requested and the installation must be aware of what the ship intends to pump up. The bridge and the engine room must each be sure that the other knows which grade is to be pumped, and which tank or tanks it is in. In other words, there must be instruction and verification in every respect. The tank valves should be double checked.

During the discharge the lower suctions should be used, and the upper suctions brought into operation only in the event of blockages of the lower suctions. The ship should be trimmed by the stern and, when discharging the wing tanks, listed in the direction of the suction.

On completion, the quantity discharged should be agreed with the installation and in the event of a discrepancy this should be investigated at the time by sounding the tanks.

If necessary, small quantities remaining should be pumped into one tank and the discharge completed.

Mud tank cleaning

The vessel's mud tanks are maintained in a brine clean condition and on the completion of a charter it is the charterer's responsibility to leave them in that state.

During the charter the state of the tanks remains the responsibility of the charterer, though he should be made aware of the possibility of blocked suction. This requires the ship to make occasional visual inspections of the tanks when empty.

Mud tank cleaning systems

The recent introduction of shipboard mud tank cleaning systems somewhat alters the last paragraph of the bulk procedures guide for vessels so fitted. Ships with these systems bear the responsibility for maintaining the condition of their mud tanks to a standard which has previously been agreed with the charterers.

Figure 39   *A tank cleaning machine in position*

Operation of mud tank cleaning systems

Anyone who is familiar with the operation of crude oil washing systems will have no difficulty in understanding the manner in which mud tank cleaning systems operate. They are intended to remove from the tanks the accumulated solids which settle out from the liquid during carriage. This settlement occurs even in vessels fitted with agitators, and gets worse in direct relation to the length of time the cargo remains on board.

Once settlement has occurred there is no means generally available to return these solids to the liquid. As a result, over a number of voyages the level of sediment increases, reducing the carrying capacity of the vessel and threatening its ability to discharge its cargo via the lower suction.

Since the liquid used to make the mud is formulated to accept the solids, the best means of reducing the sediment within the tanks is to spray it with mud, and this is what the tank cleaning machines do.

The process of returning the solids to suspension and discharging them to their eventual destination, whether it be to an offshore installation or the shore tanks of the mud supply company, ensures that none of the cargo is lost and that the mud is discharged at the correct weight.

Tank cleaning machine data

The tank cleaning machines operate in a programmed cycle: at 8 bar one cycle will take about 10 minutes, the throughput of the machines being approximately 15 m^3 per hour. It may take up to three complete cycles for every point on the surface of the tanks to be covered.

In small tanks where the area of impingement is seen to be narrow, the jet

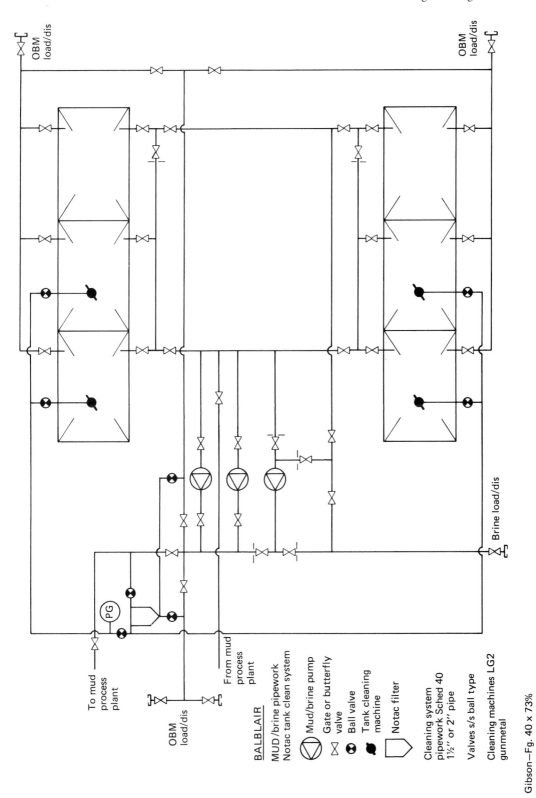

BALBLAIR

MUD/brine pipework
Notac tank clean system

⬇ Mud/brine pump

⋈ Gate or butterfly
   valve

⊗ Ball valve

● Tank cleaning
   machine

▷ Notac filter

Cleaning system
pipework Sched 40
1½″ or 2″ pipe

Valves s/s ball type

Cleaning machines LG2
gunmetal

Gibson—Fg. 40 x 73%

Figure 40   *Schematic diagram of a PSV mud system*

To mud
process
plant

OBM
load/dis

From mud
process
plant

OBM
load/dis

OBM
load/dis

Brine load/dis

width may be increased by removing one or both stream straighteners from inside the nozzles, though the removal of both stream straighteners may reduce the ability of the jets to penetrate particularly glutinous solids.

Strainers in the system

Strainers are installed to protect the cleaning machines from stones and other large objects which may be added to the mud, particularly when backloaded from the offshore installation. They also protect the system from pieces of wood and polythene which are sometimes added to the mud when it is being mixed ashore.

The cleaning operation

The tank cleaning machines are started up as soon as they are clear of the mud to give the maximum number of cycles before the tank is emptied, and on most vessel two complete cycles can take place. This will usually result in the tank walls being extremely well washed, but the cleaning jets will only have a good effect on the tank bottom when there is very little mud left in the tank, so the bottom will probably not be completely cleaned before the tank is empty.

The internal coatings of the mud tanks also have an effect on the cleaning operation. Tanks which are painted, particularly with epoxy paints, are easier to clean than uncoated tanks. Tanks where the steelwork is either completely un-treated or only covered by a primer tend to hold the mud, thereby reducing the wash effect. Hence in this type of tank all surfaces should be directly jetted, inevitably increasing the cleaning time.

Thus, as well using the basic cleaning methods, it may be necessary to carry out additional operations when circumstances permit, or use alternative methods during each discharge.

The simplest alternative technique is to commence cleaning the first tank when it is empty, and the discharge of the second has started. The cleaning machines will then be jetting a completely empty tank, and the ideal three cycles can be carried out while only putting a few cubic metres of mud back into the tank. In fact, on some vessels it may be possible to crack open the discharge valve of the tank being cleaned and so keep the tank bottom completely clear.

When discharging the last tank, the only way of carrying out an effective cleaning operation is to slow down the discharge when it is close to empty, possibly stopping it altogether and allowing the mud to circulate through the cleaning machine for a couple of cycles. However, if time does not allow this, it is only necessary to ensure that another tank is the last to be discharged next time.

Opportunities may also be found to clean the tanks when only small quantities of cargo, or part cargoes, are aboard.

Where an empty tank is available, the cleaning machines can be operated for a number of cycles and then the residues returned to the tank of origin. On some vessels it is possible to use the main discharge pump to operate the cleaning machine or machines, and for the residues to be returned to the original tank using the circulating system.

Where water-based muds are being carried, every effort should be made to operate the cleaning system during discharge in a way which will ensure that residues left aboard the vessel are minimized. These products are extremely expensive, and so far have proved less capable of holding the barytes in suspension that oil-based muds. Hence the need to deliver the product to the rig at the correct weight assumes some priority. The same may be said of the so-called 'environmentally based muds', which are non-toxic, but even more expensive.

These two products have no adverse effect on the environment and therefore may be discharged to the sea. In the event of the vessel's tanks being empty but mud clean, having carried either water-based mud or 'environmentally based mud', some water may be introduced to one of the tanks and a cleaning operation carried out to return the tanks to a brine clean condition. Before carrying out such an operation, permission to do so should be gained.

It is also possible to clean the tanks to brine standard using a small quantity of base oil. If 30 bbls or so are introduced into one tank, each tank may be cleaned in rotation until they are all brine clean and all the barytes has been returned to suspension in the base oil. It can then be retained aboard as part of the next mud cargo, or returned to the mud company for cleaning and credit.

Stability

Traditionally, supply ships have always had very large GMs, and have been very stiff at sea, and consequently during the early years of their operation some of their special stability problems were not realized.

It only took a few stability calculations for a supply ship master to see that by keeping plenty of ballast in the ship it remained theoretically very stable, with a massive righting moment. Most supply ships would go to sea right down to their marks, whether loaded with cargo or not, and carried out anchor handling operations so deep in the water that even in moderate weather conditions the crew could expect to be paddling for the majority of the time.

No account was taken of the fact that, being so deep in the water, the ships would suffer from deck edge immersion, and at that point there would be a massive reduction in the area under the curve. There was also a tendency not to carry out stability calculations at all, but to rely on previous experience, and so slack tanks were seldom taken into account. Indeed ballast tanks might be filled up, but on passage start to empty themselves through the deck vents if heavy rolling was taking place. The tanks then became slack without anyone being aware of it.

Tubulars were seldom thought about until the unique properties of supply ships were looked at by the Department of Transport when passing the ship's stability books. It was not realized that tubulars have a great capacity for entrapping water and therefore increasing the deck weight to a point where, under certain conditions, the ships will become unstable. Stability information for modern supply ships contains data on how to deal with this problem.

Modern supply ships also have a much smaller light ship GM due to the increase in accommodation size in relation to the hull. They also have larger numbers of dedicated tanks, which reduces the ballast capacity. It is therefore essential that stability calculations are made, no matter how tedious this may seem, and some estimates of the ship's condition after discharge considered.

It should be borne in mind that ballasting during discharge may result in large numbers of slack tanks which, in rough weather, with the possibility of deck edge immersion, leave the ship in a vulnerable condition.

There have been some losses of supply ships due to cargo problems, which have illustrated the absolute necessity to ensure that the ship is aware of its own stability condition, and that at all times the first point of access of water into the vessel is borne in mind. If all the access points are closed there is very little chance of a supply ship sinking; if not, it is when the first access lets water in that the stability curve becomes vertical.

In 1975 a supply ship capsized and sank while tied up to an oil rig. This was such an unusual event that the then Department of Transport canvassed the serving ship masters to try to find some explanation. The most popular theory was slack tanks.

In 1974 the *East Shore* sank after its funnel casing was penetrated by tubulars: water entered the hole and fused the electrics. Since the crew were lost, one can only assume that subsequently the engine-room gradually filled up until the vessel sank. While this loss is attributable more to shifting cargo than to loss of stability, it illustrates the importance of maintaining the integrity of the hull.

In fact, it is difficult to see how stability could be monitored during discharge without the computer, which has come to the aid of the supply ship master and provided a means by which stability calculations can be made rapidly. The best known stability program available for supply ships is that marketed by Sea Information Systems of Aberdeen (Figure 41). This program allows various situations to be analysed and will quickly show if the ship is going to be in trouble.

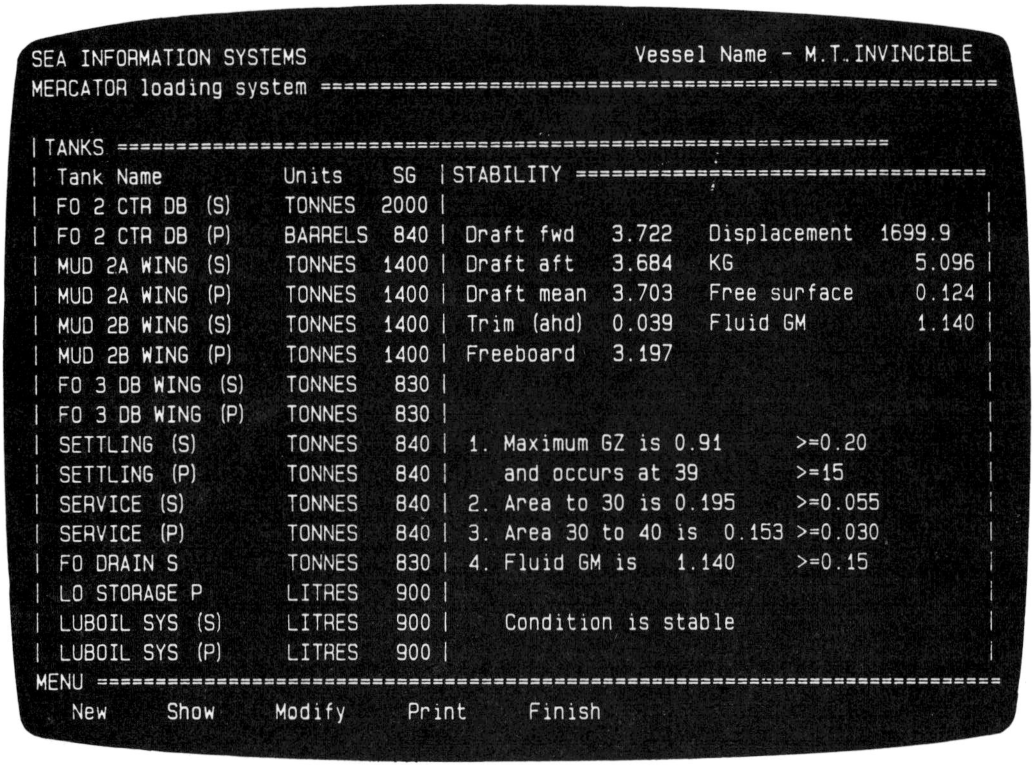

```
SEA INFORMATION SYSTEMS                      Vessel Name - M.T. INVINCIBLE
MERCATOR loading system ===============================================

| TANKS ================================================================
| Tank Name          Units    SG  | STABILITY =========================
| FO 2 CTR DB  (S)   TONNES  2000 |                                    |
| FO 2 CTR DB  (P)   BARRELS  840 | Draft fwd   3.722  Displacement 1699.9 |
| MUD 2A WING  (S)   TONNES  1400 | Draft aft   3.684  KG           5.096 |
| MUD 2A WING  (P)   TONNES  1400 | Draft mean  3.703  Free surface 0.124 |
| MUD 2B WING  (S)   TONNES  1400 | Trim (ahd)  0.039  Fluid GM     1.140 |
| MUD 2B WING  (P)   TONNES  1400 | Freeboard   3.197                  |
| FO 3 DB WING (S)   TONNES   830 |                                    |
| FO 3 DB WING (P)   TONNES   830 |                                    |
| SETTLING (S)       TONNES   840 | 1. Maximum GZ is 0.91      >=0.20  |
| SETTLING (P)       TONNES   840 |    and occurs at 39        >=15    |
| SERVICE (S)        TONNES   840 | 2. Area to 30 is 0.195     >=0.055 |
| SERVICE (P)        TONNES   840 | 3. Area 30 to 40 is  0.153 >=0.030 |
| FO DRAIN S         TONNES   830 | 4. Fluid GM is   1.140     >=0.15  |
| LO STORAGE P       LITRES   900 |                                    |
| LUBOIL SYS (S)     LITRES   900 |    Condition is stable             |
| LUBOIL SYS (P)     LITRES   900 |                                    |
MENU =================================================================
   New    Show    Modify    Print    Finish
```

Figure 41 *Typical VDU display showing actual loading conditions against the permitted limits*

Alternatively, if no proprietary program is available, a little knowledge of BASIC will allow anyone to develop their own, which, even if it does not present all the information available with professional software, will be at least as good as working it out with pencil and paper. See Appendix I.

Stability tanks

Most supply vessels are fitted with what are known as stability tanks, though they would more properly be known as stabilizing tanks since their purpose is to increase the roll period. This is done firstly by only partially filling the tanks so as to provide free surface, and therefore reduce the GM, and secondly by providing some impediment to the movement of the water from side to side, e.g. fitting them with a number of latticed grills in a fore and aft direction, or situating the tanks in a U-shape round the hull and restricting the flow of air in and out. Some are provided with charts showing the level to which they are to be filled, depending on the roll period.

In view of the foregoing, it is essential that these tanks be used with the full knowledge of the stability of the vessel.

All these tanks stretch from one side of the ship to the other, and it has been known for them to give problems when being used for the carriage of water rather than for stability. If they are filled up there is obviously no free surface, but when the ship is rolling water can sometimes overflow through the deck vents, in a similar manner to the ballast tanks described earlier. The result is similar but much worse, since loss of water from the tank will result in a great deal of free surface, fine when it is necessary but potentially disastrous when it is not.

On some supply ships where this problem has been identified the vents have been extended up to the level of the crash barrier so that there is no loss of tank contents during heavy rolling.

When deciding whether or not to use the stability tank, the filling of other tanks at the other end of the vessel must also be considered. To end up with the right trim, several hundred tonnes may have to be added to the displacement of the vessel, with a corresponding loss of freeboard. It should be borne in mind that it is really not sufficient to ensure that the vessel is not overloaded. On some supply ships there is very little freeboard when loaded down to the marks. The ship may be safe to go to sea within the terms of the Merchant Shipping Act, but may still take on board a great deal of water in heavy seas, putting the cargo and the men on the deck at risk during cargo work.

Care of the cargo on passage

On passage there is a natural requirement, as with all ships, to protect the cargo from the sea, and it is all too easy to assume that everything is well secured and that if it is possible for the ship to make headway all will be well.

Modern supply ships, particularly anchor handlers, are capable of maintaining good speed in very heavy head seas. In this situation they are extremely uncomfortable, and can ship very heavy seas on the afterdeck, putting the cargo at risk.

It is therefore first of all necessary to keep a good eye on the cargo. The watchkeeper should frequently move to the after end of the wheelhouse and look at the boxes on the deck to see how they are reacting to the movement of the vessel and the water on deck. Although opinions differ, it is probably advisable to keep the deck lights on so that the deck can be seen even at night. It must be accepted that this will reduce the ability of the watchkeeper to see the lights of other vessels, but this may be considered an acceptable drawback, given the extreme manoeuvrability of the vessels. The only exception to this may be steaming in fog, where it is most unlikely that the seas will be rough as well.

If the cargo shows any sign of moving, steps must be taken to safeguard it. Quite often an alteration of course is effective. If the seas can be put abaft the beam, the ship can proceed at full speed without any seas coming aboard. This is such an advantage that very broad alterations of course are acceptable. Alternatively, slow down and wait for the weather to improve or for the wind to change direction. This is better than losing or damaging cargo, or having to put the crew on deck to carry out a securing operation in poor weather in the dead of night.

Once on the location, even if the weather is bad, the cargo is unlikely to be threatened. Dodging — steaming very slowly into the wind, then turning and running as slowly as possible before it — is a practice which supply ships have been engaged in ever since they arrived in the North Sea. Even in the worst weather the cargo will probably remain safe, since the ship will lift over the seas rather than running into them.

Going for shelter

When the ships were smaller it was accepted practice to send them to shelter if conditions were really bad. In the worst weather this usually involved running to the lee of the Shetlands in the North Sea. Today it is almost unknown for this to happen, since the danger to the cargo would probably be greater during the passage than if the ship remained on location. Also it would be necessary to judge when the weather would improve, to make sure that the ships were back in time, and again the return journey might hazard the cargo.

However, the improvement in weather forecasting often means that vessels will be given a time when they are expected to arrive at the location and may therefore be able to steam slowly in rough weather, easing the passage and keeping the cargo safe in this manner.

5 | Towing

Introduction

Towing, which was taking place for years before the arrival of the anchor handler, has been moderately well covered in principle elsewhere. However it is a subject full of mystique and, as in the offshore business, experience is traditionally handed on from master to mate. To the early anchor handler designers, little was available in the form of scientific input to their designs. There was some doubt about the advisability of having the towing point, i.e. the winch, so close to the forward end of the ship, since it was conventional tug practice to have the towing point as close to the stern as possible, while still allowing the tug the ability to turn.

Indeed, tug designers were faced with the difficulty of the initial requirement to place the winch at the turning point of the tug so as to allow it to change course, while at the same time being aware that by doing this they might be placing it in danger, since this would allow the tug to broach very easily and turn over if it ended up beam-on to the tow.

Hence the early anchor handler crews were instructed to secure their tow-lines to a point closer to the stern of the vessel than the winch: they took no notice. The early anchor handlers were also provided with fabricated strongbacks in sections, which bolted to the crash barriers. These were supposed to be erected across the deck before long-distance tows were taken on so as to support the tow-wire in the same manner as the permanent strongbacks then fitted to tugs. Needless to say, these were never used either. In fact it is curious that almost all modern deep sea tugs owe their designs to the offshore industry, which seems to have proved inadvertently that towing is much simpler than it appears to be.

Preparing for towing

The offshore industry recognized the broaching problem by using another tug accessory, the gob-wire. This wire is shackled over the tow-wire close to the stern

Figure 42   *The towing pod on a ME303. This vessel is equipped with twin workdrums, a single tow drum and three storage drums*

and is usually the end of the workwire. While the ship is required to turn, the gob-wire is let out; while on passage, it can be kept fairly tight to ensure that the tow-wire stays in the right place. The wire is passed through a device on the deck, either a shackle secured to a point which is usually under the deck plating, or a plate with a large eye attached to it, described below.

On some ships, particularly Norwegian vessels, a towing pod is used instead of a gob-wire, or sometimes as well as a gob-wire. The towing pod is a tube on a stand which bolts to the deck and through which the tow-wire is passed. This also has the effect of moving the point of the tow towards the stern.

When preparing for a tow, on vessels with open access to the bitts at the after quarters, these must be filled in with bolt-on sections that are carried on the vessel. However, most modern ships have a rail over the top of the bitts, making this unnecessary.

The towing pod and/or gob-wire point must then be put in position. The towing pod should be pulled by tuggers to the deck plate and bolted down. Some gob-wire securing points are also positioned in this way, but simpler designs only require the removal of a plate in the deck and the addition of a large shackle.

Some vessels are also fitted with what is known as a gob plate. This is bolted down in a similar position to the towing pod and if it is fitted the gob-wire is invariably used as well. The gob plate is fitted with a short length of chain which is shackled to the tow-wire and serves more or less as a back-up to the gob-wire. Its usefulness is debatable.

It goes without saying that on vessels that use bolt-down fixtures, the bolt holes should be cleared and prepared by filling them with greased rags while the ship in still in port.

Figure 43 *Both gob plate and gob-wire in use on a UT704 towing a small ship*

Connecting the tow

There are two methods used to tow rigs, either on the bridle or on the anchor. If the latter technique is to be used, the towing vessel simply takes the anchor pennant and connects it up to the tow-wire.

Towing on the anchor is therefore simple and the connection easy, and there is a body of opinion which considers it preferable because the weight of the anchor itself acts as a spring and so reduces shock loading. The only serious argument against the technique is that the crown pennant is unlikely to be as strong as the rest of the system. The method also offends the purists because it seems somehow casual.

If the bridle is to be used, the towing vessel must back in very close to the bow of the rig and the end of the bridle will be passed down, either using a suitably positioned rig crane or, more likely, by means of a small winch under the bow or helideck.

In this case the ship must back up until the end of the bridle is against the roller where, by means of a boathook and the end of the tugger wire, the deck crew can grab it and pull it onto the deck for securing.

On vessels with a towing gate the bridle must first of all be brought aboard and secured in the tong or the pelican hook. Then the gate may be closed, with a loop of tow-wire going over the top of it and back under it to the end of the bridle. The two can then be connected and the bridle released. The bridle and the end of the loop of tow-wire will slide under the gate and the tow-wire will end up resting on the top of it, ready for the tow.

Fuse links

To use or not to use fuse links: these are short lengths of wire of smaller dimensions than the tow-wire and are put in between the bridle and the end of the ship's wire. Their purpose is to break if the weight on the tow-wire becomes excessive, ensuring that the tow-wire itself remains complete. Hence, if the fuse wire breaks, the rig can recover the bridle, the ship can recover the tow-wire, and then the two can be reconnected with the minimum of disruption.

This sounds like a really good idea, except that drifting rigs now cause a great deal of panic, and it is becoming more and more common for the excess personnel on the rig to be helicoptered off if the tow is lost. Usually the reason for the tow breaking is heavy weather, and in really heavy seas it is difficult for the towing vessel to get close enough to reconnect.

If a fuse link is not used, all these problems may possibly be avoided since the weight on the tow-wire must be that much greater before it parts. So, in this, as with many other activities in the offshore industry, opinions are divided, and there is really no scientific evidence as to which method is preferable. The writer inclines to use of the fuse link, but with the proviso that the link be provided new for each tow, and that its breaking strain be within 10% of the breaking strain of the tow-wire. The casual use of 56 mm pennants as fuse links in 72 mm systems should be avoided, since there is obviously a massive disparity between the breaking strains of the two wires.

Where there is no fuse link, the most likely breaking point for the wire is at the ship end, either at the point where the wire leaves the drum or at the point where

Figure 44   *Towing in heavy weather. The tow-wire can be seen leading down over the stern, and two anchor buoys on deck (Photo Mark Nicholson)*

it goes over the stern, the latter particularly if proper steps are not taken to protect it. Hence, 700 metres or so of wire may end up trailing under the rig which really has very little hope of recovering it. The usual answer is to leave it where it is, and hope that it does not snag on any subsea object, employing a second bridle or the anchors for the towing vessels.

The towing spring

In many ways the towing spring is approached by the industry in the same way as fuse links. The towing spring is usually made up of a doubled length of very large diameter plaited nylon with a large eye in each end. To use it at all the ship must

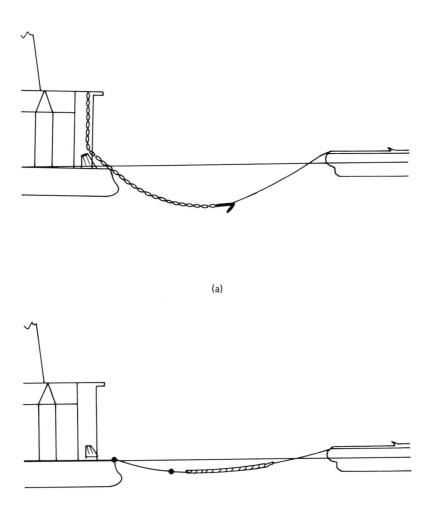

(a)

(b)

Figure 45 *(a) Towing on the anchor*
(b) Towing with a spring

also be provided with a special shackle, although a conventional 100 tonne D shackle will sometimes suffice.

Experience with towing springs has shown that these have the same tendency to break as the fuse link, though the reason for this may be the degradation of the material over the passing of time.

Where a tow is to take place in shallow water with a great deal of manoeuvring, it is possible that the spring will be useful, since it will take up shock loading when there is little catenary in the cable.

Probably the most important consideration with towing springs is that they should be kept in good condition during storage. It is acceptable to reel them onto the tow drum and to cover them with the tow-wire cover. They should not be stored in areas such as the steering gear compartment where they will soon become contaminated with hydraulic oil.

The initial stages

The tow-wire is passed through the towing pod or gob-wire shackle and secured to the pennant or bridle. The ship may then reel out the tow-wire and pull away from the rig.

At this point the other anchor handlers will still be at work lifting the remaining anchors, and the towing vessel will be able to lie quietly at the end of the tow with the engines clutched in, maintaining the rig heading. However, if the weather is poor, the rig will be tending to drift off heading and will be instructing the ship to take up different headings to hold the position. Because of the state of the job, the tow-line will also be kept short.

The first problem is the snatching of the tow-line, and the master must make an intuitive judgement as to how much weight he can afford to put on, since a big swell may put sufficient weight on the tow to break it. More tow-wires are broken during this part of the operation than at any other time.

Secondly, he will be receiving instructions to change direction for a tow which is not moving, so just turning the ship and steaming off in the new direction may not produce the required result. A better technique is to use the rudders and the bow thruster to move the ship sideways, so that the whole ship and tow-line pivot round the securing point on the rig until the new direction is taken up. This technique may also be used by ships towing on the anchor through a towing gate, which restricts the movement of the wire.

Most tows take place using two ships, one of which will be designated as the lead tow. The second ship will be connected up as the anchor recovery operation is being completed, or may be the ship which has lifted the last anchor if only two ships are involved.

Connecting the second towing vessel

The second vessel to connect up has a different set of problems to deal with. There are only a few occasions when a ship has to work to a rig which is not attached to the seabed, and this is one of them. It should be remembered that once a rig is mobile, all previous concepts are reversed: the weather side becomes the lee side, because the windage of the rig is greater than the windage of the anchor handler, and so it will drift faster.

In addition, if the anchor handler gets into the lee of the rig it will be sheltered.

The result can be a large object bearing down rapidly, and the only means of escape is to go full ahead until clear. Many ship masters getting out of this situation have found that they have had to alter course round the bow of the rig to stop the stern being run down, and have then been confronted with the tow-wire connected up to the first towing vessel. It says something for the manoeuvrability of the supply vessel that they usually manage to turn the other way in the 15 metres or so available.

One master paid the price of failure by getting the mast of his ship tangled in the bridle which was attached to the top of the legs of the rig, but was sufficiently skilled to turn onto the correct course and, once the mast had detached itself and crashed to the deck, was able to pull clear.

To minimize such difficulties, the second tug should request that the rig be turned into the wind by the first and that the ahead speed should be minimized. Then there should be little difficulty in approaching up the correct side and edging in ahead of the leg that is closest to the bridle to be passed down. Ships with fixed-pitch propellers may need to have one engine going astern, while the other is set with sufficient revolutions to maintain forward progress.

Having overcome these problems, the second towing vessel will be successfully connected and both ships will be instructed to take up a heading. The rig is now mobile, so conventional alterations of course are possible.

Initial alterations which may be quite large require the coordination of both vessels: the one on the inside of the turn must not alter course too rapidly, or the one on the outside will not be able to keep up: the one on the outside must not turn faster than the one on the inside, so as to avoid getting too close.

Once on the correct course, the lead tug will begin to pay out tow-wire and the second tug should do the same, always remaining slightly astern of the other vessel. When sufficient tow-wire has been paid out, the tugs can begin to increase speed. All this may take a couple of hours and will proceed quite naturally, the complete tow beginning to make progress along its intended path.

Increases in power should be indicated by the lead tug to the rig, who will also instruct the second tug to make increases. If sister ships are carrying out the tow, the power can easily be matched; if not, it is a matter of guesswork and will only be of importance if the tow starts to take up curious attitudes due to an imbalance of forces.

There are some ships available which would not tow at full power, having bollard pulls in excess of 150 tonnes, but on the average anchor handler it will probably be possible to go up to somewhere near maximum power.

The use of high power anchor handlers

Frequently the rig insurers will stipulate a minimum of 10 000 bhp (7500 kW) total for the towing vessels, which used to result in two ships being used. However, with the advent of many vessels having well in excess of 10 000 bhp available, one vessel may well be used.

The use of these very high powered vessels may put an unacceptable strain on the tow-wire, the bridle and the associated wires and shackles. Indeed, with some vessels having a continuous bollard pull in excess of 150 tonnes, it is difficult to see how they could be equipped with tow-wires and shackles capable both of accepting this level of strain and of being stowed on tow drums and handled by the deck crew. When these vessels are being used, some caution must be exercised to avoid breaking parts of the system.

Responsibilities of the lead tug

There is no particular precedent for the selection of the lead tug. If two anchor handlers of different powers are to tow together, the higher powered ship may be selected; if one tug is a long-term chartered vessel and the second one is a spot charter, the long-term vessel may be selected.

As far as the vessels are concerned, it would obviously be preferable for the more experienced master to take the lead, but the charterers have no idea of the difference in experience so a master who has never towed anything before may end up in charge of the operation.

The lead tug has a number of traditional tasks which are to some extent super-fluous now that enhanced navigation systems are available, but are still carried out.

The master of the lead tug first of all discusses with the tow master the route to be followed by the rig, and agrees on the reporting intervals: every hour, every two hours or every four hours. At these times the officer of the watch on the ship will call up the rig, and give the current position, the distance gone and the distance to go.

The lead tug is traditionally in charge of the tow (a fact which is often lost to all concerned) and the master of the lead tug has a positive responsibility for the tow: it is his responsibility to make sure that the tow remains safe as far as possible. However, there may be times when the tow master and his team on the rig will instruct the tugs to carry out operations with which the master of the lead tug disagrees, and this particularly relates to towing in bad weather. Obviously, if the rig is on location and has just pulled the anchors, an unexpected change in weather must be dealt with in whatever way is possible; if the rig is in a sheltered situation, a decision must be taken as to when to commence the tow on the best information available.

The lead tug's master has a problem here, in that the rig may have a more detailed weather report than is available to him; however, he can ask for it to be read to him if the rig does not volunteer the information. Thereafter someone will decide that the rig is to get under way, and as usual there will be commercial pressures on the tow master and the oil company representative for action.

If it seems to the lead tug master unwise to commence the tow he must make his feelings known to the rig personnel, and must put his view positively and directly. Technically and traditionally it would seem that he cannot be overruled, but in the end the rig may issue an instruction and here the tug master is faced with a dilemma. While it is very difficult for him to refuse the instruction, he should bear in mind that if the tow-wire is broken it remains the responsibility of his owners to replace it. At this point he may be able to say that if the tow-wire breaks it will be the responsibility of the oil company to replace it. Any conversation along these lines can be recorded for future reference. It must be stressed that this is a hypothetical situation and probably has no precedent. Whatever the result, it will certainly make those on the rig think carefully about the intended action.

In the North Sea, broken tow-wires and rigs drifting about in high seas are becoming more common, though at the time of writing no concrete reasons for this increase have been detected. It is possible that rig operators are becoming overconfident of the operating capabilities of the very high powered vessels available and are forgetting that, no matter what the bollard pull, this has to be transferred to the tow via the tow-wire.

During a particularly bad blow in 1991 a rig left the shelter of the Shetlands for a northerly location. The seas were so high that at times only the mast tops of the two very large, high power towing vessels were visible from the rig. Three tow-lines were broken before the weather finally abated, by which time the whole tow had drifted about 100 miles in the wrong direction. At the time the decision to commence the tow was taken it was possible to see and feel the weather conditions, but it was assumed that they were about to improve.

While it is easy to be wise in hindsight, it does seem likely that the operation was initiated on the basis of some misguided thinking, which eventually put at hazard the rig and, importantly for the tugs, their crews who had to go out onto the deck to reconnect the broken tows.

Towing jack-ups

Jack-up rigs have their own problems, the main one being that they are not designed to be floating objects. When under tow they have a low freeboard and a GM that is affected by the legs which protrude into the air for up to 90 metres. Jack-up towing is, then, a fine weather operation. If caught out by bad weather the legs cannot be jacked down, and so the jack-up must remain afloat until an improvement occurs.

While the tug master can do little to assist a jack-up caught in bad weather, he should be aware of a number of relevant facts. In their drilling situation jack-ups require little marine involvement, so there will probably be no mariners among the crew. The operators will assign a tow master for the move, but he will not be aware of all the systems used on the rig, and may be unable to glean the relevant information from the rig personnel. Some operators are overcoming this difficulty by insisting that the rig owners assign a marine expert to the rig during each move.

It has been the custom and practice for the rig to collect loose objects and place them on the skid deck for the move; amazingly, up until recently this has included liferafts and lifeboats. Since marine expertise is not available, loose objects, including the lifeboats and any containers on the deck, are likely to be inadequately lashed down and in bad weather will begin to move about.

In 1990 a jack-up was lost when the lifeboats started to move about on the deck due to inadequate lashing down. The weather was awful, and a wave had demolished the helideck, but the rig was lost because one of the lifeboats broke off vents into the machinery space, and finally, allowed the ingress of water.

If a jack-up tow is caught in bad weather it is therefore essential that those in charge act to minimize the movement of the rig. It may be worth considering turning the tow downwind, even if this will take it away from the intended location; moreover, since jack-ups operate in shallow water, it may be that shelter is not far away. Very positive action for the protection of the rig should be considered since it is vulnerable to high seas, and if not protected may be lost. Indeed, the figures for the loss of jack-ups under tow are horrendous.

Maintaining the tow-wire

There are a number of theories as to the manner in which the tow-wire should be maintained. It is modern practice for tow-wire manufacturers to supply them greased internally and to wipe the outer surface clean before delivery. Therefore in theory it is only the outer surface that has to be maintained.

The easiest way of maintaining the outer surface is to grease the wire with some proprietary brand of lubricant during the recovery of the wire, so that the only problems occur when the tow-wire is not used for long periods.

If the wire is not being used, the lubrication intervals should be as long as possible, since the company must balance the potential for damaging the wire when reeling it off and on against the likely extension in the life of the wire by carrying out the greasing operation. In the opinion of the writer, a wire which has not been used for towing may be left for two years between coatings, and one which has been used for towing may be left for twelve months.

In between the maintenance periods and the towing operations the reels should be covered with burlap, which will hold the grease coating in position. After four years the wires should be changed, one for the other, to extend their working life.

A method frequently used both to grease tow-wires and to change them is to stream the wire aft of the vessel, but this method may well damage the wire on the seabed and so is to be discouraged. A more effective technique is to use the ship's workdrums and reel the wire from one to the other, using some of the methods described in the section on deep water anchor handling. If the workdrum is not large enough to take the tow-wire, a powered reel should be obtained to carry out the job. If the ship owner is reluctant to provide this, the best course of action is just to coat the outer surface of the reel and leave it. More damage is likely to be done to a tow-wire by moving it inefficiently than by leaving it with a modicum of surface corrosion visible.

After reeling on a tow-wire in a non-operational situation, whether it be for maintenance or when one is being replaced for any reason, when the ship next connects up a tow the wire should be reeled out as far as possible and then recovered to the correct length. This is once more to avoid buried turns, which will cause embarrassment and damage the wire.

Wire protection during the tow

During the tow the wire moves over the metal surfaces of the ship, whether it be a rounded quarter or a towing gate, and this will eventually wear it away. To alleviate this problem, tow-wires are usually reeled onto the drum with two plastic towing sleeves in place. The wire is threaded through them before it is fitted to the drum and so they end up next to the eye.

To hold them in place during the connecting-up operation a shackle is usually placed over the wire, between the sleeves and the eye, so that the wire will run out through them, the shackle being connected to a tugger wire. When the tow has been fully extended, the tugger is slackened off until the sleeve runs down to the point of contact between the wire and the ship. Then, as the wire moves across the stern, the sleeve rotates, ensuring that no wear takes place.

Two sleeves are initially fitted so that if one wears out, or if one is lost down the tow-wire during the initial part of the operation, one remains for use.

Figure 46 *Rig under tow. The gob-wire is in position. The first nylon protector is at the roller and the spare is forward of the gob-wire*

If the tow-wire is not fitted with a sleeve, the ship must resort to more traditional techniques. Firstly, the wire must be paid out a little every hour. The amount can be as little as 1 ft (300 mm) each time, so many days towing will pass before the difference in length can be seen. Secondly, the point of contact on the ship, whether it be the shaped stern or a towing gate, must be greased thoroughly. Attention to this sort of detail may just make the difference between keeping the tow and losing it in rough weather.

Towing routine

Once the rig is under tow and the towing vessels have the required amount of wire out, the lead tug will work up to full speed and instruct the second tug to do the same. The two ships will be steaming on the required course about one cable apart, with the rig trailing directly astern. The ships can keep the correct distance from each other by setting the range marker on the radar and checking it occasionally.

There is little else to do but watch what is happening, check the distances from the other ship and the rig, and keep a good lookout for vessels which may think they have right of way. Alterations of course will be indicated by the lead tug and should be carried out as soon as the instruction is received by the second tug.

While there is really not much difficulty in the towing operation, the mystique which it has developed tends to give the ship master the impression that he must be constantly supervising everything that happens. In fact the difficult parts occur at connection and the initiation of the activity, and at the end of the tow. In good weather the parts in between are simple and can easily be dealt with by an experienced watch-keeper. This and the fact that during an anchor job the only real rest period available is when the tow is under way, mean that at this time the master should take the opportunity to get some rest. The least he should do is recline on the chartroom settee, but there is really no reason why he should not retire to bed as long as he has a telephone link with the bridge.

It is customary to have a couple of crew members available, however, since for some reason they always seem to be unable to respond rapidly to a request to go onto the deck in an emergency. This is not a problem if the M Notices are conformed to, since there will be four men available and they will be able to adopt a six on/six off routine. The watch officers will also be able to adopt the same routine, leaving the master rested for the next stage of the activity.

Slowing the rig down

As the rig approaches its new location a ship may be designated to slow it down, usually by connecting to the stern. The preamble to this may be the loading of anchor gear while the rig is moving, as described in Chapter 3.

This job is not difficult as long as no alterations of course are required. However, should the rig need to go round again, or for any reason change the direction of approach, the stern tug may be given new headings tens of degrees away from the correct heading. The only way of taking up this new heading is to reduce the weight in the tow-wire which, since the rig is moving, is making no change in direction possible.

The ship should therefore increase stern power until the tow-wire is slack, and then, when the master judges that there is a good catenary, turn the bow well past the new course and steam out in that direction. If this manoeuvre is successful he will reach the new heading, which can be checked with the radar, before the tow-wire tightens up and pulls him stern-to once more. Then, by steaming slowly on the new course, he will take his part in changing the rig direction.

Towing barges

Barge towing is an activity carried out more and more by anchor handlers as the deep seas tug fleet is reduced in numbers. Indeed, it is probably the proliferation of high power oil rig supply vessels which has caused this reduction.

The techniques used are essentially the same even though many of these tows are over extremely long distances. The use of fuse wires or towing springs is not common since the barges are usually ship shaped, and there consequently should not be any extremes of shock loading. The presence of either of these items is also likely to impede the manoeuvring capability of the tug and tow in restricted waters.

This is becoming a frequently used method of moving jack-ups for long distances since, as has already been discussed, jack-up designs do not lend themselves to being towed.

The method of loading the jack-up is to sink the barge and then float the rig over it, and it is important for the tug master to be certain that the barge hull remains sound after the operation is carried out. Boulders on the seabed can hole a barge and it will be some time after the tow is at sea that any loss of buoyancy becomes apparent. It is therefore important for the tug master to inspect the tow with the tow surveyor, and preferably to have the tanks sounded before setting out.

It is normal practice for the barge to be fitted with a second bridle with a short pennant attached. This in turn is joined to a light line which is buoyed at the end, and will float astern of the barge when under way. This arrangement should be checked before departure since, if the tow breaks, there will be no one to help with reconnection in the middle of the Atlantic.

Route planning is important, particularly the projected fuel consumption and the planned fuelling points. Fuel consumption of a medium-sized supply ship is about 30 tonnes per day, and large anchor handlers may use up to 50 tonnes per day when towing at full power. Hence, during the tow the power used should be the minimum to achieve a reasonable speed through the water, otherwise the ship may find itself running short of fuel after a couple of weeks.

Supporting heavy-lift barges

A frequent task during the construction of offshore installations is the towing of modules out to the construction site, and then placing the barge alongside the heavy-lift barge for lift-off.

It is a normal component of this operation for the ship to tow the barge out and then have to remain on the location for some time before the modules are required. Hence the tug and tow may find themselves steaming up and down at slow speed until they are required. It is almost inevitable that when they are called to go alongside that they will be in the wrong position, and the temptation therefore is to cut corners to get alongside. The tow will also almost certainly have to be placed between the jacket and the barge and even if the heavy-lift vessel has pulled off to make space, there will be very little room to manoeuvre.

It is essential that the tow make a long approach on the correct line, no matter how long this takes. By making a long approach, the effect of wind and tide can be taken into account while the tow is some way off and the course adjusted. This is important as there will really be no room for error in the final stages: you only get one shot at it.

As the tug nears the jacket the tow should be shortened up, and a second tug will attach itself to the stern of the barge to keep it correctly aligned. Indeed, much of the success of the operation will depend on the stern tug, but fortunately these vessels are usually part of the heavy-lift company operation and will be well experienced in the task.

When the tow is fully shortened up the wire may snatch at the stern, but despite this it is generally accepted that towing springs would impede the manoeuvrability of the unit and they are not normally used. The ship will ease through the gap between the platform and the barge. They will be alarmingly close, but there is no way to avoid this. Once past the barge, the stern tug will slow the tow to a stop and it will be allowed to drop alongside to be secured to the heavy-lift vessel.

It is conventional practice then to let out some of the tow wire and to remain in this position while the lift is taken off.

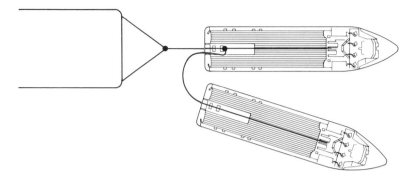

Figure 47   *Changing tow-wires at sea. The vessel to starboard is taking over the tow*

Changing tows

When the tow is on location it is not unusual for the towing vessel to be changed, for a variety of operational reasons. Like all activities involving vessels operating in close proximity at sea, this is an alarming experience. It is amazing how close one has to be to be able to throw a heaving line from one ship to another.

For this operation it is the usual practice for the vessel taking the tow to approach the other and close the sterns together as far as possible. The ship taking the tow will throw a heaving line across to the other and pull over a tugger wire. This will be connected to the tow-wire and the towing vessel will pull this across.

The ship connected to the tow now has the tow-wire from the other on board and will disconnect its own tow-wire, then connect this up to the bridle. The bridle is then released and the former towing vessel is clear. The new towing vessel is connected and may extend its wire and commence operations.

Salvage

It is the dream of all anchor handler masters to be steaming along and come across a very large ship in trouble, and to be able to carry out a salvage. The chances of this happening are similar to winning a lottery, but nevertheless supply ships do sometimes carry out salvage operations.

It is normally part of the charter requirements that one ship on the same charter as another will render salvage without making a claim. This effectively precludes the most likely salvage which statistically appears to be the standby vessel standing by the rig which the supply vessel is servicing.

In addition, should the opportunity of carrying out a salvage present itself, it is normally a requirement that permission first be obtained from the charterers. Since there is something like a 70% chance that the opportunity will occur outside normal working hours this may be difficult to obtain, but since the charterers will also receive a share of the salvage reward, the master may have to make his own judgement as to whether to engage in the activity, and then tell the charterers afterwards.

Lloyds Open Form

There have been changes in the administration of salvage awards, to make the service to be carried out more attractive to the salvor, but the principle remains the same.

Before carrying out the salvage the salvor should ask the master of the vessel being saved whether he accepts Lloyds Open Form. A verbal response either recorded or witnessed is initially sufficient, and the physical paperwork may be done later. The reason for the whole procedure should be remembered, which is to save the ship, but for the salvor to be suitably rewarded for his efforts by the insurers. It is preferable for them to have the ship saved, and to pay out for the service, rather than for them to have to pay out for a total loss.

Hence the value of the service is taken into account in making the payment. Maximum payment will be made if the vessel in distress would otherwise definitely have been lost and the salvor goes to considerable trouble and possibly hazards his own ship to carry out the service. The potential scenario for such a service is the rescue of a ship broken down and taking water in a force 12 gale in the middle of the Atlantic. Once having taken the ship in tow, the salvor has to proceed in the opposite direction to that intended and loses weeks from its intended schedule.

The other extreme might be a ship broken down a mile off the breakwater of a safe haven in flat calm with no anchoring capability, and a ship already proceeding to the port stopping for half an hour to connect up a tow and take it to safety. Obviously, in the latter case, even though the result of the service is the same — the saving of a ship which would otherwise probably be lost — the amount of effort on the part of the salvor is totally different, and this is taken into account when payment is made.

6 | Emergencies

Standby duties

The operation of standby vessels in the North Sea has become a specialized activity, and the ships involved are equipped with efficient and extensive equipment, both in terms of on-board equipment, and boats and launching davits.

Nevertheless it is possible, following the period in the 1980s when it was common for supply vessels to have standby capability under the then regulations, that a supply vessel may be equipped with a rescue boat, a crane to launch it, scrambling nets and a rescue basket. Regardless of the presence of this equipment, if possible rescue tasks should be left to the standby craft, which have the latest

Figure 48 *A modern standby vessel with one of its fast rescue craft in Aberdeen*

davits and rescue boats and whose crews are specially trained in rescue operations. However, in some parts of the world standby ships are not a requirement and so the supply ship master may of necessity have to engage in rescue activities, and if so a number of points must be considered.

The first consideration is the suitability of his inflatable, and whether this should be launched, or whether an attempt be made to recover men from the water directly onto the ship.

The condition of the rescue craft is all-important. The engine or engines must be maintained at all times, so that in the event of its having to be launched it is unlikely to break down; all too often ill-maintained engines have resulted in rescue craft breakdown adding to the disaster rather than alleviating it. Its crew should also be trained in launching and recovery. If this is not so, then it is not a

Figure 49   *A group of students on a survival course wearing survival suits and life jackets*

good idea to launch the boat, and it may be better to attempt to effect recovery with the ship.

The effect of immersion on men overboard

Initially immersion in cold water results in an increase in blood pressure, heart rate and breathing rate, and this in itself has been known to kill middle-aged or older people.

Victims will also suffer from rapid exhaustion if they try to swim, and as the length of immersion increases will progressively suffer from cramp, nausea and lethargy and will have problems with mental and physical processes. If someone in this condition is lifted from the water, particularly vertically, a 30% reduction of heart output may result, which will cause collapse or even death.

Hence casualties should not be allowed to exert themselves during rescue, which gives the rescue craft particular difficulties if they are not suitably equipped. Even where scrambling nets are part of the ship's equipment, if the vertical height to the deck is too great it may be hazardous for those in the water to attempt to use them.

It is only possible to put these points before the ship master, so that he may make his own judgement as to the most effective help he can give. However, if the decision is taken to rescue survivors directly from the water onto the ship it is possible that this task may be made easier by listing the vessel, and so reducing the freeboard.

Survivors on board the vessel

Assuming that the master is able to overcome these difficulties (and if he is the sole means of rescue he may have to), survivors need to be particularly carefully treated once aboard the vessel.

Alert and conscious survivors should be directed to a shower or bath as a means of rewarming them. If a shower is used, they should be able to sit rather than stand under it if possible, and should be carefully supervised in case they faint. Survivors suffering from serious hypothermia should not be subjected to this rapid rewarming treatment without proper medical supervision. They should then be given a warm drink, but no alcohol, and proper medical advice taken at the first opportunity.

Should the survivors be suffering from frostbite, the affected extremities should be warmed in water, then dried and covered with a dressing. This is a painful process so some painkilling drug may have to be administered.

Survivors may also suffer from 'immersion foot': the feet swell, become numb and discolored, and ulcerated due to poor blood circulation. Survivors suffering from this should have their feet gently dried without rubbing, antibiotics given to combat infection, and the feet dusted and dressed.

Evacuation of offshore installations

The primary means of evacuating personnel from offshore installations is by helicopter. If this can be done, the vessels on the location will have to stand by down-wind of the installation in the conventional manner when dealing with helicopter activities. The problem so well illustrated by the *Piper Alpha* and the *Ocean Odyssey* disasters is that events may move with such rapidity that evacuation must take place before helicopters have reached the scene.

If helicopters are not available, the next move in a controlled evacuation is for the installation personnel to be lifted by basket directly onto the support vessels. This procedure is also a somewhat long-term operation governed by the speed of the crane whipline, and the number of people capable of standing on the basket at any one time. People afraid of heights may find it a terrifying process and may only be prepared to stand on the basket in extremis. Once more, the process is fairly simple for the support vessel. It must remain within range of the crane and allow the basket to land on the deck.

Ship's crew should be available to lead the survivors into the comparative comfort of the ship's accommodation and to provide them with warm drinks. The supply ship master should be aware of the numbers of men embarking and, if other vessels are present, be prepared to move out of the way and allow the other ships to take survivors. Survivors may subsequently be reluctant to transfer from the vessel which has them on board either by basket at another installation, or by rescue boat, so an even distribution should be effected initially.

This is one procedure in which the standby vessels should defer to the supply ships, since they are less suitably equipped both to remain within range of the crane and to provide landing space for the basket. The primary requirement is, after all, to rescue the crew of the installation, and comfort and medical treatment are of secondary importance; while the comfort of the supply ship may not equal that of the standby vessel, it will be welcome enough to the survivors.

There are a few direct evacuation systems under development which use a wire from the installation to a special tension winch fitted to the standby vessel. Once the wire is under tension between the ship and the installation a survival capsule is winched back and forth carrying sixteen men at a time. So far the only vessels considered for this task have been the large in-field support craft which also carry out other duties. However, if it becomes a popular means of evacuation then standby vessels with good manoeuvring capabilities and long-term supply ships may be fitted with these winches.

The potential difficulty for the ship using this system is to maintain position while such intensive activity is taking place. While experience with it is limited, it would seem to the writer that the ship should have some means of detecting whether the tension winch is reeling out or in; if it cannot be seen visually, perhaps a readout on the console would be of assistance.

Some experiments have also taken place with specially strengthened liferafts which have been lowered from the overhanging decks of the installations directly onto the deck of a supply ship. The requirement for the supply ship in this case is simply to be very close, and in calm weather the master might take the decision to put the stern of his vessel against the legs of the installation. What minimal damage might result would probably be worth while if this assisted with the rescue.

Lower on the list of means of survival are the lifeboats, or 'totally enclosed motor propelled survival craft (TEMPSC)'. Most current models are situated about the periphery of the installation. In the event of the order to evacuate being given, and all the crew being at their allotted boat stations and capable of hearing the instruction, the boats will be loaded and, once everyone is aboard, lowered

Figure 50 *A Harding lifeboat positioned on the stern of a conventional ship*

away. The coxswains are instructed to turn the boats away from the installation, but there is a chance of their being blown back under the legs on the windward side, or being steered into them if the coxswain becomes disorientated. Some capsules can also be released from the lowering hook while still in the stowed position, and if this happens the occupants are unlikely to survive.

In an effort to improve the chances of the boats being driven directly away from the installations long glass-fibre booms known as *Prods* are available which direct the bows outwards, and experiments are under way with small torpedoes which are programmed to tow the boats away from the vicinity of the rig.

However, the most popular lifeboats in future developments are likely to be free-fall craft into which the survivors are strapped, and the boat then being released to plunge bow first into the sea.

What ever type of craft is being used, the support vessels should stand off to allow then to clear the structure. Once more, there is no precedent for such an evacuation. However, once the lifeboats are clear of the installation there is no reason why the supply ship should not approach them to within heaving line distance and then pull them alongside. The survivors may then climb up the nets, if available, or up the ship's rope ladders. This is a calm weather operation. In rougher seas transfers may possibly be better carried out by means of the standby vessel's RIB.

In extremely rough weather conditions where the survivors have managed to evacuate the rig in the lifeboats and liferafts it may be necessary for the ships on location to take them in tow until the weather improves and the survivors can be transferred.

Working with helicopters

It is possible during offshore emergencies that supply vessels may be required to work with helicopters, the most likely scenario being the dispatch of badly injured personnel to the shore.

If a helicopter operation is to take place, communication with the aircraft may be initiated on channel 16 VHF. Contact should be sparing, and should not take place while the aircraft is over the ship unless requested by the helicopter.

Prior to its approach, as large an area of deck as possible should be cleared. This may require restowing of cargo at the fore end by means of the tugger winches. This cargo should also be resecured to avoid any problems with it later during the transfer operation. Any small objects which might be blown into the air by the helicopter rotor should also be collected and stowed.

The ship should steam as required by the helicopter pilot, which will usually be into the wind, at extremely slow speed to minimize movement. The helicopter will hover overhead and a winchman will be lowered onto the deck. He should not be touched until he has landed and earthed himself on the ship, after which he will not give anyone an electric shock.

In the event of an injured man needing to be lifted into the helicopter, the winchman will secure the stretcher onto the winchwire, and will travel up with it back to the helicopter.

When survivors are lifted into the helicopter they will be helped into the lifting strop by the winchman, who will give a thumbs up sign when they are ready to be lifted. They will go up in turn. Such an evacuation must be carefully controlled on the deck, and it is suggested that the winchman will remain at the helicopter lifting position and the mate will control the movement of the men from the fore end of the deck to the winching position. On no account should they be allowed to assemble at the winching position.

Search and rescue

The most likely search and rescue operation which the supply vessel may be engaged in is man overboard emergency. If a man is seen to fall from ship or installation hopefully someone will be quick thinking enough to throw him a lifebuoy which will mark his position and allow him to be recovered rapidly.

However, SARs typically involve the loss of a man overboard at some indeterminate time, since his absence is only discovered later. Ships in the area where he may have been lost are then required to set up a search pattern and steam back and forth searching the sea for the man. The loss will be reported to the coast radio station who will in turn inform the Coastguard.

There are obviously other emergencies which may initiate a search and rescue operation: at the worst end of the scale, the abandonment of an offshore installation.

It is customary for an on-scene commander to be designated who, in the event of the emergency being concerned with or close to an offshore installation, will be the offshore installation manager. It is considered that he will be close enough to the scene to be able to monitor and coordinate developments. It is the on-scene commander's responsibility to execute the SAR mission coordinator's SAR plan, and to modify it in the light of any developments, changes in weather conditions etc. He should also deal with communication with all search units and brief any new arrivals. It is up to him to receive the reports from all search units, including the results of the searches as the units leave the scene.

In an oil field related incident the on-scene commander will normally again be the offshore installation manager, though if a decision is made to abandon the installation this role will be taken up elsewhere, and it may initially be required that the standby vessel master take on the task. However, since he will already be engaged in intensive rescue work the role may be passed onto the master of the emergency support vessel if there is one on the scene, or to the OIM of another platform or rig.

SAR radio communications

Other channels, in addition to channel 16 VHF, are used during search and rescue operations. Channel 16 is available to all vessels and aircraft both civilian and military and is therefore the basic communications channel.

Channel 6 VHF is also available to most ships and aircraft, and during an SAR mission is likely to be used between an airborne OSC and the CSS.

When numbers of vessels involved in a search are divided into groups, VHF channels 9, 10, 67 and 73 are used, one channel being assigned to each group. Channel 16 can then be used between the CSS and the group leaders.

Channel 0 is used by specialized rescue vessels and aircraft, and channel 70 is a distress channel used with Digital Selective Calling.

Emergencies concerning one's own vessel

Making the ship safe for heavy weather

Supply ships are capable of withstanding almost anything that the weather can deal out as long as proper precautions are taken to keep the ship safe, and to do this proper attention should be directed to all the openings in the vessel. In the simplest terms, this means that the master must ensure that all the openings to the deck are closed at the onset of heavy weather. Accesses to the engine-room in the winch space of anchor handlers are habitually left open, as is the steel access door to the accommodation in the same space. On PSVs the access door to the accommodation at the forward end of the deck is often left ajar for ease of entry. These should be closed.

Another easy point for the ingress of water on supply ships is the spurling pipes. On many ships these are left open, or at least only covered with canvas. On a vessel not so fitted the master should take steps to have his owners make up steel spurling pipe covers which can then be covered with canvas. Failure to do this may result in heavy seas flooding the chain lockers, gradually trimming the ship by the head, and on many vessels where the chain lockers are connected by means of non-watertight hatches to the forepeak store this space will also fill up, to make the situation even worse. Even if steel spurling pipe covers are fitted, it is a wise precaution to have the engine-room regularly pump the forepeak store bilges during very rough weather.

If the ship is shipping heavy seas forward the master should also issue instructions to close the deadlights in the forward cabins. Supply ship crews tend to rely on the glass in their portholes to withstand any seas which may come over the bow, but sadly this confidence is not always correctly placed and portholes have sometimes been pushed in to fill parts of the accommodation with water.

Cargo

The securing and the safety of the cargo have been dealt with elsewhere, but once more it must be underlined that shifting cargo can alter the trim of the vessel. Heavy items such as anchors are capable of sliding about on the deck in heavy rolling and stabilizing bars can go through the barrier to the ship's side, breaking off vent pipes and so allowing water to enter internal spaces.

Bridge windows

The supply vessel's bridge windows are extremely vulnerable to rough seas, and in the worst scenario they can be broken by heavy seas which then flood the bridge and cut off all controls by shorting out all the electrical circuits, so that the ship loses radar, steering and engine control.

All the controls should be checked, since some of them may still work even though others are non-operational. This particularly applies to the joystick, if fitted, since the wiring from the computer to the engines and rudders is frequently entirely independent of the manual controls.

Meanwhile, the ship will lie beam to the seas and will be rolling violently. Liferafts, lifeboats and loose or lightly secured items on the deck may be lost, but as long as all the accesses are closed and the cargo is secure the ship will remain safe. Hence the crew must concentrate on restoring control so that the ship may steam slowly downwind, and then securing the broken window.

If no control can be found on the bridge, an engineer should be dispatched to the steering gear to operate it from there. Communications with the bridge should be established, and one deck officer assigned to carrying out this task; another engineer should operate the engines from the control room.

The deck crew should then take steps to close the space made by the broken window. Many ships have steel plates on the bridge deck for this very purpose, in which case the task is simple. If such plates are not available, a suitable plug can usually be made up by taking up an engine-room deck plate, covering it with a couple of blankets and shoring it up against the inside of the window.

On some vessels even suitable shoring may not be available inside the accommodation, in which case the shelving from the dry store will be found to be ideal for the purpose.

Once all these tasks have been carried out, the master is in a position to assess the seaworthiness of his ship, and to decide whether to ask for outside assistance.

It can be seen from the above that proper precautions are necessary to keep the ship safe, and that it is a good idea to practise engine manoeuvring from the engine-room, and steering from the steering gear compartment.

Emergency drills

Formal emergency drills are a legal requirement of the operation of all ships, as is the posting of the emergency duties for each of the ship's crew as well as the abandon ship procedures and duties.

Unfortunately this legal requirement leads to a sort of stereotyping of both the drills and the duties, particularly since most ships are supplied with standard forms for the posting of and instruction in these duties. The result may be emergency procedures which are unsuitable for individual crews and ships.

It is suggested that one of the duties that the ship's safety committee should undertake is to review the emergency and abandon ship procedures for the vessel, and decide if they are really valid. If they are not, the committee should write new procedures tailored to that vessel and crew. Logical sequences should be set up which will allow crew members to move from the positions which they are most likely to be in while trying to save the ship to positions which they will be in when trying to save themselves, and these positions may differ, depending on whether the ship is sinking due to fire, stranding or rough weather.

If this is not done, when the real disaster occurs crew members will respond to it in a manner which differs from the assigned method and the whole emergency will be dealt with on an ad-hoc basis.

In making up new procedures the committee should consider the following:

1 Where will the master be as the emergency progresses? It seems likely that he may start on the bridge, but it is possible that in a very serious situation he may need to assign the bridge watch to a junior officer and take charge on site.

2 Where will the chief engineer be? There is a good chance that he will be in the engine-room until the last moment, either keeping the ship afloat or taking charge of the pumps which will be putting the fire out. Any emergency procedures should provide for his leaving the engine-room and, if he doesn't, someone going to get him.

3 How will the fire-fighting teams be made up? There is a tendency to assign everyone who has nothing else to do, to putting out the fires. This is not practical, and in fact small teams must be made up using the best qualified personnel to lead them. It may be that the second engineer would be the best leader of the primary fire-fighting party, since the most likely place for a fire is in the engine-room or associated spaces.

4 If the ship is equipped with both lifeboats and liferafts, which will be used in the event of abandoning ship? It is probable that this will depend on weather conditions and on the type of davits with which the ship is fitted. All possibilities should be allowed for.

5 How will the liferafts be launched? Will the rafts be launched while the crew stand about having given up their fire-fighting or ship-saving efforts? This seems unlikely. It is more probable that at some time a team will go to the rafts and prepare them, possibly even launch them, before it becomes essential that the ship be abandoned. A team should be available for this task while the ship-saving activities are still in progress.

Carrying out the emergency drill
Emergency drills should be practical and should be tailored to conform with likely events as far as possible; otherwise the drill will be little more than a token gesture which allows the master to fill in the official log book with a clear conscience.

One of the problems with supply ships is that for much of the time they are operating in poor weather conditions which make mustering outside uncomfortable. However, this is the first thing which the crew must face: the fact that abandoning ship is likely to be a cold and unpleasant event, and that all crew members should be properly clothed. Mustering on the bridge in T-shirts, jeans and flip-flops is unlikely to bring this point home.

The under-deck areas of supply ships are often labyrinthine and the recovery of an injured man from the most distant point from the engine-room access can also be very difficult. This should be practised. The fire-fighting teams should also practise under deck, though they will obviously be prevented from using real water.

The emergency fire pump should be capable of being started and put on line by any member of the crew, so during each drill a different crew member should be given this task.

Conclusion

It must be apparent from the foregoing that the most positive way of dealing with emergencies is training for them, and avoiding the 'It can't happen to me' syndrome.

In any emergency take the time to think what the best action may be and how the ship may be best operated either to save others or your own crew.

Supply ships are immensely versatile and well found craft, but to get the best from them any action taken must be considered and within the bounds of good seamanship. It is only by exercising good seamanship at all times that the limitations of the craft will be understood.

7 Miscellaneous activities

Changing anchor wires

Some semi-submersibles are fitted with wires rather than anchor chain, and these need to be changed every few years. To carry out this operation an anchor handler is fitted with a reel containing the new wire, and must go out to the rig, remove the old wire and reel on the new one.

The reel should be positioned at the fore end of the deck (Figure 51), and welded to the crash barrier and the transverse section which holds down the deck planking. This is quite adequate, and if done in this way the removal and subsequent replacement of deck planking is avoided. In this position the ship's workdrum, or one of the workdrums in the case of a twin-drum vessel, is left clear.

Having been instructed to start the job, the ship should lift and deck the anchor, stopper off the anchor wire, disconnect the anchor and then move it out of the way. The anchor wire socket should then be pulled up the deck until it is close to the workwinch, and the wire bulldogged with a couple of bulldog grips from the ship's stock. If the ship does not already carry them they should be obtained from the oil company before sailing.

These bulldog grips then become the stopper, and can be dropped back against the shark's jaw or whatever stoppering system the ship is provided with. The socket should then be burnt off the anchor wire. This is to save space, and to return the socket to the rig for further use.

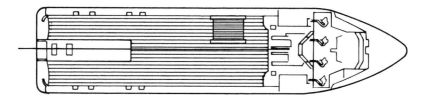

Figure 51 *The position of the anchor wire reel on the deck of an anchor handler*

The anchor wire should then be connected to the workwire with a strop and reeled onto the workdrum; obviously once a few turns are in place the bulldog grip may be removed. The anchor wire should be reeled on with great care. Every turn should be tight against the last and the wire run from side to side using tuggers or some other technique. It is important to have a smooth surface available when the drum is nearly full since at that point each wrap is worth about 15 metres.

Once the drum is full, the wire should be bulldogged once more and run back against the stopper. It can then be cut, and the first section cleared out of the way. If two workdrums are available the ship can go through the same process with the second drum, which will completely clear the old wire off the deck.

In the event of there only being one drum available, the master must decide whether to take on board the rest of the anchor wire by pulling on bights with the tugger winches, or whether to take the wire already collected off the drum, and go through the same process again with the remaining wire.

Probably the most important factor to be considered in relation to this decision is that, as the wire nears its end, the ship will be pulled in closer and closer to the rig, and inevitably during the operation the ship is already going to spend a great deal of time in the close vicinity of the leg which is having its anchor wire changed. Hence, in all but ideal weather conditions it seems advisable to strip the wire which has already been collected off the drum and lay it out on the deck, and then go through the process again with the last length of wire.

Whichever technique is used, eventually the end of the wire will be brought on deck, and shackled to a light messenger; this messenger should be shackled in turn to the end of the new wire. This is a very small shackle, which should be able to pass through the leads between the rack and the anchor winch on the rig. The messenger is also very small, so no weight can be put on it while it is being heaved back to the rig.

If events pass in the normal way, the rig will have sent down a technician on the basket, whose job it is to operate the brake of the wire spool to make sure that the new wire does not cascade to the seabed.

The small messenger wire shackled on to the anchor wire will be pulled over the stern and will gradually make its way through the leads until it reaches the deck. During this time the ship must remain very close to the rig, and the absolute minimum of cable should be paid out. While there is no doubt that a member of the ship's crew could operate the brake, by good fortune this responsibility lies with a rig mechanic, who alone must contemplate the horrors of letting too much wire out, breaking the messenger, and having to go through the whole process again, including putting a diver down to lead the messenger through the fairlead.

The wire will arrive on the rig deck, where it will be stoppered off and the messenger removed. Then they will feed it into the drum of the anchor winch and make it fast. Once the ship has received the word that it is fast, the master may give the instructions to pay out the wire, and may move away from the rig. Thereafter, the deck crew will go through the process of reeling it on, making sure that the turns are close up to each other and that each rap is put in place without causing any damage to the wire.

When the end is reached the ship may need to burn off the securing point for the socket, before which the wire should have been once more passed through the ship's stopper.

If the ship has a spare workdrum, which will only be the case if it has two drums, and if one has been stripped (somewhat unlikely), the anchor may be connected up and rerun. If not, the socket should be passed back to the rig on the crane, so releasing the ship. The ship can then stand off, strip the workdrum/ drums, and return to the rig to offload the wire. Since anchor wires weigh between 15 and 20 tonnes, half a wire may exceed the safe working load of the rig crane.

Spooling on pennants

Before an anchor job the ship is often supplied with sets of pennants, either new from the shore or sometimes in a used condition from the rig. In the latter case the symmetry of the coils cannot be guaranteed, and even in the former case unless great care is taken problems can result. Never connect up the eye and then drop the new pennant straight over the stern.

The prudent technique is to place the new coil close to the stern and connect up the eye on top to the workwire. Then turn each coil over to ensure that it is clear, until the other end of the pennant comes into view. This end may then be dropped over the stern. The rest will then follow in good order.

The pennant should then be wound on until the eye is on the deck, and the next connected, and the same process followed. When all the pennants are connected, the whole lot should be paid over the stern and recovered with the ship steaming. This will do a little to put some weight on them and make sure that there are no loose turns. However, if the opportunity occurs, possibly when the first anchor to be recovered is connected to the new pennant string, the whole lot should be paid out and recovered with some weight on.

If this is not done, it is certain that during the lifting of the anchors the pennants will bury turns on the drum. It is then something of a lottery as to whether these turns will jam tight while an anchor is being lowered to the seabed, placing the ship in an extremely embarrassing position and, worse, taking several hours to free.

Down-hole surveys

Occasionally the operators may wish to check the relationship between the hole and the substrata by carrying out a down-hole survey. The basic principle of this is to let off an explosion at a defined distance from the rig and recover data by the use of a geophone at a set distance down the hole.

The supply ship therefore is required to carry an air-gun and some form of sophisticated position fixing equipment, and fire the air-gun when instructed from the rig. Technicians will be sent aboard the ship for this operation, together with the position fixing equipment and the air-gun.

The air-gun will be attached to the end of the ship's crane wire — a ship without a crane cannot do this job — and the signal receiving equipment set up on the bridge, usually terminating in a VDU which will display a series of concentric circles within which the ship will remain while the gun is being fired.

The geophone starts near the top of the hole and is gradually lowered to the bottom, being fired at predetermined intervals. As the geophone gets deeper into the earth's crust, the ship must maintain position within a smaller and smaller circle. The easiest way of doing this job is to place the stern to the weather and, if one is available, maintain position using the joystick. In this way it should be possible to maintain position with little effort.

Once more the master should judge whether this task may be entrusted to his watch-keeping officers. It is not difficult, and does not involve the vessel operating in the proximity of fixed structures. In addition, it is good training. This is a good job for them to do and, since it will go on for many hours, the advantage of having a fresh operator at all times probably outweighs the extra skill which the master will have in manoeuvring the ship.

Basket transfers

Basket transfers now seldom take place, having been banned except for emergency or essential use, mainly because they are frightening for those who have to do them. There are no recorded accidents from them but they do seem to be an unsafe activity since they rely on the strength in the arms of those undergoing them.

The basket is a buoyant ring fitted with a conical net which is suspended from the rig crane. The passengers stand on the periphery of the ring and hold on to the netting. They are therefore on the outside of the basket and if they let go will fall into the water.

If a basket transfer is to take place the ship must ensure that there is a good area of clear deck at the aft end. For a transfer from the ship to the offshore installation, the prospective passengers should be prepared by wearing life-jackets or buoyant work vests and have any gear they are taking with them to hand.

The crane will come over with the basket and land it on the clear area of deck, leaving a little slack in the crane wire so that the netting remains vertical but the basket does not move. The passengers should throw their gear into the centre and then stand round the outside in a way that will distribute their weight evenly. A couple of crew members should stand on the deck and hold the netting to steady the basket. It is a good idea to put the arms through the netting and hold on from the inside. In this way the netting is held both by the bends in the arms and by the fingers holding directly onto the net.

If only one person is to make the ascent, the rig will often send down a man who is familiar with the system to make sure that the basket remains level during the lift, the theory being that he can manage an uneven distribution of weight but there is no knowing whether the passenger going up will be able to do so.

When the lift is ready, a crew member should indicate that they are ready to the crane driver and stand back. The crane will lift the basket into the air and away from the deck of the ship, take the basket up and then swing it over the deck of the installation.

A downward transfer takes place in exactly the same way. When the basket is landed on the deck, the crane driver will make sure that the wire is slack. The passenger will step off and while the basket is being held in position by a couple of crew members he can remove his gear from the centre of the basket.

Operating saturation diving vessels

Someone said that the function of a diving ship is to put a man on the bottom with a spanner and, stripped to its essentials, this is true. The problem is that the bottom may be 200 metres beneath the ship and the man needs to be positioned at the precise place where his work is to be carried out.

Under normal circumstances a diver returning to the surface from these depths would require many hours of decompression before he could rejoin those on the surface, so these ships are fitted with saturation chambers in which the divers live while they are resting between shifts.

Since the position of the ship must be precise and often within a couple of metres of the platform, diving ships are fitted with dynamic positioning systems which locate the craft exactly, using position fixing systems such as Artemis and Syledis, as well as taut wires and seabed beacons.

The resulting craft are complex and expensive to build and operate, and the responsibilities of the masters are extremely onerous. They are fitted with hyperbaric lifeboats into which the divers can move without being exposed to the atmosphere in the event of the ship being evacuated, though the thought of having to give such an instruction must weigh heavily on the minds of all diving ship masters.

While the ship is carrying out its diving operations the dynamic positioning system interfaces with the main engines and the thrusters to keep it in position, and so the strain on all power units is massive.

The main function of the deck officers is to monitor the position to ensure that the ship does not move away from it, and the engine-room staff must remain constantly alert for any machinery failure. All ship's staff are therefore carrying out highly stressful but normally boring activities which could be said to be the worst of all worlds.

Figure 52 *The diving ship* Wild Drake

Diving ships' staff are rightly highly paid for this essential work, but despite the financial inducements it is a role which is seldom taken up by supply ship officers who have usually become accustomed to the more active work of their craft.

Operating air diving ships

While specialized saturation diving ships that are used in deep water are all dynamically positioned and their officers are usually trained in the operation of the dynamic positioning systems, air diving vessels, which are a cheap way of maintaining platforms in shallow water, may be nothing more than supply ships with additional accommodation, a small decompression chamber and sometimes a small crane.

Their role is to drop two anchors and tie up astern to the platform so that the divers may work over the stern. Since it requires no special training, supply ship masters may find themselves carrying out this task.

Almost invariably the ships are old supply ships and are often low powered, with limited cable and, if the master is really unlucky, accommodation positioned on the afterdeck so that he cannot see the stern. He will usually be required to tie up without the assistance of the platform's cranes, since these may still be needed to receive supply ships. There will often be pipelines on or just below the seabed which must not be anchored on, but may be anchored over.

The secret of tying up these ships lies in preparation. The ship should lie off the point where the tying up is to be carried out, to allow the master to plot the direction of the pipeline in his mind. If this is insufficient, it may also be done on the radar.

The ship should be positioned bow-in at the first anchor drop point, which should be the down-wind or down-tide one. The distance of the position from the platform is determined by the amount of cable available. A distance of 150 metres will probably allow the ship to have five shackles out when tied up and still be able to carry out the operation to be described.

Having dropped the first anchor, the ship should be steamed towards the platform for at least half the distance from the drop point, then turned and steamed to the second drop point.

After the second anchor is dropped it is then possible to go astern back to the platform, paying out the second anchor cable while the first is easily dragged into the correct position (Figure 53). It can be seen that, if the ship proceeds directly from the first point to the second, both cables will have to be paid out and then, when the ship is in position, the windlass will have to drag the first cable across the seabed until it is tight. This is unlikely to be successful and will result in the first cable slackening up while the ship is tied up, giving cause for anxiety since the stern will move towards the platform.

If the stern is not visible from the bridge the master goes aft and gives helm and engine orders to the mate on the bridge by radio. This is difficult to do at first, but once a rapport has built up will be found to be successful. It is infinitely preferable to remaining on the bridge while the mate shouts up distances off, so that the apparent speed of approach will vary with his judgement of the distance.

Once tied up, the diving can commence; this may well be dependent on tide, so that the time available may be only a few hours a day. It should be remembered

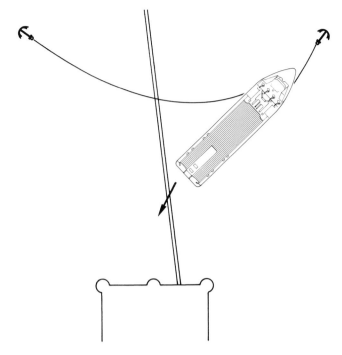

Figure 53 *An air diving ship tying up to the platform*

that, in general, the ship will be contracted to fulfil the role of a diving platform, and while it is in position its contractual obligations are being carried out.

As well as the restriction of tide there may well be times when the divers will not be working due to rough seas. This situation may well occur before the ship has to pull off from the platform; however, if the ship is not alongside the divers

Figure 54 *The air diving ship* British Enterprise I *tied up to a platform in the southern North Sea*

may say that the weather is suitable for operations before the master judges that it is calm enough to carry out the tying up operation. Hence it is a good idea to remain tied up, even if the divers are not working. It may be possible to pull off by slackening down the stern lines, and the ship will probably lie comfortably up to about a force seven gale, though naturally individual circumstances may differ.

Often the weather will ease without the ship having to let go, and the divers will be put in a position where they have to go to work at the first opportunity. This will place the master in a position of great favour with the company representative.

Operating seismic survey vessels

Seismic survey vessels are now almost exclusively operated by specialist companies, so it is unlikely that those in the supply industry will be required to serve on these craft. However, their operation is described in general so that anyone assigned to such a ship will have an idea of what to expect.

These ships were mainly former supply ships or large fishing craft, although today some extremely large and powerful ships are entering the market due to the larger arrays and greater lengths of cable which they are required to tow.

The seismic survey vessel is fitted with a large reel of cable on the stern which is used to position geophones at regular intervals astern of the ship, sometimes at distances greater than two miles. They also carry banks of air-guns which are deployed over each quarter. These are generally carried today on two rails which extend forward from the stern of the ship on either side of the reel.

The role of seismic survey vessels is to provide the oil industry with detailed data on the substrata under the seabed from which the interpretive staff can tell if there are suitable strata which might contain oil. Modern techniques require complex equipment, but as far as the mariner is concerned he is in charge of a ship which has at least two miles of cable trailing along behind it. This cable is vulnerable to passing ships, especially fishing vessels with their gear down so, as well as maintaining the predetermined track, much of the watchkeeper's time is spent looking for potential hazards which might threaten the cable.

Threatening craft are usually found by radar plotting, and if one is seen to be crossing the cable a positive attempt must be made to change its course. This is done firstly by attempting to contact it by VHF radio. Deep sea ships are usually called on channel 16, and there may or may not be any response.

The routine method used to indicate the survey vessel is to identify it by saying 'This is the seismic survey vessel in position X on course Y. I have two miles of seismic astern of me. Please keep clear. I am calling a vessel (follow with a description and then identify your position from the vessel, e.g. I am two miles on your port bow etc.)'.

If no response is received then indicate to the vessel the alteration of course which will be required for it to pass clear of the cable's marker buoy. This often produces results, which seems to indicate that many watchkeepers are either prohibited from using VHF, or do not want to use it.

Fishing vessels, particularly in the northern North Sea, cannot often be contacted on channel 16, since they tend to talk to each other on a frequency of their own. The objective is then to find this frequency and call them on that. Once more, an instruction as to what alteration to make is sometimes successful.

If all these techniques fail, it may be necessary to resort to firing white flares, all seismic vessels being provided with suitable pistols and large quantities of ammunition.

The effect of rough weather on the cable

During seismic work the cable is required to remain within certain depth parameters, and is kept at this level by what are known in the business as birds. These small winged appendages to the cable can be individually controlled so as to keep the cable, which is itself neutrally buoyant, at the correct depth.

In rough weather the ship will naturally go up and down and this puts a whip into the cable which will travel along it. If the movement becomes too great, the whip will take the cable beyond the depth parameters and the work will have to be stopped.

It is also necessary to consider recovering the cable when the weather gets bad, since too much movement during this operation will put an unacceptable strain on it. Indeed, if the cable is left out for too long there will be no chance of recovering it and it will have to be left out until the weather improves or until the ship can travel, at the moderate speed which is possible with the cable out, to a position of shelter.

Recovering the cable

The conventional method of recovery is to stop the ship and start reeling the cable in. However, because the whole length of it is being dragged through the water, this will also strain the cable: the ship should start going slowly astern, at all times keeping the cable lined up with the direction of the ship. This is not an easy task.

A simpler but less used technique is to maintain the speed of the ship at about 2 knots and then start to reel in the cable, gradually slowing down and allowing the momentum of the cable to be maintained by the reel. Eventually the ship should be stationary and the cable travelling at 2 knots through the water. Using this method the ship can more easily be kept in line and there is no great strain on the cable.

Recovering sub-sea buoys

Sub-sea buoys are those which are weighted in some way so that they sink to the seabed. When recovering them it should be a matter of approaching their position and then sending them their radio signal. They are released from their housing and bob to the surface.

There is really only one thing to watch for: the ship should not, if possible, be positioned directly over them. On at least one occasion a sub-sea buoy rose to the surface directly under the supply vessel that released it. It hit a point just aft of the engines under the propeller shafts where, as bad luck would have it, the ship was single skinned. The master ran for the nearest beach and was able to put it ashore before it sank. It was refloated on the next tide, when the hole had been patched up.

Pilotage on supply ships

The requirement to use a pilot on a supply ship varies from country to country and port to port, and is by no means as stringent as it is for deep sea ships.

When approaching a port the supply vessel master must first of all find out whether he will be required to take a pilot and, if not, whether he wants one anyway. Pilots are down to the charterers' account, and the charterer may be distressed to find that one ship takes a pilot and another does not.

It is probable that, if the master is unfamiliar with the port that he is approaching, he will have no idea where his berth is and this is often a good reason to take a pilot for the first time, and on every other occasion to do the pilotage himself.

A typical European oil port is Den Helder in The Netherlands, where the approach is by means of one of two channels (both of which are bedevilled by strong tides) into a river estuary, thence into the Dutch Naval Base, through the other side and into a canal, past a swing bridge, and finally to the supply ship common user berths. The Dutch do not require or even expect ships to take pilots either to enter or leave the port.

In places where a pilot must be taken by law, he will usually climb aboard, tell the master which berth he is allocated and then leave the rest to the master. This is the best course of action for both parties. The master knows best how his ship reacts and his driving technique is probably as individual in port as it is at sea, so any attempt by the pilot to superimpose instructions will end in chaos.

A small number of pilots will adopt exactly the opposite technique by taking the controls as soon as they arrive on the bridge. These men must be watched carefully. If they seem to know what they are doing it may be acceptable to let them carry on, but the master should be ready to take the controls if necessary to keep the ship out of danger.

Laying anchors over seabed obstacles

There are a number of situations where rigs may be positioned with their anchor wires or cables running over sub-sea cables or pipelines, particularly where they are being positioned within existing fields with sub-sea complications.

Here the operator requires that the anchors be positioned on the other side of the undersea impedimenta, and that during the laying of the cables they do not touch the seabed. This operation is normally carried out by using several ships. The first one will bring the anchor to the stern in the conventional manner and begin to steam out in the direction of the dropping point, usually under the guidance of laser direction-finders. If these are being used, the crew will be advised not to look in the direction of the rig during the operation.

A member of the rig crew operating the laser equipment will advise the ship what direction to move in; after it has moved out a predetermined distance it will be told to ease off its power and hold position. A second vessel will then approach the rig with a J-hook over the stern and hook onto the cable. The ship master should never miss the opportunity to use the J-hook in less critical circumstances since delays during this activity can be embarrassing.

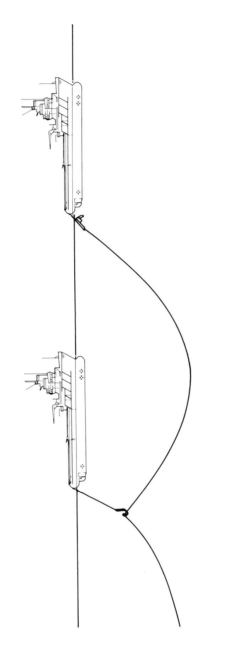

Figure 55 *Two anchor handlers running an anchor in tandem*

Once the second ship is hooked on, both vessels will be instructed to proceed outwards under laser guidance until the cable has been paid out sufficiently to hook onto yet a third ship. All three vessels will them be instructed to proceed, still being guided from the rig.

When the drop position is reached, the first ship will lower the anchor to the seabed, and the other two ships will run their J-hooks back to the rig and unhook them.

Working with chain

Anchor handlers are sometimes required to work with rig or mooring chain on the deck, and for this purpose most are fitted with chain lockers under the main winch which double as ballast or brine tanks when not in use.

The workdrums are fitted with gypsies for either 3 in or $3\frac{1}{2}$ in (76 or 89 mm) chain, and to change from one size to the other the gypsies need to be changed. This is a straightforward operation requiring only the unbolting of the securing plate from the outside of the gypsy; then, as long as suitable lugs have been welded to the deckhead immediately above the gypsy, the weight can be taken with chain blocks, the old gypsy slid off, and the new one lifted and slid into place.

If there are no lugs welded to the deckhead, do not imagine that there is some better way of doing this: it just means that the task has not been carried out before, and the shipyard forgot to fit them.

The most likely task is to change the chain of a rig. In its best organized form this is done by loading one chain ashore; going out to the rig; removing one chain from the rig; stowing it in one chain locker; then connecting up the new chain and reeling it out. To do this, the anchor is decked and removed; then the end of the chain is pulled up the deck and heaved by means of the crane or a tugger wire onto the end of the gypsy, then paid down into the chain locker. It may be prudent to send a couple of crew members down into the locker with fish-box hooks, to stow the cable and so ensure that it all goes below.

The end of the new cable is then reeled out and sent up to the rig, and then the end is connected to the anchor, which can be put back in the water in the normal manner. An essential piece of equipment for both these tasks is the 'tuning fork', a fork with two 180 degree bends in the ends which fits over a single link in the chain. As the end of the chain comes out of the locker, the tuning fork can be fitted over a link on the deck and the wire attached to it slackened off. Obviously, if this is not done the end of the chain will disappear over the stern as soon as the last link is free of the gypsy.

Permanent moorings

Anchor handlers are sometimes required to lay permanent moorings for tankers or for military purposes. The chains used in these systems are likely to be larger than $3\frac{1}{2}$ in (89 mm) and so neither the chain lockers nor the gypsies are likely to be of any use. In such situations the cables will be stowed on the deck, and paid out using the tuning forks alone. Even the tuning forks may have to be specially made up for the operation.

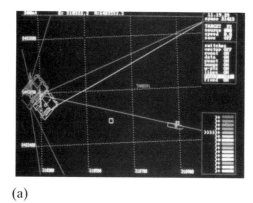

(a)

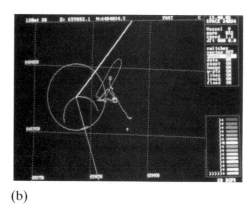

(b)

Figure 56   *The differential GPS system DIFFSIS used (a) to run a rig anchor and (b) to lay a single buoy. The display uses colour to distinguish the different vessels' tracks*

This operation will require another vessel fitted with a crane, which will lift the anchor onto the deck. The anchor can then be attached to the chain and dropped over the stern by the crane. The anchor may then be lowered to the bottom when the ship is in the correct position.

Working with rig or mooring chain is very hard work for both the deck crew and the officers on the bridge, so all hands should be prepared for at least days, and sometimes weeks, of hard work. If the ship is suitably located and if the owners are willing it is a good idea to get extra hands on board, particularly a second driver to relieve the master.

If no second driver is available, the master should be alert for periods of prolonged work on deck when he is going to be unable to contribute anything to the operation: he may then be able to take some rest. Even a couple of hours off is an advantage.

Working pipebarges

Traditional pipebarges lay pipe by taking lengths of pipe aboard, welding them together and then lowering the completed string over the stern down a sort of chute known as a stinger. As a result they move slowly along the surface by winching in the anchor wires which lead forward and letting out the ones leading aft, leaving a trail of pipe behind them on the seabed.

Anchor handlers or tugs are used to move the anchors, and one or two of these vessel are constantly employed moving the forward anchors back into a position as far from the barge as possible, then dashing astern to pick up the stern anchors and move them up to the barge.

This task is usually made simpler by the design of the mooring system, which differs from rig moorings in that the buoys have a tube through the middle of them through which the anchor pennant is threaded. The anchor handler moves up to the buoy and puts a hook fitted to the end of the workwire through the loop in the pennant. The pennant can then be heaved in and the anchor lifted without the buoy leaving the water.

8 | Trends and developments

The offshore industry is undergoing an unprecedented level of change, occasioned mainly by the increasing amount of health, environmental and safety legislation with which it must comply.

The effect of the Cullen Report on the role of the standby vessel

The standby vessel industry in the UK has been changed out of all recognition by the *Piper Alpha* disaster, of which the standby vessel *Silver Pit* was but a small part. The subsequent Cullen Report made a variety of recommendations which were incorporated in the Standby Vessel Regulations by the Department of Transport and the Health and Safety Executive.

Because the new regulations require much more from both the ships and the crews than previously, many of Britain's traditional supply ship operators are affected and some supply ships will in the future fulfil dual roles. In fact some standby vessels will also fulfil dual roles, but it seems unlikely, due to the framing of the legislation, that the two will become interchangeable.

However, mariners entering the industry should be aware of the job that the standby vessels are now required to do and the form the actual ships are likely to take.

It seems that many of the new generation of standby vessels will be capable of carrying cargo, both out to the field and between structures within the field. There is some disparity of opinion as to how far this should be allowed to take place: the mariners' unions seem to think it 'a bad idea' for the ships to carry out infield transfers, but express no opinion as to the suitability of carrying cargo out to the location.

Here it may not be appreciated that the skills required to command a standby vessel are not exactly the same as those required to command a supply ship, and that some standby vessel masters may not have gained the experience required to remain under a rig crane for long periods of time. Here may lie the reason for the union objection.

134

The operators, while apparently liking the idea of having a craft on location capable of carrying cargo, seem to have unilaterally drawn the line at having them attached by hoses to an installation. This would certainly limit their ability to manoeuvre.

There are also strict and far-reaching regulations on training in a number of areas, particularly rescue boat handling and first aid, which will eventually make the standby vessel crew member a valuable man and therefore worth keeping. This in turn necessitates a regular work/leave pattern and reasonable salaries, and, if possible, a well defined career progression. The supply ship owners who have entered this market offer all these things, and therefore prospective offshore mariners may well find themselves starting out their careers on board a standby vessel.

It is therefore advisable for mariners serving on standby boats to spend as much time as possible practising the types of manoeuvre that are more appropriate to supply ships — particularly those mariners serving on what were formerly supply ships. This is in addition to the normal practice of launching and recovering and working with their fast rescue craft.

Supply ship design

It is always difficult to predict what the future may hold for ship design in general, and for once the offshore industry is little different here. One of the exhilarating things about the industry has been the astonishing progress from the original supply ship, the *Ebb Tide* in 1953, to that of the present day, which at the time of writing is the ME303 Mk II designed by Maritime Engineering of Oslo.

Most of the advances have taken place in the North Sea, while the rest of the world has trailed along behind, broadly following current American design, where the changes are slower and everything is on a much smaller scale, reflecting the principal operating area for American vessels, the Gulf of Mexico. During 1992, Oil and Gas Rental Services of Morgan City took delivery of six platform ships. These craft were the first US supply ships to be fitted with joysticks, which had been used in the North Sea since 1979, and though dimensionally impressive for the Gulf they would look small on the Continental Shelf.

In the North Sea, design has progressed at a rapid rate to enable the operators to be efficiently served in deeper and rougher waters. Platform supply ships have become larger to reduce the number of voyages required, and anchor handlers have also increased in size both to carry more cargo and to provide better working platforms during rig shifts, and so reduce the amount of downtime due to weather. Increases in vessel size have also reduced downtime working alongside offshore installations.

The potential size of the supply ship

The first aspect of future design to approach must therefore be the optimum size of the supply ship or, in more basic terms: how big can they get? When considering the sheer size of offshore vessels, each of the three dimensions that are material to the situation, draft, beam and length, must be considered.

Limitations imposed by North Sea ports

The principal North Sea supply port, Aberdeen, has a draft limitation caused by silting up of the harbour entrance. Despite annual dredging, a draft of more than 6 metres will restrict the times when vessels can enter and leave. If the ships get much deeper this limitation may become unacceptable, since the operators have a noticeable preference for being able to sail their vessels at times convenient to themselves.

In Aberdeen there is additionally a draft limitation caused by depths of water alongside, and if the supply vessel draft exceeds 8 metres there is only one quay where it can tie up, thereby excluding it from serving several of the major operators. However, it must be said that no such limitation exists in Peterhead.

Incidentally, one of the major factors governing the size of American supply ships is also the general draft limitation in the Gulf of Mexico. A UT704, now one of the smallest supply ship types working in the North Sea, would have real difficulty in getting up the river to the principal Gulf of Mexico oil port, Morgan City.

Now that supply ships seldom tie up to offshore installations, and in fact usually opt to work beam-on rather than stern-to, the length of the working deck is of less importance. In fact the limitation is once more placed on the design by the port operations.

All supply bases in the northern European ports were designed at a time when the maximum vessel length was not more than 60 metres. Now that the maximum vessel length is likely to be over 70 metres, the capacity of the bases to take ships is being somewhat strained. Any length greater than this might mean some increase in berth size, or a reduction in the total number of ships being serviced. It is difficult to see either of these situations being acceptable.

Beam limited by offshore crane jibs

Lastly, the beam of the vessels is governed by the maximum outreach of the offshore cranes. There is never likely to be any problem with platform cranes, but exploration rig cranes do not always have very long jibs, and very wide vessels working beam-on could end up unacceptably close to the legs of the rig.

It would therefore be reasonable to say that the Maersk Master class, with a length of 82 m, a beam of 18 m and a loaded draft of 6.9 m is as large as the industry is likely to accept for the foreseeable future.

Power plant

Supply ships are, of necessity, complex mechanical creatures, all having more than one propeller and one or more thrusters. Attempts at simplification have not been acceptable to the industry.

Harrisons (Clyde) built and operated a class of vessel powered by a single azimuthing thruster aft and a single azimuthing thruster forward, but they were commercially unsuccessful despite the fact that these vessels were very manoeuvrable and well suited to the tidal conditions of the southern North Sea. It is a salutary lesson that all these ships are now standby boats. It seems that a single engine did not fit in with the industry's concept of what was needed to power a supply ship.

Screws and thrusters

All supply ships in the future are likely to be powered by not less than two propellers driven by two or four engines, though variations are possible with greater numbers of engines powering electrically driven thrusters. This is true of the Maersk Mariner class where one main propeller and two smaller azimuthing thrusters at the stern provide the ahead power as well as the after manoeuvring capability.

It has been totally accepted that the propellers should be of controllable pitch. This means that changes in direction are very rapid and that very slow speeds are possible, neither of which is available with fixed-pitch propellers.

In the 1970s many British ships were fitted with an azimuthing thruster forward which helped in situations where fixed-pitch propellers were a liability. However, the universal adoption of CP propellers has meant that tunnel thrusters are now almost always fitted, giving maximum power output/input ratio. Some new designs are also being fitted with a retractable azimuthing thruster forward, in addition to the tunnel thrusters. This type of thruster has the advantage of being usable when the ship is required to dodge on location, making reasonable manoeuvring possible for very small fuel consumption.

It seems unlikely that any North Sea supply ship will now be built with the minimum single thruster forward. The UT 734 anchor handlers built in the early 1980s were inadequately powered by a single 800 bhp (600 kW) thruster, and if constructed today would almost certainly have two of these units.

All supply ships built in the future for operations in European waters are likely to be fitted with a stern thruster. When no stern thruster is fitted, joystick controls are limited and must be programmed with this in mind. In view of what has been said about bow thrusters it would seem prudent in the future to equip all ships with 1400 bhp (1050 kW) in two bow thrusters and 700 bhp (525 kW) in a single stern thruster.

Rudders

Considerable rudder development has taken place over the years and there is little doubt that all North Sea supply ships will be fitted with Becker or similar flap rudders. The flap increases the side thrust from the rudder and the control systems increase the speed with which the rudder moves. Masters therefore should no longer be faced with the sometimes agonizing experience of pushing the tiller over in a difficult situation, to watch the rudder slowly making its way from one side to the other. There is also a case for fitting Schilling Vectwin rudders which can provide total sideways thrust from a single screw, enabling the vessel to operate efficiently with one screw down.

Main engines

Main engine requirements for modern vessels really conflict with ease of maintenance, the objective in the latter case being to have as few cylinders as possible.

Many anchor handlers are fitted with four V8s, giving a total of 32 cylinders in all. This enables them to run with one engine operating each screw, thereby reducing fuel consumption.

However, as long as lubrication can be provided for the gearboxes independent of the main engines, most supply vessels will run on one screw, so providing the economy mode, and thereby allowing even anchor handlers to be fitted with two instead of four engines. Wartsila Diesels have produced a 9 cylinder engine outputting 4500 bhp (3375 kW) fitted in some UT734s, and MAK have manufactured an 8 cylinder diesel producing 6000 bhp (4500 kW) which has been fitted to the Maersk L class anchor handlers. The latter craft also have linked shaft generators which allow one engine to drive both screws, surely providing the best of all worlds.

Pumping systems

All supply ships must have the capability to carry and pump a number of different bulk cargoes. These include (but are not limited to) gas oil, potable water, drill water, brine, oil-based mud and cement. The different systems use dedicated pumps and separate piping systems, so that the engineers on most vessels have to clamber about the engine-room and associated compartments, at sea, sometimes in rough weather, to set up the lines for discharge.

Some vessels are fitted with electric or air-driven valves with mimic boards for ease of reference, and it is obvious that all future ships should be so fitted. The advent of the UMS engine-room also suggests that it is possible that the mimic boards should be installed on the bridge, though the advantage of this to the ship's crew depends on the manning of the vessel.

Many ships already have the mimic board and switching system for the cement discharge fitted on the bridge, in part because effective discharge of this cargo depends on observation of the hoses to the installation. On vessels carrying a second mate this has proved perfectly acceptable, since a deck officer will always be available to come to the bridge to activate the system. Where the ship carries only a master and mate, the mate needs to be available to operate the system at times when he might otherwise be resting.

In the 1990s there is a move towards fitting ships with completely computerized valve and pumping systems which are activated by means of a keyboard and have their information presented on VDUs. This of course must be the ultimate system and doubtless in the passing of time the control system will be duplicated on the bridge and in the engine room.

Anchor handling equipment

The most important item of equipment on the deck of an anchor handler is the anchor handling tong — the thing that grabs the wire at the first opportunity. The three types available today are described in detail in Chapter 3, and at present there is no sign of any new design.

Each of the three has advantages, and it seems likely that enthusiasts for both the Shark's Jaw and Triplex gear may move in the direction of fitting two rather than one into the decks of their ships. Some owners who have carried out this expensive installation have reaped benefit where ships are required to recover parts of sub-sea moorings and make a connection between them on the deck.

However, these multiple hydraulic installations must suffer a little from sheer complexity, and seem a little unnecessary when the same result may be achieved by use of the much simpler Karmfork. The drawback of this system is that in the event of hydraulic failure the forks will gradually retract into the deck, opening the latch and eventually releasing the wire; however, there seems to be no reason why the designers could not fit a safety device which would stop it withdrawing in the event of hydraulic failure.

The Karmfork would appear to be the most operationally friendly, and its simplicity in operation allows it to be activated from the bridge, making it possible to clear the deck completely of crew members during the moments when wires are released.

Towing pins or pop-ups

The 'pop-ups' already mentioned also need attention. The latest installations are fitted with plates on top which turn inward as the post rises from the deck, so that when both are in position the plates butt against each other, thereby trapping the wire completely. This is an essential development which stops the wire riding up over the top of the posts, an occurrence which at least makes recovery of the wire difficult and more seriously is capable of causing damage to both the ship's structure and any personnel on the deck.

The towing pins supplied with the Triplex gear are set diagonally into the deck athwartships, so that when they rise from the deck plating they meet in a sort of inverted vee.

Quarter posts

There are times, such as the moment when an anchor is being decked, when all the methods of trapping and making wires safe must be withdrawn, and unless the vessel is correctly aligned there is a danger that the wire or chain will ride up over the side roller and along the top of the crash barrier. The danger of this event to both ship and personnel is obvious.

Some vessels are fitted with lightweight posts at the quarters, which might well prove inadequate, and it is the opinion of the writer that all anchor handlers should be fitted with heavy duty retractable posts to confine the wire or chain to the stern area.

Dollies on the deck

During anchor work much effort is expended pulling a variety of objects towards the stern. To assist in this activity there has been a gradual increase over the years in the size of tugger winches until now most have an 10 tonne safe working load. This is likely to be the minimum capability of any tuggers fitted in the future.

All supply vessels in the future are likely to be fitted with a substantial number of dollies set as close to the edge of the deck as possible without intruding on the cargo area. They should be set about 2 ft (0.6 m) above the deck to exert an upward rather than a downward pull on any objects being moved about the deck.

Many modern vessels are already adequately equipped with dollies but most lack any means of pulling aft of the pins. To assist in this activity some means of fitting portable dollies to the side rollers should be available. This need be no more complex than small posts fitted into slots in the side rollers.

Tugger winch fittings
Tugger winch wires must be fitted with at least 3 ft (1 m) of suitable chain and equipped with lightweight hooks. The chain is used to wrap round small objects and wires and the hook needs to be small enough to fit into the twist-lock points of containers, and should also be small enough to be passed through the eyes of wires and through the sizes of shackles used in anchor work.

Winches and wire storage

Some anchor handlers are fitted with two workdrums, which greatly increases the flexibility possible during anchor work. This installation is likely to become standard. A few are also fitted with two tow drums so that, in the event of a tow-wire breaking, the second may immediately be brought into operation without the necessity of the spare wire having to be reeled on from a storage drum. While this is a very worth-while improvement in specification, should the owner be in any way restrained by financial limitations it is possible that funds allocated to a second tow drum could be better spent elsewhere.

However, modern anchor handlers are likely to be provided with an increasing number of powered storage reels to provide space for the vast lengths of wire used in deep water anchor handling. Here double workdrums have the additional function of providing wire storage, as in fact do double tow drums with the tow-wires removed.

Work winches will be capable of lifting 2000 ft (600 m) of rig chain together with an anchor with a full drum, and still be able to pull the anchor over the stern; the brake should be capable of holding while the vessel is exerting maximum bollard pull under the same circumstances. Workdrums are also likely to be fitted with high and low speed gearing to save time during anchor work.

Bridge layout and controls

Bridge layout should be such that both the officer of the watch when the vessel is steaming and the officer at the controls when the vessel is working have the maximum visibility in all directions. There should also be good vision of the forepart of the vessel during docking operations. To achieve all these requirements is difficult but not impossible, though most designers only manage to get part of it right.

Over the years the funnels of supply ships have moved further and further forward. During the 1970s they moved from the afterdeck to a point on either side of the foredeck aft of the bridge, which gave the master blind spots on either quarter when at the after controls. This caused little problem when working stern-to, but once supply ships began to work beam to installations this blind spot caused numerous problems and so the funnels were moved to either side of the bridge, or even up through the middle of the wheelhouse.

Which of these positions is best depends on a number of factors. Funnels on either side of the wheelhouse obviously still have blind spots on the quarter when steaming, and a funnel through the centre of the wheelhouse stops the man at the after controls seeing all of the wheelhouse, and makes communication difficult between the forward and after ends of the space. It is also bound to generate extra work for the air conditioning system in hot climates.

On balance, the writer would recommend exterior funnels set at the sides of the wheelhouse to provide maximum vision fore and aft and a slight loss on the quarters from forward and on either bow from aft.

The forepart of the wheelhouse should be as close to triangular as possible, though it is necessary to have three forward facing windows amidships to provide a position for the forward console. Aft of the console should be the forward radar and bridge seat. The watchkeeper will therefore be able to see forward and on both bows from the chair without the intrusion of window uprights.

The wheelhouse itself should be as short in the fore and aft direction as reasonably possible and set as far back as possible from the bow. This provides more directional 'feel' from the driving position and gives some protection to the bridge windows from high seas.

The windows on either side of the console should be deep, to allow the driver to see either side of the bow during docking manoeuvres.

The after driving position, and the winch control on an anchor handler, should be set in a pod sticking out from the aft end of the wheelhouse. This provides the maximum possible vision aft and on either side. It is possible to design the after console so that all the switches, controls and telephones can be positioned within a small area and within reach of the driver, and designers should not sacrifice this convenience to the grander style of banks of instruments set over large areas of console which look impressive but are extremely inconvenient to use.

Communications

Supply vessel communications systems have probably received less attention than any other area of design. They consist at present of internal telephone systems, probably including the engine-room, a VHF telephone handset with VHF receiver, and a loud-hailer for the deck.

The master of a supply vessel when operating at an offshore installation is required to use all these systems in conjunction and often is provided with an additional VHF for use with the deck of the rig. He is therefore required to operate the controls, watch the ship, watch the cargo and pick up the appropriate handset at any time to speak to any of the areas, whether on board the ship or on board the rig, involved in the cargo operation.

The worst method of communication is by loud-hailer with the deck. While the loudspeaker may be audible at some distance from the ship, the hearing of those on deck is impeded by the competing sounds of engines and vent fans, which often make the voice from the bridge all but inaudible. Attempts at providing portable speakers have been little more successful due to the ingress of seawater into plugs and switches, making them extremely unreliable.

Communications designers should be moving towards the provision of a single headphone/microphone which can be switched in to the various communications systems, thereby avoiding multiple handsets and incorporating an entirely new approach to bridge/deck communications.

Joystick

The joystick was originally developed as little more than an aid to masters of diving vessels in moving their ships about on location or in harbour, when such movement was beyond the scope of the computer. Subsequently parts of the system have been transferred to supply ships, with varying degrees of success.

It is significant that few masters will use the joystick in preference to manual controls when moving in harbour, the main complaint being lack of sensitivity. They use it offshore because it does give a fixed heading, and the advantages of this are so great that all other shortcomings of the system become tolerable. This is particularly true when working head to wind, a situation requiring constant small movements ahead, which assist the computer to maintain the ship's heading.

On most joystick consoles it is impossible to place the joystick in the same position twice. In fact, the only position where the operator knows exactly what is happening is where the stick is in the neutral or central position — when nothing is happening. This leads drivers to propel the ship in the required direction with sudden bursts of power, subsequently returning the stick to the central position, not because that is the best place, but because it is the only one where they can predict what is going to happen to the ship next.

Where stern thrusters are fitted the situation is improved, the main engines being used by the computer purely to drive the ship ahead or astern and the thruster to provide sideways thrust. This means that the stick can be placed in a definite position in relation to the main engines, the unknown being what the thrusters are doing.

However, probably the two most serious faults inherent in today's joysticks are lack of sensitivity, and dissimilar power response to different directions of joystick. If the stick is moved to the limit of its travel athwartships, a reasonable and controllable 3 knots sideways will be the result. If it is moved to the limit of its travel fore or aft, full power surge will result, with black smoke from the funnels, churning propellers, and heart failure on the bridge.

It would appear that the best way of improving the control system would be to dispense with the joystick altogether but to retain the computer. The joystick should be replaced by two controls, one for fore and aft and one for sideways movement.

In operating a supply ship offshore, the driver judges by eye the distance and position from a fixed object and resolves the forces acting on the ship onto fore-and-aft and athwartships components. Currently he either applies countering forces by using the controls, or counters them by 'recombining' them and opposing them with the joystick. By using two individual levers, the fore-and-aft and athwartships forces could be balanced, leaving the ship stationary, the heading being maintained as always by the computer.

Most importantly the driver would then know exactly what forces he was applying to the ship, and be able to make small adjustments to maintain position.

Conclusion

The operation of the supply ship is unique in the marine world. The tendency to take standard marine equipment and adapt it for the offshore task should be avoided: the industry needs equipment developed for its particular needs. Other fields that may well offer suitable technology include aircraft, hovercraft etc. Even agricultural machinery has something to contribute, modern tractor seats being in every way superior to anything provided so far for the ship master to sit on.

Quality assurance

The last few years have seen an increase in the requirement for quality assurance throughout industry, and shipping has been almost the last to pick up this particular ball and run with it. It could be said that the supply ship industry has operated totally 'by the seat of its pants' making it an unlikely candidate for the application of quality assurance. However, the same might be said of the oil industry, yet in 1991 Amerada Hess became the first UK operator to be certified to BS 5750.

More and more operators are auditing the craft they employ, and the companies running them, against their own predetermined standards and it is therefore natural that ship owners will be moving towards accreditation so that the standards that will be demanded by their customers will already be shown to be in place. Seafarers should take quality assurance to their hearts and do their best to make the quality management system work. The systems their management will be putting in place will, once the paperwork is understood, be of immense benefit to them.

The heart of quality management is self regulation and positive communication. The ships will receive quality manuals, which will probably contain all their previous manuals suitably rewritten, and there will be a time during the implementation of the system when they can comment on, and alter if necessary, their own manuals. It is obviously essential to take proper notice of the system at this stage to ensure that the ship is not saddled with unworkable procedures.

The manuals will set the standards to which the vessels should be maintained, and the procedures for all operations. At intervals an auditor from the company will appear to audit the ship. The auditor will have been appointed from within the staff and will have been suitably trained to carry out the audit. It should be borne in mind that the office will be audited as well, and even the QA manager will be audited to ensure that he or she is doing the correct job.

QA, if operated properly on board ship, offers the ship master a genuine tool for the management of his vessel. Where the correct operation of the ship depends on input from the shore back-up, and where this is not forthcoming, the QA system is a formidable weapon.

The basis for the QA operation is more than anything self regulation and the ships will be expected to audit themselves, and hold QA meetings to keep the ship on par. The practical advice here is to accept the procedures and make them work, rather than overlay existing systems with paperwork that has no function other than to satisfy the QA manager.

The global positioning system

The American military satellite system known as GPS was developed for military reasons and is claimed to be capable of providing individual personnel with their own positions anywhere on the earth's surface with an accuracy of one metre, using handheld equipment. To prevent similar military use of the system by other nations, the satellite positions are electronically displaced as far as commercial equipment is concerned: actual positions may differ from the apparent positions by as much as 50 metres.

This, of course, does not affect ships on the high seas but precludes use of the system for the purposes of oil industry surveying, and rig and anchor positioning. As a result, a number of survey companies have produced what are known as differential GPS systems, which use a base station at a known position to measure the differential between the real and the theoretical position, and then to transmit this differential to the mobiles on board the craft whose positions need to be fixed. Some differential GPS systems are so compact and simple to operate that they do not require survey personnel, and as a consequence not only can the rig being moved be fitted, so can every anchor handler involved, so that all can see exactly what they are doing no matter what the visibility.

In conjunction with computer driven plotting systems, rig moves may be planned and drawn before execution and then can be carried out by following lines on the VDU. Anchor handlers can follow the cable runs to the anchor position and drop the anchor on the correct spot, and every aspect of the operation can be recorded and played back later in the office. It may be assumed that in the passing of time all rig moves will be carried out in this manner, so that the vessels involved in the operation will have a totally accurate means of carrying out their tasks; a quality record of the operation will be made at the same time.

Limits of responsibility

The offshore industry is currently attempting to tackle the knotty problems of master's responsibility and working hours for masters and crews. The positions of the oil companies on what exactly they require in terms of working hours from their ships vary from one to another, and some have no defined position at all, but leave it to their rig and platform personnel to deal with the ships.

Some operators accept that the ships are not crewed up for working 24 hours a day alongside installations and consequently stipulate a maximum number of working hours before rest is taken, and some require 24 hour working. In the latter case they may accept the ship owner's assurance that his ship is able to work continuously, whether it can or not, and in others they will pay for an extra deck officer over and above the charter rate, so that their requirements can be carried out.

If the ship is on a charter where the working hours are limited, the master may safely remain at the controls for the whole period, and then rest when the ship is pulled off from the platform. If he is on a 24 hour operation he has more difficult problems. If he hands over the control of the ship to the mate, and the mate then runs into the installation, what exactly is the master's responsibility in the situation? Diving ships have overcome this problem by having a day master and a night master and actually signing over the ship. It is unlikely that the question of responsibility will be resolved until a case or two come to law, and in the meantime one can only speculate. However, one may draw logical conclusions.

There is absolutely nothing that says that a suitably trained mate may not drive a supply ship close to an installation. This is after all the ship's normal work and could be considered to be part of the mate's duties. It is not the fault of the ship master that there is no formal training or examination in this marine skill, and he therefore must make his own judgement.

The master is essentially in the same position as the master of a deep sea vessel. Firstly he is controlled by his owners' instructions and organization. If the owners say that in no situation should the mate drive the ship, then his course is clear. If the owners accept a requirement for 24 hour working, but do not provide an extra master, they are accepting that a second officer must drive the ship, and therefore they have some responsibility.

It is the writer's view that the ship master must identify the times when he must be driving, and when one of his assistants can be driving, in the same way as a deep sea ship master identifies the times when he must be in charge on the bridge, and when the job may be left to the officer of the watch. Other factors should also be taken into account, particularly the experience of the officer.

This is only an opinion, but it seems likely that should the master have been on the bridge for 16 hours, and then delegate a simple pumping operation to a mate with years of experience of ship handling in calm weather at a problem-free installation, and then by some misfortune such as mechanical failure the ship and/or rig were damaged, he would suffer little censure. However, given circumstances such as high winds or strong tide, he would not walk away without bearing most of the responsibility.

In the UK the oil companies and the ship owners have got together to produce what is currently known as the UKOOA/BOSVA Code which they hope will improve safety standards on supply vessels and increase the efficiency of offshore marine activities in general. This document gives formal backing to the manning levels recommended in M Notice 781, allies itself to regulations concerning hours of work and makes a number of other fairly revolutionary statements. It is printed in full in Appendix 2.

Appendix 1
Useful computer programs in BASIC

Many supply vessels now carry computers for some purpose, and by one means or another the BASIC language is usually available.

There is a tendency for owners to supply the computer already provided with a hard disc suitably programmed to show a menu when switched on. The uninitiated may be cautious about breaking into this presentation; since the computer will have been provided with a DOS operating system, it is just a matter of getting a copy of the command files from this plus a copy of the computer supplier's version of BASIC, which will probably be a clone of IBM BASIC.

With these programs on disc, inserted in the disc drive before switching on, the computer will boot up from the disc, and will provide paths to that disc, i.e. A>. Type in BASICA, and the computer will allow you to run BASIC. It is then just a matter of typing in the lines on the following pages. It is a long and tedious business, but the programs can be saved at any time under a name of up to eight letters.

When the programs are to be run the names can be checked by typing in FILES and then ENTER. The one required should then be loaded and can be "RUN.

Errors, and there will be some, will be indicated by the computer. The line with the error should be listed and the typing checked against the book copy. This is correct, being a direct print of the program.

The first program provides a means of calculating the stability of any supply vessel, and is self-explanatory once running. In the form presented it is for data taken from even keel hydrostatic information. To include the ability to use different trim conditions, two lines have to be added:

```
995 LOCATE 13,22:PRINT"TRIM TABLE     ";TRTAB
1085 LOCATE 13,40:PRINT"     ":LOCATE 13,40:INPUT;TRTAB
```

Amend end of 2300 as follows:

```
2300    TTRIM=TRTAB+((TMOM/MCTC)/100)
```

The second program, TOWDIP, is a simple means of calculating the catenary of the tow-wire using existing formulae. It is, once more, self-explanatory when running, and will assist the tug master with the decisions that must be made when shortening up in shallow water.

The third program provides a means of converting all the well-known oil industry measurements to well-known marine measurements.

Simplified stability program

```
10 REM SIMPLIFIED STABILITY PROGRAM
20 :
30 COLOR 7,1,4
40 DEF FNA(X,Y)=INT((X*Y)+.5)/Y
50 CLS:LOCATE 1,20:PRINT "SIMPLIFIED STABILITY PROGRAM"
60 LOCATE 10,30:INPUT "SHIP'S NAME";S$
70 LOCATE 14,30:INPUT"Length B.P. ";LBP
80 CLS:LOCATE 2,20:PRINT "SIMPLIFIED STABILITY PROGRAM FOR ";S$ :PRINT:PRINT
90 LOCATE 5,20:INPUT "HAVE YOU ALREADY INPUT TANK NAMES y/n";X$
100 IF X$="y" THEN GOTO 370
110 :
120 :
130 LOCATE 5,20:PRINT "TYPE IN LIST OF FRESH WATER TANKS     - PRESS ENTER WHEN C
OMPLETE"
140 Y=0:GOSUB 1840
150 CLS:LOCATE 5,20:PRINT "TYPE IN LIST OF BALL/DRILL WATER TANKS "
160 Y=10:GOSUB 1840
170 CLS:LOCATE 5,20:PRINT "TYPE IN LIST OF GAS OIL TANKS        "
180 Y=20:GOSUB 1840
190 CLS:LOCATE 5,20:PRINT "TYPE IN LIST OF HFO TANKS            "
200 Y=30:GOSUB 1840
210 CLS:LOCATE 5,20:PRINT "TYPE IN LIST OF MUD TANKS            "
220 Y=40:GOSUB 1840
230 CLS:LOCATE 5,20:PRINT "TYPE IN LIST OF BRINE TANKS          "
240 Y=50:GOSUB 1840
250 CLS:LOCATE 5,20: PRINT "TYPE IN LIST OF CEMENT TANKS           "
260 Y=60:GOSUB 1840
270 REM filing deck cargo names
280 Y=70:GOSUB 1960
290 REM filing miscellaneous names
300 Y=80:GOSUB 1960
310 REM filing Totals names
320 GOSUB 2070
330 REM filing page titles
340 GOSUB 2170
350 :
360 :
370 CLS:LOCATE 3,36:PRINT"* MENU *"
380 LOCATE 5,18:PRINT"Title";TAB(60)"Page"
390 OPEN "R",#3,"Titles",25
400 FIELD #3,25 AS TIT$
410 LOCATE 7,18:FOR X%=1 TO 12
420 GET #3,X%
430 PRINT TAB(18)TIT$;TAB(60)X%
440 NEXT X%
450 CLOSE #3
460 :
470 LOCATE 21,5:INPUT"Enter Page Number Required      ";N$
480 :
490 IF N$="1" THEN Y=0:D=1:Z%=1:GOTO 1300
500 IF N$="2" THEN Y=10:D=1.025:Z%=2:GOTO 1300
510 IF N$="3" THEN Y=20:D=.89:Z%=3:GOTO 1300
520 IF N$="4" THEN Y=30:D=.89:Z%=4:GOTO 1300
530 IF N$="5" THEN Y=40:Z%=5:LOCATE 21,60:INPUT"What SG    ";D:GOTO 1300
540 IF N$="6" THEN Y=50:Z%=6:LOCATE 21,60:INPUT"What SG    ";D:GOTO 1300
550 IF N$="7" THEN Y=60:D=0:Z%=7:GOTO 1300
560 IF N$="8" THEN Y=70:D=0:Z%=8:GOTO 1300
570 IF N$="9" THEN Y=80:D=0:Z%=9:GOTO 1300
580 IF N$="10" THEN GOTO 640
590 IF N$="11" THEN GOTO 940
600 IF N$="12" THEN GOTO 1130
610 GOTO 370
620 :
630 :
640 CLS:PRINT "COMMODITY";TAB(17) "WEIGHT";TAB(33) "T.V-MOM";TAB(49)"T.L-MOM" ;T
AB(63) "T.FR.SUR"
650 TW=0:TVM=0:TLM=0:TFS=0
660 OPEN "R",#2,"TOTALS",51
```

```
670 FIELD #2,11 AS SSNM$,10 AS SSW$,10 AS SSVM$,10 AS SSLM$,10 AS SSFS$
680 FOR Z%=1 TO 9
690 GET #2,Z%
700 SW=CVS(SSW$):SVM=CVS(SSVM$):SLM=CVS(SSLM$):SFS=CVS(SSFS$)
710 PRINT SSNM$;TAB(17)SW;TAB(33)SVM;TAB(49)SLM;TAB(63)SFS
720 TW=TW+SW:TVM=TVM+SVM:TLM=TLM+SLM:TFS=TFS+SFS
730 NEXT Z%
740 PRINT:PRINT "DEADWEIGHT";TAB(17)TW;TAB(33)TVM;TAB(49)TLM;TAB(63)TFS
750 PRINT:Z%=10
760 GET #2,Z%
770 SW=CVS(SSW$):SVM=CVS(SSVM$):SLM=CVS(SSLM$):SFS=CVS(SSFS$)
780 PRINT SSNM$;TAB(17)SW;TAB(33)SVM;TAB(49)SLM;TAB(63)SFS
790 PRINT:
800 TW=TW+SW:TVM=TVM+SVM:TLM=TLM+SLM:TFS=TFS+SFS
810 PRINT "DISPLACEMENT";TAB(17)TW;TAB(33)TVM;TAB(49)TLM;TAB(63)TFS
820 LOCATE 20,20:INPUT "DO YOU WISH TO CHANGE LIGHT SHIP DETAILS y/n";X$
830 IF X$="n" THEN CLOSE #2:GOTO 370
840 LOCATE 20,20:PRINT "                                             "
850 LOCATE 21,20:INPUT "LIGHT SHIP WEIGHT";SW
860 LOCATE 22,20:INPUT "                  VCG";V
870 LOCATE 23,20:INPUT "                  LCG";L
880 SVM=V*SW:SLM=L*SW
890 LSET SSNM$=SSNM$:LSET SSW$=MKS$(SW):LSET SSVM$=MKS$(SVM):LSET SSLM$=MKS$(SLM
)
900 PUT #2,Z%:CLOSE #2: GOTO 640
910 :
920 :
930 REM Hydrostatic Page Next
940 CLS:LOCATE 5,25:PRINT"DATA  from  Vessel's   Hydrostatic Tables"
950 LOCATE 8,30:PRINT "KM";TAB(40)KM
960 LOCATE 9,29:PRINT "LCF";TAB(40)LCF
970 LOCATE 10,29:PRINT "LCB";TAB(40)LCB
980 LOCATE 11,28:PRINT "MCTC";TAB(40)MCTC
990 LOCATE 12,22:PRINT "Mean Draft";TAB(40)MDR
1000 :
1010 LOCATE 18,20:INPUT"Do You Wish to Change HYDROSTATIC DATA - y/n  ";N$
1020 IF N$="n" THEN GOTO 370
1030 :
1040 LOCATE 8,40:PRINT"       ":LOCATE 8,40:INPUT;KM
1050 LOCATE 9,40:PRINT"       ":LOCATE 9,40:INPUT;LCF
1060 LOCATE 10,40:PRINT"       ":LOCATE 10,40:INPUT;LCB
1070 LOCATE 11,40:PRINT"       ":LOCATE 11,40:INPUT;MCTC
1080 LOCATE 12,40:PRINT"       ":LOCATE 12,40:INPUT;MDR
1090 GOTO 940
1100 :
1110 :
1120 REM Results Page Next
1130 CLS:GOSUB 2260
1140 CLS:LOCATE 4,25:PRINT"* GM  Trim  Draught *"
1150 LOCATE 7,12:PRINT"KM     ";FNA(KM,1000)
1160 LOCATE 8,11:PRINT"VCG    ";FNA(VCG,1000)
1170 LOCATE 9,6:PRINT"Solid GM  ";FNA(GMS,1000)
1180 LOCATE 10,11:PRINT"fse    ";FNA(FSE,1000)
1190 LOCATE 11,6:PRINT"Fluid GM   ";FNA(GMF,1000)
1200 LOCATE 10,35:PRINT"Total Trim  ";FNA(TTRIM,1000);TAB(53)"Metres"
1210 LOCATE 15,32:PRINT "AFT";TAB(46)"FOR'D"
1220 LOCATE 16,15:PRINT"Mean Draft";TAB(30)MDR;TAB(45)MDR
1230 LOCATE 17,21:PRINT"Trim";TAB(30)FNA(ATR,1000);TAB(45)FNA(FTR,1000)
1240 LOCATE 18,14:PRINT"Final Draft";TAB(30);FNA(ADR,1000);TAB(45)FNA(FDR,1000)
1250 LOCATE 21,20:PRINT"Press Any Key to Return to MENU""
1260 IF INKEY$="" THEN GOTO 1260
1270 GOTO 370
1280 :
1290 :
1300 REM present list of tanks and input data
1310 CLS:LOCATE 2,1:PRINT "NAME";TAB(17)"WEIGHT";TAB(25)"VCG";TAB(33)"V-MOM";TAB
(41)"LCG";TAB(49)"L-MOM";TAB(57)"FR.SURF"
1320 OPEN "R",#1,"STAB",48
1330 FIELD #1,16 AS NME$,8 AS WT$,8 AS VCG$,8 AS LCG$,8 AS FS$
1340 X=2:SW=0:SVM=0:SLM=0:SFS=0
1350 FOR CODE%=Y+1 TO Y+9
1360 X=X+1
1370 GET #1,CODE%
1380 N$=NME$:W=CVS(WT$):V=CVS(VCG$):L=CVS(LCG$):F=CVS(FS$)
1390 VM=W*V:LM=W*L:FS=F*D
1400 SW=SW+W:SVM=SVM+VM:SLM=SLM+LM:SFS=SFS+FS
1410 LOCATE X,1:PRINT "
                      "
```

```
1420 LOCATE X,1:PRINT N$;TAB(17)W;TAB(25)V;TAB(33)VM;TAB(41)L;TAB(49)LM;TAB(57)F
S
1430 NEXT CODE%
1440 GOSUB 1780
1450 :
1460 LOCATE 15,1:PRINT "TOTALS";TAB(17)SW;TAB(33)SVM;TAB(49)SLM;TAB(57)SFS
1470 LOCATE 20,20:INPUT " DO YOU WISH TO ALTER DATA y/n";X$
1480 IF X$="n" THEN CLOSE #1:GOTO 370
1490 :
1500 X=X-9
1510 Y=Y+1:X=X+1
1520 CODE%=Y:GET #1,CODE%
1530 W=CVS(WT$):V=CVS(VCG$):L=CVS(LCG$):F=CVS(FS$)
1540 LOCATE X,17:PRINT "          "
1550 LOCATE X,17:INPUT;B$
1560 IF B$="" THEN PRINT W
1570 IF X=11 THEN CLOSE #1:Y=Y-9:GOTO 1300
1580 IF B$="" THEN GOTO 1510
1590 B=VAL(B$)
1600 W=B
1610 IF W=0 THEN V=0 AND L=0 AND F=0:LSET WT$=MKS$(W):LSET VM$=MKS$(V):LSET LM$=
MKS$(L):LSET FS$=MKS$(F):PUT #1,CODE%:GOTO 1510
1620 LSET WT$=MKS$(W)
1630 LOCATE X,25:PRINT "          ":LOCATE X,25:INPUT;C
1640 IF C=0 THEN PRINT V: GOTO 1660
1650 V=C
1660 LSET VCG$=MKS$(V)
1670 LOCATE X,41:PRINT "          ":LOCATE X,41:INPUT;E
1680 IF E=0 THEN PRINT L: GOTO 1700
1690 L=E
1700 LSET LCG$=MKS$(L)
1710 LOCATE X,57:PRINT "          ":LOCATE X,57: INPUT;F
1720 LSET FS$=MKS$(F)
1730 PUT #1,CODE%
1740 IF X=11 THEN CLOSE #1:GOTO 1300
1750 GOTO 1510
1760 :
1770 :
1780 OPEN "R",#2,"TOTALS",51
1790 FIELD #2,11 AS SSNM$,10 AS SSW$,10 AS SSVM$,10 AS SSLM$,10 AS SSFS$
1800 GET #2,Z%
1810 LSET SSW$=MKS$(SW):LSET SSVM$=MKS$(SVM):LSET SSLM$=MKS$(SLM):LSET SSFS$=MKS
$(SFS)
1820 PUT #2,Z%:CLOSE #2:RETURN
1830 :
1840 REM filing list of tank names
1850 OPEN "R",#1,"Stab",48
1860 FIELD #1,16 AS NME$,8 AS WT$,8 AS VCG$,8 AS LCG$,8 AS FS$
1870 X=6
1880 FOR XX=Y TO Y+8
1890 X=X+1:Y=Y+1
1900 LOCATE X,20:INPUT;N$
1910 LSET NME$=N$
1920 CODE%=Y:PUT #1,CODE%:NEXT XX
1930 CLOSE #1:RETURN
1940 :
1950 :
1960 REM filing compartment names
1970 OPEN "R",#1,"Stab",48
1980 FIELD #1,16 AS NME$,8 AS WT$,8 AS VCG$,8 AS LCG$,8 AS FS$
1990 FOR X=Y TO Y+8
2000 Y=Y+1
2010 READ N$
2020 LSET NME$=N$
2030 CODE%=Y:PUT #1,CODE%:NEXT X
2040 CLOSE #1:RETURN
2050 :
2060 :
2070 OPEN "R",#2,"Totals",51
2080 FIELD #2,11 AS SSNM$,10 AS SSW$,10 AS SSVM$,10 AS SSLM$,10 AS SSF$
2090 FOR Z%=1 TO 10
2100 READ N$
2110 LSET SSNM$=N$
2120 PUT #2,Z%
2130 NEXT Z%
2140 CLOSE #2:RETURN
2150 :
```

```
2160 :
2170 OPEN "R",#3,"Titles",25
2180 FIELD #3,25 AS TIT$
2190 FOR X%=1 TO 12
2200 READ N$:LSET TIT$=N$
2210 PUT #3,X%
2220 NEXT X%
2230 CLOSE #3:RETURN
2240 :
2250 :
2260 VCG=TVM/TW
2270 GMS=KM-VCG
2280 FSE=TFS/TW
2290 GMF=GMS-FSE
2300 LCG=TLM/TW:LGB=LCG-LCB:TMOM=LGB*TW:TTRIM=(TMOM/MCTC)/100
2310 ATR=(((LBP/2)+LCF)/LBP)*TTRIM*(-1)
2320 FTR=(((LBP/2)-LCF)/LBP)*TTRIM
2330 ADR=MDR+ATR
2340 FDR=MDR+FTR
2350 RETURN
2360 DATA Dk No.1,Dk No.2,Dk No.3,Dk No.4,Dk No.5,Dk No.6,Dk No.7,Dk No.8,Dk No.
9
2370 DATA For'd Dk,Mid Dk,Aft Dk,Sewage,Hyd Oil,Towwire,Strs,Crew,Misc
2380 DATA FRESH-WATER,BALL/DRILL,GAS-OIL,HFO,MUD,BRINE,CEMENT,DECK-CARGO,MISC,LI
GHT-SHIP
2390 DATA FRESH WATER TANKS,BALLAST/DRILL WATER TANKS,GAS OIL TANKS,HFO TANKS,MU
D TANKS,BRINE TANKS,CEMENT TANKS,DECK CARGO,MISCELLANEOUS,COMPARTMENT-DISP-TOTAL
S,HYDROSTATIC INPUT,RESULTS
```

Catenary program

```
10 REM CATENARY PROGRAM.TOWDIP
15 SCREEN 2:WIDTH 40 :KEY OFF
20 CLS:LOCATE 5,11:PRINT "CATENARY PROGRAM"
30 OPEN "R",#1,"DATA",127
40 FIELD #1,15 AS NM$,2 AS DI$,40 AS LL$,30 AS FF$,40 AS DD$
50 CODE%=1:GET #1,CODE%
60 N$=NM$
70 LOCATE 10,11:PRINT N$
80 X=CVI(DI$)
82 LOCATE 15,7: PRINT "Tow-wire diameter in mm" X
90 LOCATE 20,1:INPUT "Alterations to Name or Wire dia y/n";A$
100 IF A$="n" THEN GOTO 210
110 LOCATE 10,11:PRINT "                         "
120 LOCATE 10,11:INPUT;M$
130 IF M$="" THEN LOCATE 10,11:PRINT N$:GOTO 150
135 N$=M$
140 LSET NM$=N$
150 LOCATE 15,31:PRINT "   "
160 LOCATE 15,32:INPUT;Y
165 IF Y=>79 OR Y=<48 THEN LOCATE 20,1:PRINT "        Wire size out of range
   ": GOTO 150
170 IF Y=0 THEN LOCATE 15,32:PRINT X: GOTO 190
180 X=Y
190 LSET DI$=MKI$(X)
200 PUT #1,CODE%
210 GET #1,CODE%
211 L=CVI(LL$):F=CVI(FF$):D=CVI(DD$)
220 CLS:IF X=79 AND X=>73 THEN W=16.2626
230 IF X=<72 AND X=>67 THEN W=13.6651
240 IF X=<66 AND X=>61 THEN W=11.2935
250 IF X=<60 AND X=>55 THEN W=9.1474
260 IF X=<54 AND X=>49 THEN W=7.2278
270 LOCATE 4,4:PRINT "Length of Tow-wire Metres";INT(L)
280 LOCATE 6,4 :PRINT "Bollard Pull Tonnes      ";INT(F)
290 LOCATE 8,4 : PRINT "Dip of Tow-wire Metres   ";(INT(D/.3281))/10
292 LOCATE 12,4: PRINT "Press 1 to continue - 2 to finish"
293 X$=INKEY$
294 IF X$="1" THEN GOTO 298
295 IF X$="2" THEN GOTO 650
296 GOTO 293
```

```
298 LOCATE 12,4:PRINT "Leave space where new fig.required"
300 LOCATE 4,29:PRINT "          ":LOCATE 4,30:INPUT;L
310 LOCATE 6,29:PRINT "          ":LOCATE 6,30:INPUT;F
320 LOCATE 8,29:PRINT "          ":LOCATE 8,30:INPUT;D :D=D*3.281
330 IF L=0 THEN GOTO 360
340 IF F=0 THEN GOTO 440
350 IF D=0 THEN GOTO 500
355 STOP
360 F=F*2240
370 Y=F/W
380 C=Y-D
390 Q=C/W
400 S=SQR((D*(2*C+D)))
420 L=2*S/3.281
430 LOCATE 4,27:PRINT INT(L) :F=F/2240:GOTO 590
440 S=L*3.289/2
450 C=((S*S/D)-D)/2
460 Y=C+D
470 F=(Y*W)/2240
480 LOCATE 6,27:PRINT INT(F):GOTO 590
500 F=F*2240
510 S=L*3.281/2
520 V=S*W
530 Q=SQR(F*F-V*V)
540 Y=F/W
550 C=Q/W
560 D=(Y-C)
570 LOCATE 8,27:PRINT INT(D):F=F/2240:GOTO 590
590 L=INT(L):F=INT(F):D=INT(D)
600 LSET LL$=MKI$(L)
610 LSET FF$=MKI$(F)
620 LSET DD$=MKI$(D)
630 PUT #1,CODE%
640 GOTO 210
650 END
```

Conversion program

```
5 REM CONVERSION PROGRAM. CONVERS.
10 CLS
20 LOCATE 10,30
30 PRINT "CONVERSION PROGRAM"
40 LOCATE 20,30:PRINT "PRESS ANY KEY TO CONTINUE"
50 IF INKEY$="" THEN GOTO 50
60 CLS
70 PRINT:PRINT: PRINT TAB(30) "CONVERSIONS"
80 PRINT TAB(10) "From"; TAB(20) "Code";TAB(50) "To";TAB(60)"code"
100 PRINT TAB(10)"M3";TAB(20)"1";TAB(50)"M3";TAB(60)"1"
110 PRINT TAB(10)"Litres";TAB(20)"2";TAB(50) "Litres";TAB(60)"2"
120 PRINT TAB(10)"Barrels";TAB(20)"3";TAB(50)"Barrels";TAB(60)"3"
130 PRINT TAB(10)"Tonnes";TAB(20)"4";TAB(50)"Tonnes";TAB(60)"4"
132 PRINT TAB(10)"Metres";TAB(20)"5";TAB(50)"Feet";TAB(60)"5"
134 PRINT TAB(10) "Feet"; TAB(20) "6";TAB(50) "Metres"; TAB(60) "6"
140 LOCATE 12,15 :PRINT "Press code numbers for conversions"
145 LOCATE 15,40:PRINT "="
150 LET X$=INKEY$
160 IF X$="1" THEN LOCATE 15,20:PRINT "....M3":GOTO 300
170 IF X$="2" THEN LOCATE 15,20:PRINT "....Litres":GOTO 400
180 IF X$="3" THEN LOCATE 15,20:PRINT "....Barrels":GOTO 500
190 IF X$="4" THEN LOCATE 15,20:PRINT "....Tonnes":GOTO 600
192 IF X$="5" THEN LOCATE 15,20:PRINT "....Metres":GOTO 650
194 IF X$="6" THEN LOCATE 15,20:PRINT "....Feet":GOTO 685
200 GOTO 150
300 LET Y$=INKEY$
310 IF Y$="2" THEN LOCATE 15,60:PRINT "....Litres":GOTO 700
320 IF Y$="3" THEN LOCATE 15,60:PRINT "....Barrels":GOTO 800
330 IF Y$="4" THEN LOCATE 15,60:PRINT "....Tonnes ":GOTO 900
340 GOTO 300
400 LET Y$=INKEY$
410 IF Y$="1" THEN LOCATE 15,60:PRINT "....M3    ":GOTO 1000
420 IF Y$="3" THEN LOCATE 15,60:PRINT "....Barrels":GOTO 1100
430 IF Y$="4" THEN LOCATE 15,60:PRINT "....Tonnes":GOTO 1200
```

```
440 GOTO 400
500 LET Y$=INKEY$
510 IF Y$="1" THEN LOCATE 15,60:PRINT "....M3":GOTO 1300
520 IF Y$="2" THEN LOCATE 15,60:PRINT "....Litres":GOTO 1400
530 IF Y$="4" THEN LOCATE 15,60:PRINT "....Tonnes ":GOTO 1500
540 GOTO 500
600 LET Y$=INKEY$
610 IF Y$="1"THEN LOCATE 15,60:PRINT "....M3":GOTO 1600
620 IF Y$="2" THEN LOCATE 15,60:PRINT "....Litres":GOTO 1700
630 IF Y$="3" THEN LOCATE 15,60:PRINT "....Barrels":GOTO 1800
640 GOTO 600
650 LET Y$=INKEY$
660 IF Y$="5" THEN LOCATE 15,60:PRINT "....Feet":LOCATE 15,10:INPUT A: GOTO 1850
670 GOTO 650
680 LET Y$=INKEY$
685 IF Y$="6" THEN LOCATE 15,60:PRINT "....Metres":LOCATE 15,10:INPUT A: GOTO 18
60
690 GOTO 680
700 LOCATE 15,10:INPUT;A
710 B=A*1000
720 LOCATE 15,40:PRINT B
730 GOTO 2000
800 LOCATE 15,10:INPUT;A
810 B=A*6.2898
820 LOCATE 15,50:PRINT B
830 GOTO 2000
900 LOCATE 15,10:INPUT;A
910 LOCATE 20,10:INPUT "What is the S.G.";C
920 B=A*C
930 LOCATE 15,50:PRINT B
1000 LOCATE 15,10:INPUT;A
1010 B=A/1000
1020 LOCATE 15,50:PRINT B
1030 GOTO 2000
1100 LOCATE 15,10:INPUT A
1120 B=A*6.2898/1000
1130 LOCATE 15,50:PRINT B
1140 GOTO 2000
1200 LOCATE 15,10:INPUT A
1210 LOCATE 20,10:INPUT "What is the S.G.";C
1220 B=A*C/1000
1230 LOCATE 15,50:PRINT B
1240 GOTO 2000
1300 LOCATE 15,10:INPUT;A
1310 B=A/6.2898
1320 LOCATE 15,50:PRINT B
1330 GOTO 2000
1400 LOCATE 15,10:INPUT;A
1410 B=A*1000/6.2898
1420 LOCATE 15.5:PRINT B
1430 GOTO 2000
1500 LOCATE 15,10:INPUT A
1510 LOCATE 20,10:INPUT "What is the S.G.";C
1520 B=A*C/6.2898
1530 LOCATE 15,50:PRINT B
1540 GOTO 2000
1600 LOCATE 15,10:INPUT A
1610 LOCATE 20,10:INPUT "What is the S.G.";C
1620 B=A/C
1630 LOCATE 15,50:PRINT B
1640 GOTO 2000
1700 LOCATE 15,10:INPUT;A
1710 LOCATE 20,10:INPUT "What is the S.G."; C
1720 B=A*1000/C
1730 LOCATE 15,50:PRINT B
1740 GOTO 2000
1800 LOCATE 15,10:INPUT;A
1810 LOCATE 20,10:INPUT "What is the S.G.";C
1820 B=A*6.2898/C
1830 LOCATE 15,50:PRINT B
1840 GOTO 2000
1850 B=A*3.28083:GOTO 1890
1860 B=A*.3048 :GOTO 1890
1890 LOCATE 15,50: PRINT B
2000 LOCATE 20,10:INPUT "Do you require further conversions";F$
2015 IF F$="n" THEN CLS:END
2020 IF F$="y" THEN LOCATE 15,10:PRINT "
                          "
2030 LOCATE 20,10:PRINT "                                        "
2040 GOTO 150
```

```
┌─────────────────────────────────────────────────────────┐
│                                                           │
│  Appendix 2                                               │
│  The UKOOA/BOSVA Code                                     │
│                                                           │
│                                                           │
└─────────────────────────────────────────────────────────┘
```

This code is the first serious attempt by the offshore industry to regulate the working of supply vessels at the interface with offshore installations.

Oil company managers have for years been aware of the sometimes arbitrary way in which supply vessels have been instructed to carry out their tasks. The code, developed over a period of two years, is intended to improve the dialogue between installation management and supply ship masters.

During its development considerable interest was expressed by supply ship operators and oil companies all over the world. It is printed in full here, primarily as a means of making it available to readers outside the United Kingdom. The version given here is the second draft dated February 1992.

UKOOA/BOSVA Code of Conduct:
Supply Vessel Operations at Offshore Installations

Contents

1 Introduction

This Code of Conduct is issued by the United Kingdom Offshore Operators Association (UKOOA) and the British Offshore Support Vessels Association (BOSVA) to provide guidance to Operators, Offshore Installation Managers, Masters and Owners of offshore support vessels so as to avoid or reduce to a minimum the hazards which affect offshore vessels in their daily interface with offshore installations. Where the Code specifies master and/or OIM, it is assumed that this includes their nominated representatives.

This document is not intended to conflict with or replace any existing legislation, contractual obligations or guidance notes issued by regulatory bodies or trade associations. Where installation operators or vessel owners issue their own safety or operating procedures, it is recommended that this Code of Conduct be incorporated.

Although jointly agreed by UKOOA and BOSVA Members, it is recommended that this Code of Conduct apply to all offshore operations regardless of Association membership.

UKOOA and BOSVA will keep this Code of Conduct under review. It is the intention to issue amendments from time to time.

Usage of the male gender in the text is for brevity only. It should be read as meaning male or female, as appropriate to the individual involved.

2 Responsibilities

The Master is responsible for the safety of his crew and vessel. He has the authority to decide whether any operation affecting his vessel should proceed or terminate.

He should question any instructions from installation personnel which potentially hazard his crew or vessel.

The OIM has overall responsibility for operations within the 500 metre safety zone and may demand the modification/termination of any operation he considers hazardous.

3 Applicable regulations

The following are some of the Regulations affecting supply vessel operations:

The Health and Safety at Work Act 1974.
SI 1019 (1976) The Offshore Installations (Operational Safety, Health and Welfare) Regulations 1976.
SI 1890 (1984) The Freight Containers (Safety Convention) Regulations 1984.
SI 1655 (1988) The Docks Regulations 1988 and approved Code of Practice.
SI 37 (1987) The Dangerous Substances in Harbour Areas Regulations 1987 and approved Code of Practice.
SI 1657 (1988) The Control of Substances Hazardous to Health Regulations 1988.
SI 2605 (1990) The Merchant shipping (Dangerous Goods and Marine Pollutants) Regulations 1990 with supporting 'M' Notices.
Merchant shipping 'M' Notice M. 781 'Manning of Oil Rig Supply Vessels'.
Merchant Shipping 'M' Notice M. 117.8 'Manning of Merchant Ships Registered in the United Kingdom'.
Merchant Shipping 'M' Notice M. 1231 'Safe Cargo Handling Operations on Offshore Supply Vessels'.
Dept. of Energy Safety Notice PED 5 1/90 'Working Hours' (on Offshore Installations).
The Code of Safe Working Practices for Merchant Seamen.
The British Standards Institution (BSI) Code of Practice for Offshore Containers (BS 7072 1989).

This list is not exhaustive and is subject to change as applicable regulations change.

4 Containers and lifting gear

4.1 General

The Operator is responsible for ensuring that all cargo containers and lifting gear used to ship materials to or from offshore installations are correctly chosen for the purpose in terms of type, size and load-carrying capacity, that all certification is fully in date at the time of use, and that the load to be carried is properly secured. General recommendations are contained in the BSI Code of Practice for Offshore Containers.

4.2 Cargo handling equipment

As a minimum, all cargo handling equipment (slings, strops, shackles, hooks etc.) is to be tested, marked and examined in accordance with the relevant Regulations.

All strops and slings should be of the correct size and length for the intended use. Bulldog grips must not be used in the manufacture or length adjustment of strops or slings, but may be used for locking purposes on pipe slings. Where applicable, all containers, baskets etc. shall be pre-slung with a four leg sling arrangement terminating in a single ring with pennant line. All shackles used should have the means to prevent slackening due to vibration.

Container doors must be adequately secured and a means to prevent dislodging of the door-securing mechanism provided. Where applicable, the identification number should appear on the roof of the container. Anti-slip coating should be applied to the upper surface.

Skips or open cargo baskets containing loose equipment or rubbish should be provided with safety nets to retain the cargo. Care must be taken to prevent them being overloaded, particularly when scrap metal or shot blasting materials are stowed within. Consideration should be given to the length of lifting gear fitted to skips. The practice of multiple stacking as one unit should be discouraged unless lifting gear is modified, so avoiding the need for a ship's crew having to climb into the skip to hook on the lift.

Building industry design skips present a hazard to supply vessel crews. They should be phased out in favour of a suitable alternative.

4.3 Pre-shipment inspection

It is essential that all lifting appliances, slings and containers are fit for purpose prior to shipment offshore. Operators should have in place a testing and inspection procedure which meets the applicable Regulations. Ideally, this will include a visual inspection before each usage.

5 Carriage of cargo

It is essential that liaison is established between the Operator and Master prior to loading or backloading any cargo.

5.1 Containers

The Operator shall ensure that cargo within containers is adequately stowed and well secured. A packing certificate is required for all dangerous cargo or marine pollutants packed into containers and cargo of this nature must be stowed and segregated as per the relevant Regulations. This is equally applicable to offshore backloading. The Master has the authority to carry out random inspections and, if such an inspection of any container reveals inadequate marking/labelling of dangerous goods or marine pollutants, or he is in any doubt as to the safety status of the container, then he has a right to refuse it. Operators should ensure that as much cargo as possible/practicable is containerized to allow safer stowage and securing on deck.

5.2 Portable tanks

All portable tanks used for the carriage of dangerous substances must be approved for use by a competent authority, tested, and marked in accordance with the International Maritime Dangerous Goods Code (IMDG Code). Prior to placing on board a vessel all tanks are to be carefully checked for damage and leakage. Guidance is contained in 'M' Notice No. M1437.

5.3 Deck cargo

All cargo on deck is to be stowed to the Master's satisfaction, the Master being responsible for ensuring it is correctly stowed and adequately secured for the intended voyage. Areas on the deck which are not to be used for cargo stowage should be clearly marked (or otherwise indicated). All cargo operations, on and off shore, are to be supervised by a responsible officer on the vessel at all times. The Master has the authority to decide the sequence of cargo discharge to the installation.

5.4 Dangerous goods and marine pollutants

The carriage of dangerous goods and marine pollutants is governed by the Merchant Shipping (Dangerous Goods and Marine Pollutants) Regulations 1990, the International Maritime Dangerous Goods Code (IMDG Code) 1990 edition, and supporting DTp 'M' Notices.

Vessel Masters, Offshore Installations, and Operators should have available an up-to-date full set of IMDG volumes for reference as required. All requirements laid down in the IMDG Code must be followed, where applicable.

The Operator and Master must ensure that all dangerous goods and marine pollutants are properly declared, packaged, marked, stowed, and segregated in accordance with the Regulations. Masters must be given advance warning prior to loading or backloading dangerous goods.

Masters must receive from the Operator full details of all dangerous goods and marine pollutants to avoid legal liabilities.

The Master should consult with the Operator when in any doubt regarding shipping of dangerous goods and marine pollutants, and he has the authority to refuse to load these cargoes if the regulations are not being correctly observed.

5.5 Order of stowage

When possible and practicable, the order of loading, discharging and stowage arrangements is to be pre-planned in order to avoid the 'slotting' of containers and the necessity for ships' crews to climb on top of cargo. The Master should be provided with details of any unusual items of cargo, cargoes requiring special sea fastening arrrangements, or heavy lifts before loading.

5.6 Documentation and marking

All cargo should be accompanied by a cargo manifest clearly identifying the goods and giving details regarding the contents, destination and weight. If the Master of the vessel is unable to obtain full details of cargo to be shipped prior to loading at any port or backloading at an offshore installation, an outline list giving brief details shall be drawn up before loading is permitted to commence. All cargo should be marked so as to be readily identifiable from the manifest.

The Master has the authority to refuse cargo if insufficient information is given, the cargo is incorrectly manifested, or if he has reason to believe dangerous goods are contained in unmarked cargo.

The description and weight of loaded containers must be individually declared on the manifest. Operators should provide facilities at the shore base to verify weights during loading operations. Where weighing facilities are not available offshore installation personnel should be careful not to underestimate the weight of individual lifts.

6 Cargo handling and general procedures offshore

6.1 Master/OIM information exchange

Prior to commencing cargo operations, the programme should be discussed and agreed by radio between the OIM and Master to ensure that the installation and vessel are ready in all respects.

Any factors limiting the vessel's expected performance must be indicated to the installation, and the vessel Master should, in turn, receive information on limitations of the installation which may affect the operation.

Installations and vessels will have in place operating procedures designed to assist this. A suggested operating procedure ship/installation checklist is contained as Appendix 1.

6.2 Hours of work/manning

It is recognised that fatigue could be a hazard to personnel within the offshore industry and a threat to offshore safety. The improved capability of modern vessels to work in adverse weather conditions has increased vessel utilization. The OIM and Master should discuss the intended operation, taking into consideration the expected period of work and the prevailing conditions so as to minimize, as far as possible, the problem of fatigue.

For safety reasons, the attention of owners and operators is drawn to the manning levels laid down in M.781 and the general Principles of Safe Manning endorsed by the IMO.

Masters of vessels involved in operations alongside offshore installations have responsibilities to ensure that they and their crew achieve adequate rest periods.

The OIM has an overall responsibility for safety extending to the 500 m Safety Zone.

The advice on working hours limitations applicable to offshore installations is contained in DEn Notice PED 5 1/90.

6.3 Communications

An effective radio communication link on one channel shall be maintained at all times while a vessel is working cargo alongside an offshore installation. Masters of vessels should observe periods of radio silence which will be communicated to the vessel concerned. Effective communications between the Master, the Installation Staff and the deck crew are vital to safety. For this reason it should be ensured that key personnel have a good knowledge of the English language.

6.4 Work programme

The Master of the vessel should be advised of expected delays to operations so that the vessel's work programme may be synchronized with that of the installation. Excessive waiting time alongside the installation should be avoided.

6.5 Crane operations

In all cargo work involving crane operations, the crane driver should have a clear view of the vessel's deck.

In exceptional situations where the crane driver cannot see the vessel's deck, then a 'banksman' who does have a clear view of the deck must be appointed.

The use of swivel self-locking safety hooks is mandatory unless previously agreed and discussed between Master and OIM. The crane driver should have direct radio communication to the Master of the vessel.

Hi-visibility crane pennants can be used below the main cargo hook of the crane to assist deck crews in cargo handling operations.

The limitations of working of the crane should be formally passed to the Master of the vessel prior to operations commencing.

6.6 Platform overboard discharges

All non-essential overboard discharges that could hamper vessel operations alongside should be shut down prior to commencing cargo operations. Should the Master feel an overboard discharge causes distress to personnel or imposes danger upon the vessel, then he has the authority to cease operations and stand off until the discharge has ceased or prevailing conditions keep the discharge clear of the vessel.

6.7 Under-platform and column lighting

In some cases, lighting below platforms and around columns is of a low standard. Where the Master of the vessel does not have a clear view of the overall operation or the installation structure, operations will be restricted to daylight hours or until full visibility has been restored. In certain circumstances, the vessel's own searchlight may be utilized.

6.8 Protective clothing

The crew of a supply vessel involved in cargo operations alongside an installation must wear safety and protective clothing suitable for the work being undertaken as per the relevant Regulations. Outer clothing for all crew on deck should be of a high visibility colour. Lifesaving equipment should be readily available.

6.9 Heavy lifts

All heavy-lift cargo should be indicated to the installation prior to the vessel's arrival. All operations involving heavy lifts will require reasonable weather criteria and should be discussed and agreed prior to commencement. Other operations, bulk handling etc. may have to be suspended whilst heavy lifts are handled. Subject to agreement with the Master, taglines should be attached to heavy or large lifts to facilitate handling.

6.10 Backloading of cargo offshore

All backloading operations should be pre-planned to assist safe operations. Offloading from, and backloading into, slots is prohibited unless the Master deems it safe.

All tubular backloads should be indicated to the vessel in good time to allow for planning of stowage. Tubular cargoes should be slung in safe bundles (and bulldogged) or singly, as required by their weight. Varying lengths of sling in one lift must be avoided. Taglines should be provided as required to increase overall safety when landing cargo on the vessel's deck.

All cargo to be backloaded must be inspected by a responsible and competent person to ensure that it is in a safe and secure condition and will not create a hazard to the crew or vessel. All lifts should be inspected to ensure there are no loose items on top of or inside the cargo, that they are properly slung, that all doors, lids etc. are properly secured, and that open skips or cargo baskets are fitted with nets. Open skips/baskets should be drained of loose water prior to backloading to the vessel.

Dangerous cargo labels on empty cleaned containers must be removed prior to backloading to the vessel.

6.11 Bulk transfer procedures

Agreed procedures covering the transfer of all bulk products should be followed — see Appendix 2.

7 Rig moves/anchor handling operations

7.1 General

All vessels involved in anchor handling operations should comply with the relevant section of the Code of Safe Working Practices for Merchant Seamen.

7.2 Agreed procedures and responsibilities

Full procedures for rig move operations should be agreed by operators and their Mobile Installation Contractors and clear instructions laid down in writing. Where particular installations have detailed procedures for anchor handling, these should be passed to the relevant vessels via the operator as required, so that Masters are fully briefed on the operation to be conducted. If at all possible, Masters should be briefed prior to leaving port or, failing that, on location prior to rig move operations.

The procedures should identify the responsibilities of key personnel and identify who is the person in charge of the move. Attention is drawn to 'M' Notice 1406.

7.3 Equipment

Sufficient equipment is to be available as required for the intended operation. The Master of each vessel is responsible for the ship's own equipment.

The person in charge of the installation is responsible for all installation equipment, including equipment hired specifically for the move, and all towing gear on the installation.

The responsibility for each person extends to a full inspection of all equipment prior to the rig move operations, with appropriate log entries made, and maintenance procedures carried out.

Equipment provided by Operators should be inspected prior to shipment.

All equipment should be identified fully to all involved in the operation.

7.4 Mooring equipment

There should be agreement as to responsibility for providing mooring equipment for the move and agreement as to the amount and specification of such equipment, taking account of the anticipated holding ground on location. Sufficient piggy anchors, buoys and associated pennant systems should be available in the field as required. Attention is drawn to CONSOP Notice No. 42.

7.5 Weather limitations

Weather forecast should be available during all rig move operations, and operations planned accordingly. In marginal weather conditions the Master of each vessel and the person in charge of the move should agree to terminate/commence operations. Each vessel Master has the responsibility to decide whether or not conditions allow his vessel to operate safely.

7.6 Pipelines/sub-sea obstructions

It must be ensured that all relevant personnel involved have full details of the location, including pipeline plans and sub-sea obstructions.

Where it is known that anchor handling operations will be conducted near to pipelines or sub-sea structures, then full written procedures are to be agreed by all parties.

7.7 Safety equipment

Full safety equipment should be readily available on deck during all anchor handling operations. Crew on exposed decks should wear approved buoyancy aids or workvests and safety head protection and footwear. Lifebuoys with lines are to be readily available. The standby vessel should be informed of all operations in progress.

7.8 Hours of work/manning

Attention is drawn to Section 6.2 of this Code of Conduct.

7.9 Radio communications

Due to the nature of the operation, it is recommended that a dedicated VHF working channel is identified purely for anchor handling operations.

7.10 Anchor handling operations

No hard and fast procedures can be formally laid down with regard to anchor-handling operations, as there are so many variable factors. Offshore personnel should be aware of the operational limitations of the various vessels utilized, including their power and freeboard, with the safety of crews being of paramount importance.

Vessel owners have a responsibility to ensure that vessels involved in anchor handling operations are fit for purpose and manned to M Notice M781 levels by personnel with adequate experience and ability.

Offshore Installation personnel should ensure that whenever pennants are passed to vessels close alongside, crane drivers are experienced in this operation, effective communication has established agreed procedures for the pennant transfer, and adequate supervision is available.

When running anchors, the anchor handling vessel Master should be advised where the Installation winches have payout limitations, so that speed can be controlled. Effective communication must be established between the Master and the winch driver.

7.11 Towing operations

A safe method of passing the main towing pennant from the Installation to the towing vessel should be established, with a clear understanding of the procedures to be used by all parties.

The secondary towing system must be identified, method of retrieval of the main towing gear established, and safe method of passing the secondary towing system established.

Towing vessels should ensure that the Installation personnel are aware of the time that may be required to rig their spare towing wire. Where an additional vessel is available as reserve tug whilst on passage, it should be rigged for towing.

8 Communications between operators and vessel owners/masters

It is important that a direct line of communication is established between Owners and Operators to enable all matters of safety to be raised and, where appropriate, action taken. Individuals should be nominated for this purpose. This direct line shall not replace the first line of offshore communication between the Master of the vessel and the OIM, but will complement it where on-going safety issues cannot be resolved or where fundamental issues require to be progressed by owners and Operators. Owners and Masters will be able to raise and discuss any safety matter without fear, recrimination or adverse repercussion.

Masters should ensure that all hazards or incidents affecting safety involving their vessels and the offshore Installation are formally reported to the Operator and Owner. Use should be made of the safety officer's record book for this purpose, and relevant safety committee minutes should be forwarded to the Operator (in accordance with the Owner's in-house procedures) for all items having an effect on the Operator's operation.

UKOOA and BOSVA shall maintain a formal line for communication through their respective secretaries to ensure that this Code of Conduct shall be regularly up-dated and maintained as a definitive Code to the safe operation of rigs, platforms and support vessels.

Appendix 1: Checklist for supply vessel/installation operations

Ship

- All propulsion, control, and back-up systems operational.
- Vessel staff are sufficiently rested.
- Deck crew are briefed and correctly dressed.
- Vessel's programme has been advised/agreed.
- Communications with the installation are working.
- Internal communications on vessel are working.
- Bulk transfer operations have been agreed.
- Full details of cargo discussed/agreed.

Installation

- The required working zone alongside is clear of other vessels.
- Overside discharges in the working zone have been stopped.
- Standby vessel has been briefed on the operation.
- Installation staff are sufficiently rested.
- Deck crew and crane driver are briefed.

- Vessel's programme has been advised/agreed.
- Crane limitations have been advised to master.
- Permission given to offload during diving operations.
- Bulk transfer operations have been agreed.
- Full details of cargo discussed/agreed.

Appendix 2: Bulk transfer procedures

The following procedures should be used prior to and during any transfer offshore of bulk cargo to or from the vessel.

1 Prior to start of operations, hoses should be visually inspected and doubtful lengths replaced. Slings and lifting points should also be visually checked and replaced if required. Hoses are only to be lifted by a certified wire strop on a certified hook eye fitting.

2 The following information should be requested by the Installation (or by the Master if bulk is to be transferred from the Installation to the vessel):

Estimated pumping rate for each product.
Length of warning/estimate of time required to stop.
Emergency stop procedure.
Confirmation that the lines can be drained back to the vessel's tanks where necessary.

3 The Master should be provided with the following information:
Size of hoses, connections.
Length of hose available.
Colour scheme in operation (hose and/or product).
Maximum loading rate/pressure permitted.
Quantities of each product required, the order in which they are required, and an estimate of the time at which they will be required.

4 When the hose is connected and installation lines are set, the supply vessel should be directed to start pumping at a slow rate. For dry bulk transfers, purge air is to be utilized prior to bulk transfer to clear lines and prove connections.

5 If all is well and no leaks are observed, the supply vessel should be advised to increase pumping up to the full delivery rate.

6 When pumping has finished, both the installation and the supply vessel should set their lines to allow the hose to be drained back to the vessel's tank. If the installation has a vacuum breaker fitted to the line, this should be used to aid draining.
Lines may also be blown through with air, if available, to ensure that they are properly cleared. In suitable conditions the crane should also be used to lift the hose to aid draining.

7 When the hose is disconnected, the end should be fitted with a cap or blank in accordance with Continental Shelf Operations Notice No. 20.

8 Every bulk liquid hose should, as far as practicable, be drained back to the vessel's tank(s).

9 Hoses used for potable water should not be used for transferring other bulk liquids, including ordinary fresh water.

10 During periods of darkness, adequate illumination should be available over the hose and supply vessel throughout the operation. To facilitate identification, hoses should be fitted with hi-vis bands or hi-vis tape.

11 Hoses are normally colour-coded for manufacturers' identification and approval, frequently by use of spiral coloured bands within the *hose structure*. This colour scheme is optional. The *hose terminations* should be colour coded by use of a coloured band to mark the product, and all support vessels and installations should adopt a universal colour and connection scheme as follows:

Product	Coloured band	Connection
Potable water	Blue	4 inch hammer lug or quick release self-sealing coupling
Drill water	Green	4 inch hammer lug or quick release self-sealing coupling
Fuel	Brown	4 inch quick release self-sealing coupling
Dry bulk	Yellow cement Orange baryte/ bentonite	5 inch hammer lug union
Brine/oil-based mud	Black	4 inch hammer lug with ball valve or air blowdown facility
Dedicated base oil	Optional	4 inch quick release self-sealing coupling

12 All bulk hoses used offshore are to be type approved by the appropriate certifying authority as per DOE safety notice No. 12/88 and SI No. 289 of 1974.

13 All bulk hoses used offshore are to be of sufficient length for safe operation, and have internally swaged or other approved clamp fittings. Unapproved repairs must not be made.

14 Consideration should be given to the use of hose floats, where practicable, and where agreed by masters and installation personnel. If used, they must be correctly fitted to the appropriate portion of the hose system and be hi-vis in colour.

15 Passing hoses to vessels is a hazardous operation and it must be supervised by a responsible person on the installation with direct communication to the vessel Master.

16 During the period a vessel is connected to bulk hoses, continuous radio communication must be maintained, and the crane driver must be immediately available. Also, relevant installation personnel should stand by appropriate valves so as to act quickly in event of an emergency.

Appendix 3
Rig chain data

Rig moorings are made up of oil rig quality (ORQ) chain, which anchor handlers may find themselves carrying as cargo, either in the chain lockers or on deck. The following tables may be of use in this operation.

Data on oil rig quality (ORQ) chain — metric sizes

1 shot = 27.5 m (90 ft)

mm	Weight (kg per shot)	Proof load (tonnes)	Breaking load (tonnes)	No. of links per shot
50	1555	144	217	137
54	1809	166	251	125
56	1946	178	269	123
58	2100	190	287	119
60	2253	203	306	113
64	2573	227	343	107
66	2742	240	360	105
70	3097	270	404	97
73	3374	290	438	93
76	3681	313	472	89
81	4187	352	531	85
87	4832	405	611	79
92	5385	463	710	73
95	5723	508	794	71
102	6613	594	910	67

Data on oil rig quality (ORQ) chain — imperial sizes

1 shot = 90 ft (27.5 m)

Inches	Weight (lb per shot)	Proof load (tons)	Breaking load (tons)	No. of links per shot
2	3528	144	218	137
$2\frac{1}{8}$	3971	162	245	125
$2\frac{3}{16}$	4212	171	258	123
$2\frac{5}{16}$	4735	190	287	119
$2\frac{3}{8}$	5016	200	301	113
$2\frac{1}{2}$	5581	219	332	107
$2\frac{5}{8}$	6176	241	363	105
$2\frac{3}{4}$	6783	263	395	97
$2\frac{7}{8}$	7435	286	431	93
3	8118	309	465	89
$3\frac{3}{16}$	9180	346	522	85
$3\frac{7}{16}$	10708	398	598	79
$3\frac{5}{8}$	11874	456	699	73
$3\frac{3}{4}$	12360	500	781	71
4	14579	579	892	67

Appendix 4
Glossary of terms

A-FRAME   A hinged frame on the stern of offshore vessels used for the launching and recovery of manned submersibles, and initially for the recovery of anchors.

AGITATORS   Propeller shaped units fitted inside the mud tanks of supply vessels to keep the solids in suspension.

AHTS   Anchor handling tug supply vessel. See ANCHOR HANDLER.

AIR GUN   A device using high pressure compressed air to produce an underwater explosion for seismic work.

ANCHOR HANDLER   A supply vessel equipped for the deployment of anchors and for towing.

ANCHOR HANDLING TONG   Hydraulically operated equipment for holding anchor wires and chains on the deck of an anchor handler.

ANCHOR JOB   The complete operation of moving an oil rig.

ANCHOR SPREAD   The deployed anchors of a semi-submersible.

ARTEMIS   A short-range positioning system used by dynamically positioned vessels.

AVERY-HARDOLL   A hose connection used for fuel transfer which is self sealing when disconnected.

AZIMUTHING THRUSTER   An omnidirectional thruster which can be steered from the bridge.

BACK-UP ANCHOR   An additional anchor attached to the main anchor to improve holding.

BANKSMAN   A man who signals to the crane driver when the hook is out of his sight.

BARREL   A measurement of liquid used in the oil industry. 6.3 bbls = 1 m^3.

BARYTES   A mineral used to weight mud.

BASE OIL   The basic oil from which oil-based mud is produced.

BASKET TRANSFER   The movement of personnel between offshore installations and marine craft by means of the 'basket' on the crane.

BECKER RUDDER   A proprietary brand of flap rudder. See FLAP RUDDER.

BENTONITE   A mineral used in the manufacture of drilling fluid.

BIRD   An electronically controlled vane used to regulate the depth of a seismic cable.

BLOWOUT PREVENTER   A device consisting of pistons within the Christmas tree, which close together, severing the drill string and cutting off the well.

BOLLARD PULL   The measurement of the pulling capability of tugs, defined in tonnes.

BOLSTER   The fabricated rack at the bottom of the legs of semi-submersibles on which the anchor rests.

BOP   See BLOWOUT PREVENTER.

BOWTHRUSTER   Azimuthing or tunnel thruster situated at the bow of the vessel.

BREAKING OUT   The moment when the anchor handler pulls the rig anchor out of the seabed.

BRIDLE   The short single or double wire on the barge or semi-submersible to which the tow-wire is attached.

BRINE   Chemically formulated solution of considerable weight, used in drilling instead of mud.

BRUCE ANCHOR   High-holding-power fabricated anchor.

BULK   Oil industry term for any sort of bulk powder cargo.

BURIED TURNS   Turns on the workdrum tightened irregularly when weight is put on a loosely reeled wire.

CAMLOCK   A hose connection used in the road transport industry, but now not much at sea.

CAPPING   The procedure of shutting down a well for later re-entry.

CARPENTER'S STOPPER   A stopper which, by means of sliding wedges, allows a wire to be stoppered off at a point other than a splice.

CASING   The piping, in various sizes, used to line the well.

CEMENT   Standard cement, carried in the bulk tanks of supply vessels and used to fix the casing in place.

CIRCULATING SYSTEM   The system for circulating oil-based mud in an effort to keep the barytes in suspension.

COORDINATOR SURFACE SEARCH   A surface vessel whose responsibility is to delegate to the various search group leaders.

CRABBING   Moving sideways by using the main engines, rudders and thrusters.

CRANE LEG   A lighter wire and hook fitted to the main crane wire.

CRASH BARRIER   The rails along the sides of supply vessels behind which the crew can shelter from moving cargo etc.

CROSSING THE STICKS   Putting one engine ahead and one astern, usually as part of the crabbing manoeuvre.

CROWN CHAIN   A short length of chain from the crown of a rig anchor to the first pennant.

CSS   See COORDINATOR SURFACE SEARCH.

CULLEN REPORT   The report on the enquiry into the Piper Alpha disaster.

D-SHACKLE   Conventionally shaped shackle use in anchor work.

DECK SHEATHING   The wooden planking fitted to the decks of all supply vessels.

DELTA FLIPPER   A type of high-holding-power anchor.

DEVIATED DRILLING   Drilling holes away from the vertical to extend the recovery area of an oil field.

DIFFERENTIAL GPS   Precise position fixing system using the GPS system with base stations which compare actual and theoretical positions, and transmit this data to the mobiles.

DIVING SHIP   Any ship whose primary function is the deployment of divers.

DIVING SPREAD   All the paraphernalia used in diving: the bell, the umbilicals, the saturation chamber etc.

DODGING Steaming slowly up and down on location, waiting for something to happen — much used in rough weather.

DOLLY Rotating sleeve mounted on the crash barrier for altering the direction of pull of the tugger wires.

DOWN-HOLE SURVEY Survey carried out with an airgun on a support vessel and a geophone down the well.

DP See DYNAMIC POSITIONING.

DRILL PIPE The individual lengths of pipe used to make up the drill string.

DRILL STRING The complete length of drill pipe being used at any time.

DRILL WATER Fresh water used for drilling mud, usually carried in supply vessel ballast tanks.

DRILLING DERRICK The actual structure from which the drill string hangs.

DRILLING FLUID Any fluid used to provide the hydrostatic head and recover the drilling slurry. Includes brine and all sorts of mud.

DRIVING The term used in the industry for manoeuvring supply vessels.

DRY HOLE A well within which no oil is found.

DSV Dive Support Vessel. See DIVING SHIP.

DYNAMIC POSITIONING Any positioning system which involves direct interface between a position fixing system, a computer and the engines and thrusters.

ELEPHANT'S FEET Horizontal plates on top of the towing pins which turn inwards to trap the wire in the resulting rectangular space.

ENVIRONMENTALLY-BASED MUD A type of mud with the same properties as oil-based mud, but which is environmentally safe.

EXPLORATION RIG Any mobile platform on which the drilling derrick is mounted.

FAST RESCUE CRAFT Small craft deployed from support craft for the purposes of personnel recovery.

FISH BOX HOOK Length of heavy wire with a hook in the end used for moving things round the deck of support vessels.

FISHBASKET A wicker basket used in the fishing industry, useful for holding small tools during anchor jobs.

FLAP RUDDER A rudder with a hinged flap at the trailing edge to increase the turning effect.

FLARE BOOM Long boom for flaring gas on production platforms, or shorter boom on exploration rigs used for flaring oil during testing.

FLOATING STORAGE UNIT Hull, usually an ex-tanker, moored at the bow, and used for storing oil on small fields.

FLOTATION COLLAR Collar fitted to rig hoses to give them buoyancy.

FLOTEL Accommodation unit placed on a semi-submersible hull.

FRC See FAST RESCUE CRAFT.

FREE FALL LIFEBOAT A lifeboat which is launched without restraint into the sea.

FSU See FLOATING STORAGE UNIT.

FUSE LINK A short wire fitted between the bridle and the towline which is of slightly lower breaking strain than the rest of the set-up.

GEOPHONE Receiver for the sound waves generated by the airguns used in seismic survey. Set at intervals along the cable.

GOB PLATE A plate bolted to the deck to which is attached a short chain with a shackle which goes round the tow-wire.

GOB-WIRE Usually a workwire fed through a point in the deck near the stern of an AHTS and shackled round the tow-wire.

GPS   Global Positioning System. A US Government set of satellites giving precise position fixing world wide.

GROUT   A type of cement carried in supply vessel bulk tanks.

GUIDE BASE   The first fitting attached to the end of the 30 inch (762 mm) casing, onto which the rest of the wellhead equipment is fitted.

GUN ARRAY   One set of airguns deployed from a seismic survey vessel.

HEAVY LIFT BARGE   Semi-submersible barge fitted with one or two very large cranes.

HELIDECK   The landing area for helicopters on rigs and large support vessels.

HINGE LINK   A joining link often used instead of a D-shackle to connect pennants, since less damage to the wires results.

HOLE   Common term for the well being drilled.

HYPERBARIC LIFEBOAT   A lifeboat capable of being pressurized, for rescuing divers from sinking DSVs.

J-HOOK   Chaser used for recovering anchors whose buoys have been lost.

JACK-UP   Drilling rig which jacks itself out of the water on three or four legs.

JACKET   The steel base structure of a platform.

JEWELRY   The hardware used in the make-up of rig anchoring and chasing systems.

JOYSTICK   Single stick manoeuvring equipment interfacing a computer with engines and thrusters.

KARMFORK   Wire handling equipment consisting of hydraulic posts slotted at the top to receive the pennants or chains.

KIP   A measurement of tension: 1000 lbf or 4.448 kN.

KORT NOZZLE   Fabricated tube round the propellers of tugs which increases the bollard pull.

LASSO   Length of wire, usually fitted with a short length of chain in the centre, thrown over the anchor buoy from the AHTS.

LEAD TUG   The towing vessel nominally in charge of the tow, and followed by the second tug.

LOADING LIST   List of items to be loaded in port on a supply vessel.

LWT   Standard US Navy lightweight anchor.

MANNED SUBMERSIBLE   Submarine deployed from mother ship, usually capable of carrying up to five personnel.

MARGINAL WEATHER   Weather that requires a decision from the master as to whether work can safely proceed.

MARINE RISER   The tube between the wellhead and the rig that protects the drill string and carries the drilling fluid.

MIMIC BOARD   An instrument panel that controls the electrical operation of valves, and shows graphically whether they are open or closed.

MOONPOOL   A space in the centre of diving ships through which the bell is lowered.

MULTI-ROLE SUPPORT VESSEL (MSV)   Usually semi-submersible vessel, fitted with thrusters and moorings. Can provide accommodation and diving, emergency and firefighting services.

OFFSHORE INSTALLATION MANAGER (OIM)   The manager of a platform responsible for all aspects of its operations.

OIL-BASED MUD (OBM)   Drilling fluid consisting of detoxified gas oil to which barytes and other chemicals are added.

ONE-FOR-ONE   The practice of lifting a container out of the stow of a support vessel and returning another to the same space.

ON-SCENE COMMANDER (OSC)   The person locally in charge of a marine emergency: either an OIM or a military aircraft officer.

OPERATOR   The oil company that carries out the operation of an exploration well or producing field on behalf of the owners.

PELICAN HOOK   A wire-securing device.

PENNANT   Term for any wire used in the string between the surface buoy and the crown of the rig anchor.

PIGTAIL   The short wire from the underside of the surface buoy to the first pennant.

PILE   The tubulars used to pin the jacket to the seabed.

PIPE CARRIER   A type of support vessel designed to carry pipe for the pipe barges.

PIPE LAYING BARGE   A barge equipped to weld lengths of pipe together and then to feed them over the stern as a pipeline.

PLATFORM   See PRODUCTION PLATFORM.

PLATFORM SUPPLY VESSEL (PSV)   Today this usually means any support vessel not fitted with a winch, i.e. one designed for the carriage of cargo only.

PONTOON   The lower horizontal buoyant structure which supports the vertical columns of semi-submersibles.

POP-UPS   See TOWING PINS.

POTABLE WATER   Water suitable for drinking, carried in dedicated tanks on supply vessels.

PRODUCTION PLATFORM   A steel or concrete structure, resting on, and attached to, the seabed, supporting all the facilities necessary for the recovery of oil from an offshore oilfield.

PULSE 8   Early Decca positioning system which used mobile stations.

RACKING   The action of bringing the rig anchor onto the bolster.

RESCUE BASKET   A large buoyant ring which may be deployed overside by the deck crane of the standby vessel, for the recovery of survivors from the sea.

RESERVOIR   The oil-bearing strata tapped by the hole.

RIG CHAIN LOCKER   Compartments beneath the winch of an anchor handler for storage of rig chain.

RIGID INFLATABLE BOAT (RIB)   Rigid hull with inflatable rubber sides, often used as FRC.

ROLLER   The roller on the stern of the anchor handler which allows the wires and eventually the anchor free passage aboard.

SAFETY HOOK   A latched hook used by rig cranes to avoid hooking on to the ship's structure.

SATELLITE WELL   A well some distance from the main platform of a field, with a sub-sea completion and control and pipelines to the main platform.

SATURATION DIVING   Diving operations in which the divers remain at the pressure of the seabed in a pressure vessel on board the ship.

SBV   See STANDBY VESSEL.

SCRAMBLING NET   Net hung over the side of an SBV up which survivors might be able to scramble.

SEDIMENT   The solids which are left in the mud tanks of supply vessels after cargo discharge.

SEMI-SUBMERSIBLE   Craft, usually an exploration rig, with a shallow draft for moving and a deep draft which gives a stable platform and reduces wave action while drilling.

SHARK'S JAW   Type of anchor handling tong — usually the Ulstein type.

SHEPHERD'S CROOK   See J-HOOK.

SLIDES   Heavy canvas panels in the lower sections of cement tanks, through which air is blown to assist in the discharge.

SLOTTING   See ONE-FOR-ONE.

SNATCHING   Maintaining position under the rig crane by means of engines and thrusters.

SOAKING   Allowing the anchors of a rig to settle for several hours.

SPOOLING ON   Reeling pennants from coils or drums onto the workdrum.

SPOT CHARTER   Short-term hire: ships taken short term may receive no more than one hour's notice, and the hire period ends whenever the oil company has finished with them.

SPRING BUOY   Spring buoys are sometimes fitted part way down a pennant string to keep the crown pennant clear of the seabed.

SPUDDING IN   The initial breaking of the surface with the largest drill bit at the commencement of a hole.

STANDBY VESSEL   The craft standing by offshore installations for the purpose of rescuing personnel from the water.

STERN ROLLER   See ROLLER.

STEVIN ANCHOR   Conventionally shaped but fabricated anchor often used as a piggy-back.

STEVPRIS ANCHOR   Very large parallel-fluke twin-shank anchor with good holding power.

SUBMERSIBLE DRILLING RIG   A drilling rig which is sunk to the seabed when in drilling position.

SUB-SEA BUOY   Buoy secured to the seabed and released by a radio signal.

SUB-SEA COMPLETION   A wellhead or number of wellheads terminating on the seabed rather than on a platform, and connected to the platform by umbilicals.

SURFACE BUOY   The buoy holding up the pennant string from a rig anchor.

SWOPS VESSEL   Tanker capable of connecting up to a suitably installed wellhead and extracting the oil therefrom. (Only one exists.)

SYLEDIS   Position fixing system using mobile stations, mainly used by seismic ships.

TAG LINES   Lines hanging from the ends of tubulars to steady them, either on the ship or the rig.

TAUT WIRE   A position fixing system used by diving ships: a weight is lowered to the seabed and the computer monitors the angle of its attached wire.

TEMPLATE   A structure lowered to the seabed through which the wells of a production field may be drilled by a semi-submersible.

TEMPSC   Totally Enclosed Motor Propelled Survival Craft: a rig lifeboat.

TENSION LEG PLATFORM (TLP)   A semi-submersible platform attached to the seabed by heavy wires tensioned against the buoyancy of the unit.

TERM CHARTER   A negotiated period of supply vessel hire, from one month to 5 years.

TOPSIDES   The working part of a platform including the living, drilling and production modules.

TOW MASTER   Expert employed by the oil company to take charge of rig moves.

TOWING GATE   A gate on older anchor handlers which was closed under the tow-wire so as to allow the wire free movement.

TOWING PINS   A pair of hydraulic pins on an anchor handler, which rise from the deck, trapping between them the wire on which the deck crew are to work.

TOWING POD   A large tube bolted at tow-wire height into the middle of the deck, the tow-wire then being passed through it.

TOWING SLEEVE   A nylon sleeve on the tow-wire, positioned at the point of contact with the stern to obviate wear.

TOWING SPRING   A multi-stranded heavy duty nylon spring fitted between the bridle and the tow-wire to reduce shock loading.

TRIPLEX GEAR   Wire-securing equipment, the most elaborate of the types available.

TUBULARS   Any form of pipe supplied to offshore operations.

TUGGER   Small winch at the fore end of the supply vessel deck. The name is taken from small winches used on exploration rigs.

TUNING FORK   Twin pronged hook, used to handle chain, fitted to the end of the work-wire.

VICENAY   Manufacturer of LWT anchor.

WATER-BASED MUD   The most basic drilling fluid using drill water and barytes mixed on the rig.

WECO   A hose connection used throughout the oil industry.

Appendix 5
Further reading

Not a great deal has been published on the subject of supply vessels. The list below includes works issued by maritime organizations and publishers, as well as selected M Notices, all of which deal with one or more of the topics discussed in this book.

Anchor Manual, available free from Vryhof Ankers BV, Meerkoestraat 83a, PO Box 105, 2920 AC Krimpen ad Yssel, The Netherlands.

The Oil Rig Moorings Handbook, Captain J. Vendrell, published by Brown Son and Ferguson, 4–10 Darnley Street, Glasgow G41 2SD.

Introduction to Marine Drilling, Malcolm McLachlan, published by Oilfield Publications Ltd, PO Box 11, Ledbury, Herefordshire HR8 1BN.

Modern Towing, J.F. Blank III, published by Cornell Maritime Press, PO Box 456, Centreville, Maryland.

Ship Handling with Tugs, G.H. Reid, Published by Cornell Maritime Press.

Tugs and Towing, M.J. Gaston, published by Patrick Stephens Ltd, Sparkford, Yeovil BA22 7JJ.

PUBLISHED BY THE NAUTICAL INSTITUTE, 202 LAMBETH ROAD, LONDON SE1 7LQ:

Operating Offshore and Supply Vessels, Captain K. Appleby.

Dynamic Positioning Operator Training — Meeting the Need, Captain M. Williams J.S.S. Daniel and C.J. Parker.

The Handling of Offshore Supply Vessels, Captain S. Chaudhuri.

Proceedings of the Nautical Institute Seminar: Offshore Support Services — Initiatives and Developments.

PUBLISHED BY THE INTERNATIONAL MARITIME ORGANIZATION:

IMO Publication No. A67316: *Guidelines for the Transport and Handling of Limited Amounts of Hazardous and Noxious Liquid Substances, in Bulk, on Offshore Support Vessels.*

M Notices:

M718. Mooring, Towing and Hauling.

M748. Safety of Tugs While Towing.

M781. Recommended Manning for Offshore Support Vessels.

M1204. Helicopter Assistance.

M1221. Dynamically Positioned Vessels and Divers.

M1231. Cargo Handling Offshore.

M1234. Oil Recovery Vessels.

M1290. Offshore Installation Safety Zones.

M1406. Safety of Towed Ships.

M1458. Chemicals on Offshore Support Vessels.

Appendix 6
Other mariners' views

This appendix contains two documents which shed further light on subjects discussed in this book.

The first is a letter from an experienced towmaster on the subject of the use of high-power anchor handlers, and goes into some detail as to the possible requirements of semi-submersibles which are to be towed by these vessels.

The second is an extract from a report to the Norwegian Maritime Directorate on the rescue of personnel from the oil rig *West Gamma*. It is included to illustrate the point that, if possible, the supply vessels should leave the rescue of survivors to the standby ships, who have trained for just this purpose.

Letter from Captain N. Hancox, MNI, of Hancox Marine Services, Ocean Towage and Salvage Consultants, Westbury, Wilts, published in *Seaways*, February 1992

Sir — In October's storms in the Northern North Sea oilfields, a number of drilling units once again broke their tows which resulted in some of these units having to be partially evacuated as well as posing considerable risks to themselves, other installations and some potential risk to sub-sea equipment.

I suggest that some of these incidents are occurring as a result of poor seamanship and inadequate towing arrangements, both in the planning of the tow and the gear being used.

We — myself and others engaged in constant rig moving in this area — are fortunate to have at our disposal some of the largest and most powerful anchor handling/towing vessels in the world. It is now common to be utilising 10 to 14,000-hp vessels capable of bollard pulls in excess of 150 tonnes and I contend that some of the losses of tow gear are occurring because:

- Most semi-submersible drilling units have inadequately sized towing bridles for these high horsepower AHTs.
- Most semi-submersible drilling units and other similar vessels do not have an emergency towing bridle rigged and ready for immediate deployment should the main gear fail.

- Some vessels are using towing arrangements — for example, towing on anchor chains without fuse pennants and without any recovery gear if the tow wire parts — which are dangerous and allow for no back-up in the event of loss of tow.
- In the majority of cases the recovery gear fitted to the towing bridles is undersized in terms of winch power, poorly rigged and useless if, as is often the case, the tow parts on the stern of the tow vessel such that the rig has to heave back to main deck level weights which can exceed 20 tonnes (3 to 5 tonnes of bridle and 800/1000 metres of 70 mm wire: 15 tonnes). The gear must be hove up to above the surface in order to cut away the broken tow wire so that the bridle can be redeployed.
- Tow route planning and contingency planning is uniformly of a low standard for normal rig moves and discussion of alternative tow arrangements, action plans, etc., is rarely carried out with the towing vessels until the problems occur.
- I am dismayed at the general level of competence and towing knowledge of many of the rig masters and AHT masters and officers. This manifests itself in the following ways:

1 The use of too much power in relation to the strength of the towing gear.
2 The neglect by some boats to use chafing gear on their tow wires.
3 The unquestioning obedience of the AHT to the rig during towing operations, often to the detriment of the AHT — for example, running too long before deteriorating weather to the point where the tug is unable to turn up head to wind and is thus trapped in a most dangerous position.
4 The neglect of the severe bending and chafing forces that the tow wire is subjected to because of the design of many AHTs — a long vessel, therefore heavy pitching, scored rollers. It is very common to part the wire at the stern of an AHT and mostly it is because of neglect of good seamanship as applied to towing practice.
5 The deployment by some rig masters of towing gear whose condition is dubious — for example, the use of anchor pennants attached to anchor chains, neglect of proper checks on towing bridle shackles and wires. I have also noted that many rig masters have a poor grasp of the limitations of the AHT as a towing unit and are overawed by horsepower and bollard pull, expecting far too much of the tug.
6 Many rig masters place too much reliance on their thruster systems, if fitted. It is common for rig thrusters to fail just when they are most needed. They are a piece of equipment used only intermittently during the working life of a rig. When required to give full power for prolonged periods their reliability is variable.

I suggest that it is time to consider what should be standard towing arrangements for the majority of the North Sea fleet of heavy duty semi-submersibles. This should consist of the following basic outfit of towing gear.

- Main bridle: wire size 76 mm diameter.
- Bridle fore pennant: wire size 76 mm diameter.
- Connecting shackles: Smit D type, 100 tonnes SWL.
- Emergency bridle: same as main bridle.
- Messengers: 2 × 100 mm 76 mm diameter multiplait Polypropelene.

● Retrieving wires: 2 × 24 mm from bridle fish plate to A frames with a SWL of 20 tonnes, through snatch blocks with a SWL of 20 tonnes to 7 tonnes SWL winches. There should also be lead blocks and arrangements worked out so that the retrieving wires can be rove off the winches and led back to a point where more powerful pulling gear is readily available — for example, anchor winch warping drums or to cellar deck drill floor areas where multiple winches can be used.

● Carpenter stoppers for 24 mm wire: at least four, to be used in the event of recovery when the two retrieving winches are inadequate and alternative arrangements have to be rigged.

● Towing arrangement plans: these should be drawings and text detailing the unit's main and emergency towing systems, the method of deployment and recovery. There should also be drawings of the hull obstructions and anchor pennant positions with the radius of operation of cranes and their SWL at the maximum radii. This data should be passed to the vessels which are going to tow as a matter of course.

In conclusion it is clear that the North Sea is becoming more and more crowded with fixed and moored installations and a greater amount of sub-sea equipment is being deployed. The risks of collision are therefore also increasing and the consequences of breaking towing gear and being unable to reconnect quickly should make all those involved in towing operations consider carefully whether they are carrying out the work with due regard to the highest standards of seamanship.

Towing and anchor handling operations in the offshore oilfield require the exercise of skill and experience matched to equipment worked within the limitations imposed by weather. It is apparent that some of these limitations are being neglected.

Yours, etc.

Extracts from the observations of Captain Asbjørn Rislaa on the foundering of the *West Gamma*, supplied by the Norwegian Maritime Directorate to The Nautical Institute and published in *Seaways*, February 1992

On Tuesday 21 August 1990, the jack-up rig West Gamma *foundered in the North Sea. On board was Captain Asbjørn Rislaa, who wrote a personal account of the incident. He followed this up with some pertinent observations on matters of detail appertaining to the rescue, which are reproduced here.*

On the morning of 20 August, Captain Rislaa noticed that the wind was increasing and the sea getting rougher, the rig was moving and by the time he went for lunch things were beginning to fall off the messroom tables. After lunch, the alarm was given, and all hands were called to the bridge as the tow line had snapped and the helicopter deck had been washed overboard. Weather conditions continued to deteriorate and damage occurred to the platform. During the afternoon and evening, the rig listed more and more to port and sank deeper. By 03.00 on 21 August, the engineroom was flooding and the platform was heeling seriously, with the starboard side of the after deck being deep under the surface.

Preparations for evacuating the West Gamma *were made and the crew jumped into the sea in groups and were quickly picked up by pick-up boats from the* Normann Drott *and the* Esvagt Omega. *Captain Rislaa was rescued by a boat from the* Normann Drott, *but this boat was capsized either by a sudden wave or by being caught on a rescue net. He and others were then picked up by a boat from the* Esvagt Omega *and taken to that vessel, where they received very good treatment.*

Captain Rislaa comments: 'I would like to praise the Danish rescuers. Nothing they did from start to finish could have been done better.' (A copy of Captain Rislaa's complete manuscript is held at NI HQ. His observations on points of detail follow below.)

Survival suits

I USED the new type of helicopter suit from FCO Maritime. The suit was exactly the right size for my height. It fitted closely, was soft, elastic and did not hinder me in my movements on the platform or in the water. I had a normal amount of clothes on: a shirt, a thin sweater and jeans, although I had on two pairs of ordinary socks. I also had on protective boots instead of shoes.

It was mentioned in a circular from PPCo that on the platform, not only should the suit be hanging up where it is readily accessible, but that suitable footwear should also be kept nearby. This is important of course, as this suit has no fixed boots.

On the *West Gamma* we had plenty of time to prepare, but I can well imagine the situation if I didn't have time to think of this. Just walking/running on gratings could have put holes in nylon socks. I had heard that your feet could get cold in this suit and had therefore put on an extra pair of socks. The opening at the foot-end of the suit, allowing water to get in, would not have helped.

Suitable footwear is important

We had summer temperatures and no part of me felt the cold while I was in the water. At a guess, I was in the water for about 25 minutes. Even if it had been winter, I don't think I would have suffered any discomfort, even if I had been in the water for a longer period. It was easy to inflate the collar while I lay in the water and I can't see any reason why anyone would feel tempted to do this before — e.g., leaving a helicopter in the sea. As is well known, this would lead to problems if the helicopter is full of water.

As I said earlier, the suit was very comfortable and easy to move about in. On some other suits, the gusset is so long that swimming becomes difficult. When I was picked up the second time, I almost managed to climb into the boat without assistance. I lifted my arms over the collar and caught hold of the boat, and managed to lift one leg right over the side. This was not least thanks to the close fit of the suit.

My gloves were thin, close-fitting and very elastic and not at all cumbersome. My only criticism would have to be that the palms were smooth. I easily lost my grip when trying to hold on to a wet railing. I wonder if they had been sewn together incorrectly. The palms were smooth while the backs of the gloves were rough. My conclusion after this involuntary dip in the sea is that this suit was a pleasant surprise. My fairly wide experience of most of the suits on the market gives me a good basis for comparison.

After discussions with the Danish rescuers on the way in to Esbjerg, I have a comment about all suits. It is not easy to pull a person up out of the sea and into a boat and they were hampered by the lack of a strap over the shoulders or on the back to catch hold of. I was involved in a heated discussion on this subject a few years ago with a production manager. My conclusion is that many production managers have decided that a strap like this cannot be fitted because of the danger of it getting caught on various objects. Try again!

The rescuers pulled people up by holding on to the collar of their lifevests. They said the collar was torn right off on several occasions.

Otherwise, I believe that most people working offshore are not particularly concerned about the fact that the suit is obligatory for a reason. I now have experience of what it means to have a suit in which it was perfectly possible to survive. Many people treat their suits carelessly and leave them for long periods of time without laundering or servicing. It is also clear that those who dispense the suits do not take sufficient note of the fact that the receivers are often inexperienced. I am referring here to size.

There was one person in particular out of the 49 [on the *West Gamma*] who had a suit that was far too big. The boots were at least two sizes too big. There were holes in the suit as well. Just imagine the situation with 20−30 litres of water in each leg of the suit. When the rescuers tried to haul this person up into a boat, these heavy boots came up half-a-yard after the person in the suit. This person was working offshore for the first time and had been at work for a week. After an experience like this, it is difficult to have faith in a survival suit. Otherwise, I think most of the suits functioned as intended.

Pick-up boats

In 1978/79, I had the pleasure of participating in rigorous testing of the boat which is probably the predecessor of today's pick-up boats. It was called *Vido* and had been developed by two SAS pilots. It was a 22-footer with outboard engines, not unlike the boats used by the Danish rescuers in this rescue operation.

At that time, I was asked if I would like to test the boat against a moderate gale and rough seas and see if it would break up. I had to give up the attempt after breaking two ribs myself and winding a passenger. The boat didn't have a scratch. Some time later, I was involved in the sale of the three first pick-up boats with water jets on the Norwegian Continental shelf. I was also able to test these boats thoroughly.

My experience with this type of pick-up boat is more in the line of pleasure than a realistic rescue operation. On the other hand, I have heard many comments over the years from people who have used both types, with outboard engines or with waterjets, in rescue operations. Their comments were not in favour of the waterjet, due to its manoeuvring and reversing capabilities and the fact that the waterjet does not perform very well in very rough seas.

I had the opportunity to observe these points for myself and to discuss them with the boatmen from both boats on the way in to Esbjerg. One of the boats had a waterjet, the other two outboard engines. I saw that the waterjet boat had difficulty keeping close to the side of the ship when we tried to board *Normann Drott*, while the other boat made the same operation look quite simple when we later boarded the *Esvagt Omega*.

These points should be looked into and discussed with the boatmen, as it is obviously a question of two different classes of boat.

Boarding of mother vessel

This part of the rescue operation should be subject to closer attention in the future. I think the climbing net let down over the side of the ship in the rescue zone must be a relic from the days of sailing ships, or at least from the war. In the situation we were in, with modern equipment both in the water and on deck, this net was more a source of annoyance than any use to us. This was due primarily to the fact that it was hanging flat against the side of the ship. It would have been dangerous to climb the net because of violent seas and the degree of movement between the pick-up boat and the mother vessel.

When we attempted to board the *Normann Drott*, the boatman was unable to keep the boat close to the side of the ship. A totally unsuccessful attempt was made to attach a bowline. Next, an attempt was made to haul the boat up, but it was impossible to attach the lifting wire on to the boat. Even if this operation had been successful, the lifting device would not have been suitable for the purpose in that kind of weather. The lifting gear was too high up and as far as I could see consisted of a lifeboat davit with a slow winch.

The rescue net (rescue basket) that was swung out would have provided a solution if the boat hadn't capsized before we had a chance to use it. The Norwegian Maritime Directorate stated some years ago that this type of equipment was to be 'some kind of device for lifting people out of the sea.' Someone should have added 'dead or alive'.

As far as I could see, the crane in use did not have a wave compensator and there were quite a few yards of wire plus the wire hook that one minute crashed down into the net, only to be jerked up with great force the next. I dread to think of the consequences if more people had been in that net. I can't remember if there was a climbing net down the side of the *Esvagt Omega*, but I do remember that the boatman kept the boat 'stuck' to the side of the ship.

The rescuer told us 'keep down in the boat and don't try to help me'. It wasn't long before the hook was in place and we were lifted up to the railings. The boat would be going out again and was only lifted as far as the railings this time, but there was a proper crib on deck for the boat to land in. I stood watching when the boat was lifted in for the last time and could see that the crib had been specially designed for the purpose. It had been made as part of the rescue equipment and could receive the boat no matter how much the vessel was rolling. Other cribs I have seen are only storage spaces for the boat when not in use.

Drills

I asked the Danish rescuers how often they practised rescue operations, and was told 'once a week, irrespective of weather conditions'. Having seen the professional way they worked, I have no doubt that this is the case.

For the crew from the *Normann Drott* it was a different thing. The thought struck me while the operation was in progress, 'they haven't practised this'. I didn't have the opportunity to ask the crew from the *Normann Drott* whether this was in fact the case. It could be that I got this impression because all their attempts failed due to inadequate equipment.

When pick-up boats are in the water in order to pick up people, the mother vessels must keep a proper distance away. These vessels are of course very manoeuvrable, but even for them this capability is reduced in the kind of weather we experienced in this situation.

It's frightening enough to be in the sea under these conditions without having a violently rolling and pitching vessel trying to manoeuvre closer to you. The people in the sea feel small and helpless and the vessel appears even larger and more frightening. However, situations can of course arise where manoeuvring as close as possible is the only way to make a rescue. The climbing net would be of use here.

I don't mean by the above the any equipment is superfluous, but that all the equipment must be reassessed and not least be included in realistic drills. The rescue crews would then have a better chance of weighing up equipment and methods against each other in a rescue operation. I repeat, the above is not meant as a criticism. I am just attempting to pick out some points that are worth thinking about. I have tried at the same time to draw attention to those details which without a doubt were praiseworthy.

Everyone did their level best to bring the situation to a happy conclusion. It was impressive to see with my own eyes what a professional apparatus can be set in motion if needs be.

Index